Materializing Thailand

Materializing Culture

Series Editors: Paul Gilroy, Michael Herzfeld and Danny Miller

Materializing Thailand

Penny Van Esterik

Oxford • New York

First published in 2000 by
Berg
Editorial offices:
150 Cowley Road, Oxford, OX4 1JJ, UK
838 Broadway, Third Floor, New York, NY 10003-4812, USA

Berg is the imprint of Oxford International Publishers Ltd.

Library of Congress Cataloging-in-Publication Data

A catalogue record for this book is available from the Library of
Congress.

British Library Cataloguing-in-Publication Data

A catalogue record for this book is available from the British Library.

ISBN 1 85973 306 9 (Cloth)
      1 85973 311 5 (Paper)

Typeset by JS Typesetting, Wellingborough, Northants.
Printed in the United Kingdom by Biddles Ltd, Guildford and
King's Lynn.

Contents

Preface

We ride on the shoulders of our teachers and our students. I thank all those who have taught and inspired me in Thailand and North America in the process of researching this book. Rather than select a few to name and risk offending by naming or failure to name, I would like this dedication to A. Thomas Kirsch (1930–1999) to stand as an acknowledgement and thank you to all those who take the time to support others, personally and professionally.

Although I was never a student at Cornell, Tom Kirsch was my teacher in many ways, responding to questions, commenting, commending, correcting. Every few months over the last three years, Tom would gently probe, 'have you finished your book on Thai gender yet'? I would offer excuses, only to be buoyed up by Tom's faith in anthropology, Thai studies (and me). There is no greater gift that a mentor can give than the utter confidence that a task will be completed. Tom critiqued early chapter drafts, seeing connections to draw arguments together, pointing out contradictions, and inspiring insights that were as much his as mine.

In his own work, he saw historical context as integral to anthropological analysis, and incorporated gender as part of good ethnography in a logically elegant, unselfconscious manner into his work long before the subject became popular. His intellectual excitement was infectious.

This book is therefore dedicated to the life and scholarship of A. Thomas Kirsch, whose sensitive approach to history and gender in Thai anthropology inspired so many students and colleagues. His legacy endures in their work.

I acknowledge with thanks a York University, Faculty of Arts Research Fellowship (1992) that allowed me to spend several months at Thai Khadi Research Institute, Thammasat University, Bangkok. Stimulating visits to Southeast Asian Programs at Michigan, Wisconsin, Hawaii and Cornell made up for the isolation of writing in a school, indeed a country where Thai studies is not prominent. I would also like to thank Michael Herzfeld who introduced me to Kathryn Earle and Berg Publishers, and Kim Glaze whose computer skills saved this manuscript from near disaster.

In this work, I have transliterated words from standard Thai as a guide to pronunciation, based on a modification of the system used in Mary Haas' Thai-English dictionary. However, I have also used altern-ative spellings of words that are widely known and used by other authors. Buddhist terms are based on Thai transcriptions of Pali.

And finally, I have broken a promise to Tom that I would write this book without using the word 'discourse', but it crept in while he was otherwise engaged. Sorry Tom.

Penny Van Esterik

List of Figures

Part I

Orientations

Crafting Thailand

Amazing Thailand

Everyone knows something about Thailand. The country is known to many as the home of a wonderful cuisine, great package tours, child prostitution, fabulous silk, fake Rolex watches and magnificent temples. We learn about the country through tourist advertising, business and educational exchanges, films and news reports; these fragments reinforce the country's seductive appeal. For Thailand does not permit distancing, but rather sucks us into a sensual world of exotic sights, sounds, tastes, and smells.

Attraction to Thailand is partly aesthetic – the beauty of the country's natural and constructed environments; the Thai enjoyment of things beautiful – orchids, textiles, temples, people; the civility and grace of its peoples; their appreciation of the present moment, and the ease with which the ugly and painful is slipped out of sight. Only within the ascetic system of Theravada Buddhism is sensual pleasure denied, drawing even more attention to the beauty of ascetic simplicity made more striking beside baroque extravagance. Even the dramatic contrasts between wealth and poverty, between Buddhist denial and total indulgence, fascinate rather than repulse. There are no rewards for suppressing beauty or pleasure. This has been in the past and continues to be the fascination of Thailand for travellers and analysts alike.

'Amazing Thailand Year' was celebrated in 1998. Even in the midst of financial crisis, Thailand amazes. Tourist materials for this campaign feature beautiful men and women wearing the heritage of Thailand on elaborate headdresses including flowers, Thai food, women from upland minorities, boats, Buddhist monks and Buddha images, flanked by Ban Chiang burial pottery, orchids, painted umbrellas, elephants and waterfalls. New Year's cards celebrating Amazing Thailand Year contained cardboard cutouts of miniature monuments including the Giant Swing, temple of the Emerald Buddha, temple of the Dawn, a

3

guardian deity, and the reclining Buddha, all Bangkok-based tourist attractions.

You can buy anything in Bangkok. Women and representations of the feminine circulate much as other commodities in this very global market. As the cultural, economic and political centre of Thailand, Bangkok has a unique role in establishing cultural and gender hegemonies for the whole country. But Thailand also has a fluid, transnational identity that ranges beyond its national borders. Beauty contestants, factory workers, people with HIV/AIDS and prostitutes affect the representation of the Thai nation state, and of Thai women in Thailand and elsewhere.

Thailand encourages an essentialism of appearances or surfaces. These surfaces are gendered, and easily materialized and transformed through display, presentations, and everyday practices focussed on women as visual icons. Gendered practices such as beauty contests and state rituals fetishize national images which serve both to exoticize and reify the essence of Thainess, enhancing the country's international reputation and tourist appeal. That is why the surface is so effective, the essence quickly grasped; the real is hidden and unchallenged. The surface is taken for the real. In the absence of critical examination of the discourses constructing these gendered surfaces, we all feel we know the real 'Amazing Thailand'.

In contemporary Thailand, two processes collide – those globalizing forces that draw Thailand and Thai people and events onto the world stage, and those localizing forces that reify, exoticize and box Thai culture into opposition against global processes. This play between the surface exoticism of locality and global transnational processes creates the set of paradoxes and contradictions explored in this book. For the importance of fluidity, of surfaces and appearances belies the essentialism that makes it possible for outsiders – analysts and tourists alike – to grasp the essence of Thainess with such speed, certainty and satisfaction. This interpretive arrogance on the part of non-Thai is made possible because of well-developed cultural strategies and skills for constructing and maintaining this reified Thai essence through displays and representations which materialize Thai national identity.

This book examines the historical and cultural processes that make the 'Amazing Thailand' campaign possible and plausible, including the construction of Thai public culture and how gender is materialized. It is based on my research and participant observation in Thailand over a thirty-year period, and a critical engagement with Thai studies and feminist anthropology. It also emerges from the interplay between my sensual attraction to the essence of Thainess and things Thai, the respect

I have for Thai women, and the anger I feel at conditions that exploit women and others in Thai communities. I seek the origins of both emotions in the process of writing.

Gendered Surfaces

Why surfaces? Surface is the inevitable level of understanding available to an outside analyst observing other people, other places. It is linked to the dictionary meaning of superficiality, what is apprehended upon a casual view, without depth. This fear of inevitable superficiality is the Achille's heel of anthropology, a vulnerability that should not keep us from trying. Surface also draws attention to the outermost boundary of any material body, its smooth, polished outer appearance which provides the canvas available for creating new appearances. Consider also the surface tension of a liquid, that elastic enveloping membrane that causes particles to cohese – shades of culture.

The importance of surface appearance emerges in Thai novels and short stories. Boonrot, the heroine of Botan's novel and subsequent film of northeast Thailand in the 1960s, complains of being considered a sex worker because she dressed in bright clothes, wore sunglasses and swaggered. She is reminded that women must dress carefully so that others will not question their respectability. 'We only look at the outside form and structure of one another. We never look inside'.

Concern with appearances also emerges in the political protests lead by women students carrying photos of the royal family to demonstrate national loyalty and to make the claim that the protesters are good Thai. The following chapters recount the public relation campaigns following the 1992 democracy protests, tourist promotions, and efforts to clean up Thailand's international image concerning sex tourism as examples of Thai concern and skill with controlling public face.

Surfaces also relate to Thai concepts of temporal and spatial order that put primacy on how events and relationships come together in an impermanent world in constant flux. Rituals, both religious and secular, and codes of conduct that regulate the social cosmetic such as *kalatesa*, try to pin down points of reference in this flux. Attention to surfaces and appearances are the observable results of this pattern of adaptation.

Organization

The book is organized in three parts, titled Orientations, Representations and Interpretations. Part I orients the reader to knowledge produced about Thailand, past and present. This first chapter develops three trajectories of change: the transformation of Thailand over the last thirty years, changes in the disciplines of Thai studies and Cultural Anthropology, and my personal experience in Thailand over the same years. Although Thai studies stresses the uniqueness of Thailand, it is important to consider how Thai gender studies relate to Southeast Asian gender research, although the detailed comparisons must be left for other researchers in other texts.

In the second chapter, I introduce two orienting metaphors that emerge out of Thai experience: *kalatesa* (time/space) and palimpsest. *Kalatesa* draws attention to order and surface appearances, a theme developed further throughout the book. Palimpsest is a metaphor from Western literary traditions used here to link historical and ethnographic knowledge. The term palimpsest refers to parchment or slate from which old writing has been nearly erased to make room for new writing. The act of writing over an earlier draft version of something that has been wiped out suggests that the original version has disappeared. But palimpsests are never completely erased; nor are historical and literary representations of Thai women. I ask how Thai women have come to bear the burden of signifying Thainess both within the country and globally and explore the response of the Thai women's movement to the position and condition of Thai women, asking if Thai feminism has been shaped by global feminism. But the Thai women's movement is a pragmatic one, addressing the consequences of gender inequities and poverty often without theorizing about their historical and cultural causes.[1]

Chapter 3 explores the various linkages that have been made between Buddhism and gender in Thai society. Theravada Buddhism, the dominant religion in Thailand, provides an ideological reference system that is both liberating and confining for women. Buddhism is important to Thai identity because it is part of the logic of everyday life, not only because its texts and rituals structure gender hierarchies. Ideological orientations toward non-self and impermanence discourage essentialisms, particularly fixed binary gender identities. I develop the commonalities and contrasts between Buddhist and feminist ways of knowing, arguing that these two perspectives are both compatible and powerful explanatory frameworks for exploring Thai gender relations.

Part II, Representations, examines the logic and paradox of public culture at several sites of gender negotiation in Thailand. Each site requires rethinking cultural context, as contextual sensitivity determines how gender is read. Current practices are shaped and constrained

by earlier ones, requiring analytical frameworks that incorporate both
historical evidence and the selective inventions of imagined pasts to
interpret the present. Hence, my concern with palimpsests that are
incompletely erased.

Chapter 4 looks at gendered nationalism and how the state requires
the display of women as icons that express Thai national identity and
confirm Thai masculinity. The imposition of order is also materialized
through heritage sites – objects and buildings recreated to conform to
an imagined past. These concrete palimpsests raise questions about Thai
and Western approaches to authenticity. The representations of gender
and national identity in Thai public culture – past and present – have
the added benefit of forming the heart of Thai tourist attractions.

Beauty contests, both local and global, exemplify the display of
women as visual icons and are examined in Chapter 5. Juxtaposed to
the display of femininity in the 1992 Miss Universe contest in Bangkok,
the political protests and subsequent killings in May 1992 draw attention
to the military and masculinity. The political economy of Thailand
frames the discussion of prostitution and is one result of these national
displays of women's beauty. Chapter 6 considers how these sex practices
are attached to national and international power structures, and to
the nature of Thai marriage.

The choice of the contexts elaborated in Part II, over the infinite
possibilities of other contexts can be justified by their particular effectiveness for interpreting the contemporary Thai gender system. Each
context adds to the density, 'thickness' and complexity of the picture.
Beauty contests, temple fairs, shopping malls, Patpong disco bars and
sex shows, fake Gucci watches and Thai tourist attractions are all
elements of public culture, all localities, objects and events that demonstrate Thailand's accessibility to an internationally constituted 'public'.
They are also particular sociocultural settings where gender is most
visibly constructed, negotiated and displayed. They reveal contradictions and tensions in the representations of Thai gender, and require
stretching the boundaries of Thai to include transnational contexts
where overseas Thai communities recreate Thai contexts in Europe,
Australia and North America. Thainess is easily deterritorialized and
taken away with immigrants and exiles as they create Thai communities
in Los Angeles, Chicago, and London. But the essence of Thainess is
also reproduced in the wife-buying schemes of Japan, the Los Angeles
born 'Thai' beauty contestants, the mail order brides, prostitutes in
the cities of Europe and North America, and even in the Thai women
workers imprisoned in the toy and garment factories of southern

California. Everything is exportable, including contradictory attitudes towards women and gender existing within Thailand as a nation state.

Part III, Interpretations, explores how these understandings of Thai cultural contexts can be used to rethink a Thai model of gender relations. In Chapter 7, I propose a theory of gender relations that draws on Thai interpretations of gender as explored in the ethnographic sites of Part II, rather than on Western gender categories. Here disguise and transgendering add to the difficulty in fixing essential categories. Chapter 8 concludes with observations on how Thai studies might contribute to rethinking cultural context and feminist anthropology.

Thailand has undergone enormous changes over the last thirty years. Locating Thailand provides an opportunity to present, selectively and briefly, foundational information about the country, its history, political economy and culture. My work in the field has been shaped by the disciplines of Thai studies and cultural anthropology. Just as my experiences in Thailand have changed over the years, so too have these fields of study. These three trajectories of locality, disciplinary and personal transformations provide orientations to the later chapters.

Locating Thailand

Before Thongchai Winichakul (1994) argued for the power of the map in creating and defining Thai national identity, locating Thailand was an easy task; it is surrounded by other nation states. It is north of Malaysia, east of Burma (Myanmar), west of Lao PDR and Cambodia, and south of China. How do we locate Thailand now, while acknowledging that the old story that told how a patriotic elite modernized to save the nation from Western colonialism is itself a modern invention (O'Connor 1997:280)? The old story represented Thailand as a stable, homogeneous, Buddhist constitutional monarchy, transformed by an enlightened coup in 1932 which ended the power of the absolute monarchy, the Lords of Life of the Chakri dynasty. Founded, along with Bangkok in 1782, the Chakri dynasty is represented today in the beloved person of Rama IX, King Bhumibol Adulyadej, who, at his coronation in May, 1950 recited the ancient oath of accession: 'We will reign with righteousness, for the benefits and happiness of the Siamese people.' As a symbol of national unity, the royal family reinforces the primacy of Bangkok as the cosmological, religious, political and economic centre of the nation.

Royal authority draws legitimacy from a succession of large and small kingdoms of Tai,[2] Mon or Khmer origin from the ninth century onwards.

Most significant are the thirteenth century kingdom of Sukhothai (1240–1438) and the fifteenth century kingdom of Ayutthaya, (1351–1767), models of *dhammaraja* (righteous king) and *devaraja* (god king) political authority. Before the Burmese destroyed Ayutthaya in 1767, occasional missionaries, traders and diplomats visited the city state. The court gained some familiarity with the Portuguese, Dutch, French, Persian, and Japanese; but it was the British who succeeded in opening up trade with European countries following the Bowring treaty of 1855.

By the fourth reign of the Chakri dynasty, King Mongkut was sufficiently familiar with French and British colonial power that he recognized the need for centralizing Bangkok's control over peripheral princedoms and adopting European institutions of rule.

Thailand is the one nation in Southeast Asia that was never colonized by European powers. This historical fact, proudly asserted by Thais, is often attributed to the Chakri administration's skills at compromise and negotiation. Thailand emerges as the space in-between British and French colonies. Lack of direct colonial experience does not mean that Thai modes of production were not shaped by external forces nor that there was no interference in the internal affairs of the Thai state. 'The French were reorganizing the country's legal system, the British its treasury and the Germans its army' (Copeland 1993:93). In the nineteenth century, most commercial enterprises were in white hands and the rulers preserved independence by allowing colonial powers to exploit the nation and its resources (Copeland 1993:159). Thailand has the characteristics of an indirectly ruled colonial state with a politicized military used as a means of internal consolidation and control rather than external protection.

The internal reforms following the turn of the century were not sufficient to transform an absolute monarchy to a constitutional one, and in 1932 a small group of civil servants and military officers staged a coup and forced Rama VII to become Thailand's first constitutional monarch. Political changes and World War II strengthened efforts to develop a Thai national identity, and selectively borrow Western paths to modernity and progress.

The military has had a great influence on Thailand through its involvement in the many coups and political crises since 1932. Through the 1950s and 1960s, Thailand was transformed from a subsistence-based agricultural economy to a market-oriented rice economy and by the eighties, to an industrializing economy. While the Thai military with American support provided the stability to make this economic transformation possible, military ambitions had other consequences.

The military suppressed attempts to form a constitutional democracy in 1972, but was unable to suppress the public outrage at the oppression, corruption and ineptitude of the government of Prime Minister Thanom Kittikachorn in 1973. The student-led revolution heralded a period of democratic rule (1973–6) which was ruthlessly crushed in 1976. Stable governments in the 1980s encouraged programs of economic development, including international tourism, an immensely successful earner of foreign exchange.

Thailand experienced an exceptionally high rate of economic growth between 1985 and 1996 due to the dynamic growth of urban manufacturing, tourism and the service industry. The booming economy was growing by 8 percent a year in the late 1980s, and even 6.4 percent in 1996. Thailand is now facing a financial crisis of major proportions, and did not even reach its revised projection of 0.6 percent growth in 1997. Land prices soared in the boom years, and developers overextended themselves, building condominiums and housing estates for the new urban middle class. Banks and finance companies were stuck with huge foreign loans to these developers, at the same time that the central bank was no longer willing to prop up the local currency (*baht*). Investors, local businesses, and consumers all suffered after the currency was allowed to float in July 1997. By October, the baht had fallen 40 percent in value. Higher prices and unemployment worsened the situation. The October 1997 collapse of the Thai financial markets prompted Prime Minister Chavalit Yongchayudh to remind investors that they should not leave a country where they could get three caddies on any Thai golf course: 'one to carry your clubs, one to hold your umbrella, and one to massage your back' (*Globe and Mail*, 5 November 1997). Other approaches to encourage investors to continue to support Thailand include promotional messages in the Thai Airways magazine, *Sawasdee* (November 1997:41): 'Those who look behind the headlines, however, are finding that Thailand's growing pains can mean substantial gains for investors. Out of the country's crisis, opportunity has arisen.' The government's mismanagement of the crisis increased political instability, resulting in the resignation of Prime Minister Chavalit Yongchayudh on 30 October 1997. The $17 billion (US) bailout from the International Monetary Fund offered the country financial support, contingent on following a recovery plan that included checking inflation and reducing public spending such as halting the construction of Bangkok's $4.5 (US) billion expressway.

The new 'people's constitution' passed by parliament in September of 1997 began the process of political reform designed to deliver transparency and good governance and end corruption. One now needs a

BA to be Member of Parliament, setting up a whole new arena for potential corruption. Ironically, it was the military that forced political reform to proceed, easing public tensions and siding with a popular cause against an 'unusually corrupt' and incompetent government. For example, 123 members of the Thai parliament received envelopes containing fifty 1000 *baht* notes from the Minister of Education during a 6 February 1997 meeting about reform of the education system. This was not unusual or unacceptable behavior, although some complained it was not enough to buy an MP. Even Prime Minister Chavalit Yong-chayudh defended his minister, pointing out that 'he did not secretly distribute the money in the toilet' (*Economist*, 15 February 1997:36).

Thailand's public face obscures the power of the military, the marginalization of minority groups, the factions within Buddhism, the treatment of minority religions, the growing disparity between rich and poor, the high murder rate,[3] and other costs of rapid modernization. As Thailand began its tourist theme for 1998 – Amazing Thailand – the speed with which such facts are forgotten attests to how well the government of Thailand represents itself to the international community. Even the spread of HIV/AIDS in the country, an epidemic of staggering proportions, does not taint the international image of the country. Thailand remains a popular tourist destination. Tourists to Thailand revel in the opportunity provided by the devaluation of the *baht* for bargain shopping. 'You will love the country,' I say, and they will, they do. And so too do academics working in Thailand who are attracted back again and again, reinforcing their loyalty to Thai studies.

Disciplining Thailand: Thai Studies and Anthropology

How has Thai studies been disciplined? How has it enlarged the universe of human discourse and contributed to anthropology? Thai studies is a particular way of knowing about Thailand, where Thailand is viewed as an object of knowledge. Only recently has it been possible to describe Thai studies as a definable entity. It flourishes in Thailand, North America, Australia, Europe, India and Japan. Thai studies began in Japan after World War II, although student exchanges began earlier in 1942 during the Japanese occupation of Thailand. In North America, Thai studies is lodged within the study of Southeast Asia, itself a region with no clearly demarcated boundaries, although a product of colonial boundary making exercises. Southeast Asian studies is part of Asian studies – in North America, the smallest most peripheral part, in the boundary conscious area studies of the 1960s and 1970s. Tongchai Winichakul (1994) has convincingly demonstrated that this academic 'mapping' is also a colonial construction of great historical complexity. Area studies defined 'ethnological fields of study' (Josselin de Jong 1965), and divided up clearly bounded objects of study in the world system, treating geographical divisions, cultural differences and national boundaries as if they were isomorphic (Appadurai 1996:16).[4] For all the critiques of area studies as being too narrowly focussed on the particular, too obsessed with philology and history, and too driven by foreign-policy needs, '. . . area studies has provided the major counterpoint to the delusions of the view from nowhere that underwrites much canonical social science' (Appadurai 1996:16). Area studies, like feminist studies demands a view from somewhere.

Thai studies is the study of the nation state of Thailand, and of Tai groups speaking languages in the Tai language family residing outside Thailand's borders. Thai studies has remained firmly in the model of area studies. Broader associated groupings of countries such as ASEAN (Association of Southeast Asian Nations), APEC (Asia Pacific Economic Co-operation) and AFTA (ASEAN Free Trade Area) influenced disciplines such as economics and political science more than anthropology. These overlapping rubrics of Southeast Asian studies, Thai studies, ASEAN, APEC and AFTA underscore the difficulties analysts would encounter if they considered local Thai communities in isolation from national and transnational processes. This text emerges from the space left by area studies, where place and local geographies and histories still matter, but the boundaries of locality do not.[5]

Most foreign Thai specialists might be identified as those people who subscribe (or who have subscribed) to the Journal of the Siam Society, the Thai orientalist association founded in 1904, where elite, Western-educated Thai and visiting researchers exchange texts and talks, often in English. The objectives of the society include 'the investigation and encouragement of the Arts and Sciences in relation to Thailand and neighbouring countries' (from the rules of the Siam Society, Article 2).

Recently, foreign and Thai scholars have interacted more energetically at the international Thai studies conferences, held first in New Delhi (1981), and subsequently in Bangkok (1984), Canberra, Australia (1987), Kunming, China (1990), London (1993), Chiang Mai (1996) and Amsterdam (1999). International Thai studies conferences are visible evidence of the power of dominant discourses and the people who shape them.

International Thai studies conferences explore the foundational knowledge in Thai studies, and define the categories for organizing that knowledge. Neither women nor gender were part of the foundational knowledge imparted at the early conferences. 'Thai Women' in the later conferences were relegated to studies of fertility and contraception, discussions on HIV/AIDS (women as prostitutes and carriers of infection), and in analyses of classical Thai literature (as fictional models of Thai femininity). Gendered knowledge was less apparent in domains where resources were contested and power was at stake – as if it were somehow natural that women or gender differences do not matter when it comes to discussions of politics, ethnic relations, economic development, or even sexuality.

Craig Reynolds' plenary address to the fifth conference at London reviewed the process by which sets of differences became problematized within Thai studies. While issues of race and class are now accepted as significant, the body of knowledge related to differences in gender remains marginalized. Reynolds called for gender studies not to reproduce the history of Thai women, but to mobilize to challenge the dominant model of the Thai grand epic narrative. The voices of resistance should be heard, the subaltern version of history examined and used to reveal a new version of the narrative that is Thai studies (Reynolds 1994).

As if in answer to that call, the Thai studies conferences held in Chiang Mai in October, 1996, and in Amsterdam in July 1999 dedicated a conference theme to gender. Gender cross-cuts many other theme areas. Gender was particularly difficult to separate from discussions of sexuality and sexual sub-cultures in the AIDS era.

The last few decades have seen much scholarly and activist attention paid to Thai women, particularly during the UN Decade for Women (1975–1985), but less attention to gender. To date, the subject of gender in Thai studies has been undertheorized, as have other aspects of Thai studies. Gender research in Thailand has been almost all about women, not about men or relations between men and women. Emphasis has been on the role and status of women, women in development, or provision of services to women with little concern for articulating gender theory. Gender relations are considered primarily in the context of prostitution and sex tourism. Thai women's groups and other NGOs have addressed these pragmatic concerns, but they have kept Thai insights and practices a local matter, removed from Western academic theorizing.

Considerations of gender in Thai studies have not generated simplifying concepts but have thrown up contradictions and paradoxes requiring further examination – for example, women entrepreneurs or women meditation teachers (J. Van Esterik 1982). Considerations of gender have often been done from the perspective of texts or rituals as texts. In reviewing evidence from northern Thailand, Tanabe calls for 'a theory which encompasses the whole range of gender representations and practices, not simply those confined in "cosmological" texts' (Tanabe 1991:183). I use texts – anthropological, historical, popular, Thai and English – as works that stand in particular relations to history, ideology and power, but I struggle to avoid reading Thai culture as text, on the assumption that such readings are not only inadequate but also distorting of experience.

Thai studies has shaped the kinds of questions we ask and the categories we use to understand gender in Thailand. What are those received categories for understanding Thai gender relations?

1. Thailand is an area characterized by relative gender complementarity. (J. and L. Hanks 1963)
2. Thai women are not an undifferentiated oppressed category: there is great variability by region, class, and ethnicity. (Eberhardt 1988, Hutheesing 1990)
3. The relative advantage of Thai women in matters of social structure (including bilateral kinship, matrilocality and inheritance by youngest daughter) are lodged primarily in material conditions and social relations developed in rural rice farming communities that are changing rapidly. (Potter 1977, Karim 1995)
4. Changes in the industrial labour force have benefitted some women, but gender inequality exists in workplaces. (Mills 1999)

A model of Thai gender relations will probably have a specifiable relation to gender models in other parts of Southeast Asia, a deductive task suitable for the regional anthropology O'Connor proposes (1995), but beyond the scope of this already wide-ranging book.

Research on gender in Thailand is overwhelmingly concerned with women, and tends to describe and count rather than analyze and synthesize. Gordon and Srisambhand point out that most research conducted up to the mid-1980s on Thai women focused on family planning, fertility, health and migration (1987:1).

In a discipline like anthropology that is based on fieldwork, it matters where you go, and how far from home. For anthropologists, place is not trivial but central; localities become showcases for issues. Geertz argues that the settings of one's fieldwork shape one's work more than theories, texts, methods or 'commitments to intellectual creeds' (1995: 134).

Places have also been married to ideas and images (Appadurai 1988b: 39). Certain ideas have become 'metonymic prisons' or 'gatekeeping concepts', shaping and guiding anthropological theorizing about places where fieldwork is conducted (Appadurai 1986:357). Ideas become hegemonic in these places, summarizing past work, shaping key debates and framing new questions. In Thai studies, they also succeed in essentializing, exoticizing and totalizing Thai society and culture. These foundational ideas are slow to change and retain a special authority with regard to the theoretical issue in question (Appadurai 1986:358). The source of many familiar interpretations of Thai society is the inability of the analyst to discard the pleasure and comfort of these foundational ideas, and challenge their validity: in Thai studies these include patron-client relations, entourages, loose structure, personalized relations, gender complementarity and the 'hind legs of the elephant'. Yet, as Hertzfeld argues (1997:26), essentializing is key to both the work of anthropology and the work of nation building.

Anthropologists are prominent in Thai studies. How has the anthropology of Thailand contributed to anthropological theory and methods? If it has not, why has it not? Why have so few works on Thailand been designated theoretical, and why has Thai ethnography not informed anthropological theory nor become part of the canon? Hewison refers to Thai studies as a theoretical backwater (1983). Anderson made a similar argument for the state of Thai studies as long ago as 1978:

> . . . there is, to my knowledge, no self-conscious or self-critical literature about the larger problems of approach or method – not to say paradigm – in Western (or American) writing about modern Thai history and politics. (Anderson 1978a:194)

One possible reason for this is that Thailand has not figured prominently in many comparative studies. Since Embree's comparison between Japan and Thailand, there have been few attempts to understand Thailand through comparative analysis. A significant exception is the work of Mulder who compared Thailand with Java and the Philippines in a number of publications (1983, 1992).

If, as Lutz (1995) argues, theory is masculine, it becomes even more interesting to ask why so few works on Thailand have been designated as theoretical. Theory texts in anthropology are unlikely to mention Thai ethnographic work; if they mention anything Thai it is likely to be the 'loosely structured social system' described by Embree in 1950 and critiqued thereafter by Hans-Dieter Evers and others in 1969. One of the most persistent theoretical remnants in Thai studies, loose structure is more a sign that marks the work of anthropologists in Thailand in the 1950s and 1960s than a gatekeeping concept that guided research. In fact, by 1969 when Evers published a book of essays revisiting the concept, almost all authors criticized it or had long since abandoned it. Yet no one has challenged or tested ethnographically the observations Embree made (Kirsch 1969). As a sign of having read key works in Thai anthropology, loose-structure persists. As a founding work, the concept of loose-structure could be cited and perpetuated to demonstrate how Thai studies has contributed to anthropological theory. Unfortunately, it simply focuses attention on the gender bias and theoretical void in Thai studies.

Instead of producing critical theory we are seduced by Thailand, taken in by its nationalist representation, decrying the shortages of panels on Thailand at anthropology meetings or Asian Studies meetings, and behaving appropriately at Thai sponsored conferences, careful not to critique Thailand or at least citing Thai colleagues to legitimize our critiques. Doing fieldwork in such an open accessible society as Thailand means that outside observers are shaped by existing discourses before they have the knowledge to impose new or critique existing conceptual frameworks. Not all are taken in. NGO workers on HIV/AIDS projects, or sex tourism projects, and ethnographers of minority groups critique the centre from their perspective at the periphery of Thai society.

'If each world region has its own style of anthropological analysis, then surely Southeast Asia has come to be the place where interpretive approaches to culture have reigned, whether in anthropology, history, or politics' (Bowen 1995:1047). Bowen (1995) looks specifically at what style of anthropology emerges out of Southeast Asia, and identifies the accessibility of publicly displayed performances read by a diversity of actors as a focus for interpretist anthropologists. This orientation persists through the whims of theoretical fashions in anthropology with the result that theatricality might be considered a hegemonic concept in the region. Gatekeepers themselves play a key role in preserving these gatekeeping concepts, as Bowen (1995:1067) points out the influence of 'teacher-to-student chains of research' (Hanks' students in Thailand; Geertz' students in Indonesia; Conklin's students in the Philippines).

Becoming an anthropologist requires inheriting and critiquing the world views, methods, and theories of that profession, learned from the written work of other anthropologists. In the 1960s, in North

America, that written work was usually about Africa, New Guinea, and occasionally about Native Americans. Only rarely did Southeast Asia inform that work, with the exception of the work of Leach on the Kachin Hills (1965), and Geertz (1960) on Java. I began fieldwork in Thailand knowing more about the Nuer, the Trobrianders, and the Tikopia, than the Vietnamese, Akha and Chin. Students – myself included – prepared for fieldwork in Thailand with no idea how the production of ethnographic knowledge about Thailand would find its way into the corpus of anthropological knowledge. And the materials I produced over the years? Relevant to Thai studies, yes; but shaping the larger discourses of anthropology, hardly. How different it must be to work in a locality that is presumed to contribute to our understanding of human nature, to be an integral part of telling the human myth (cf. Richardson 1975).

Experiencing Thailand[6]

Other than seeing *The King and I*, my first impressions of Southeast Asia came from two undergraduate courses taken in my fourth year in anthropology, and participation in teach-ins and protests against the Vietnam war. Thailand took shape for me as the place where American troops recovered from bombing raids on Vietnam originating from Thai air bases.

My first direct contact with Thailand came in 1967 to 1969 when I taught Anthropology and English as a CUSO volunteer at Thammasat University, Bangkok. Those years provided a painful but enlightening view of university life in Thailand. My earliest knowledge of rural Thailand came from participating in the field training for Thai students studying the villages around Ayutthaya in central Thailand in the initial placements for what turned out to be the first long-term study of that region by the newly-formed Chulalongkorn University Social Research Institute (CUSRI). Here, I saw Bangkok students seeing rural Thai communities as unfamiliar places, and realized that it was not just foreigners who viewed rural Thai villages as exotic objects of study. Many Thai students idealized and romanticized rural life without acknowledging their lack of knowledge or experience of rural life. Few students had both respect for and a genuine interest in rural Thai communities. Many students were fascinated by objects such as fish nets, amulets, and wooden kitchen utensils. The discarded, worn, rabbit-shaped coconut graters under rural houses now sell for hundreds of dollars in Bangkok antique stores.

Over those years in Thailand, my husband and I lived in several Bangkok neighbourhoods, and were robbed in all of them. When our house was broken into in Indiana, we reacted with anger and a feeling of violation at being robbed. But in Bangkok, colleagues and neighbours provided explanations and took up collections to compensate for our losses, and robberies became just another feature of Bangkok life. A few Western goods were redistributed in the streets of Bangkok. We made friends and learned to live acceptably as foreigners in Thailand on a low income.

At Thammasat University, most of my contacts were with women professors. It was always a Thai woman who would help me when I faced problems. Consequently, I viewed Thai women as unusually competent, and thought that they viewed themselves and were viewed by their male colleagues that way also. Bonds between women seemed close – both within families, and at work, and I learned to hold hands with women without sweaty palms revealing my discomfort.

Among the most striking of my accumulated memories of Thailand are the faces of beautiful prostitutes – both men and women – among the vacant, fearful and disease-ravaged faces, in the localities where prostitution flourished – on Patpong Road and Soi Cowboy in Bangkok, at rural temple fairs in central Thailand, in the makeshift bars near the American bases in northeast Thailand, in the short-term hotels through-out the country where alert staff draw curtains around the government cars (and where I once accidentally booked my college friend, and met a number of my male university students taking a break from their studies). The university milieu may have kept me from significant encounters with prostitution, or prostitution may have been much less flagrant and public in Bangkok in 1969. With the realization that my students considered these visits to be a normal part of urban life, I began to question assumptions about the American military and tourism as explanations for the growth of prostitution in Thai society.

As a Canadian, my contact with the American military in Bangkok was minimal – seeing GIs in restaurants, feasting once on American steaks and beer that a Peace Corps volunteer had smuggled out of the American PX, an invitation to lunch in an officer's mess in a luxury hotel taken over by the American military. Nevertheless, the conflict in Indochina was on our minds in the late 1960s.

Following two years in Thailand, we entered graduate school at the University of Illinois (Urbana) with the intention of doing doctoral work in anthropology on Thailand. My first research project was on Buddhism and village religion, and explored the relation between

Buddhism and Brahmanism through a study of tonsure rituals where children had topknots ceremonially removed (P. Van Esterik 1973). During predoctoral fieldwork, we lived in a large village in Suphanburi province. I would ask women about Buddhism; and they would always say, 'Ask a man, ask a monk.' Unfortunately, I did. As a result, my early writing on women and Buddhism was not sensitive to gender relations, only to 'the role of women'. At least it is convenient to find citations for inadequate approaches to Thai gender studies. In Suphanburi, we followed the American Thai studies tradition of immersing ourselves in the day to day activities of a prosperous rice and sugar cane growing village. We were well tolerated by most community members, with a few individuals concerned that we were communist. Their antagonistic questions, and a few events we were discouraged from attending, were easily dismissed at the time. In retrospect, I realize we were probably in the presence of initial recruitment for the reactionary village scout movement (cf Bowie 1997).

My next field project concerned painted pottery from Ban Chiang, northeast Thailand, objects that have become closely identified with Thai national identity. Having offended both an American archaeologist and a Thai archaeologist for reasons quite connected to my gender, I shifted my doctoral dissertation from a study of the late period-painted pottery in situ at Ban Chiang to a theoretical study of the design system as revealed by an examination of fakes and looted collections of Ban Chiang painted pottery in the hands and homes of the Thai elite (P. Van Esterik 1979, 1981). The study of Ban Chiang painted pottery seemed an easier object of study to integrate with the care of our infant daughter. But this theoretical work on Ban Chiang design marginalized me from the dominant discourse in Thai archaeology and defined me as a liminal being, handling archaeological materials that I had not excavated myself, and asking questions more properly anchored in cultural anthropology. In hindsight, this marginalization paid off, as it paved the way for asking different questions about authenticity and the production and consumption of Thai objects as representations of Thai identity (P. Van Esterik 1985a, 1994).

Working in the early 1970s from photographs and museum collections of Ban Chiang painted pottery, and coming home to a reasonably comfortable Bangkok house eased somewhat my experience of the political and social chaos that eventually erupted in the student demonstrations in October 1973 that successfully toppled the corrupt regime of Prime Minister Thanom Kittikachorn. Thammasat University was centrally placed in these demonstrations, and I recall clearly the mixture of fear and pride that accompanied the sight of young Thai men burning down police stations, and gently helping old women across the streets and out of harm's way.

The new government ushered in an unprecedented but short-lived period of liberal, democratic consciousness raising, and an outpouring of radical, critical expressions in the form of songs, plays, books and poetry – referred to as 'literature for life'. It was in this brief three-year period that many Thai non-governmental organizations (NGOs) began. But the experiments with democracy and critical creativity were all but destroyed in the military orchestrated mob violence of 6 October 1976, centred once again at Thammasat University, which ushered in a series of repressive military regimes. The contrast between these two confrontations at Thammasat University was horrific, as right-wing groups burned and mutilated unarmed students lead by the village scouts and other right-wing groups under the direction of the military.

Perhaps my optimistic view of Thailand stems from not being at Thammasat University in October of 1976, and from my six years' absence from the country from 1975 to 1981. I read of the new NGOs, the founding of the Friends of Women and other women's groups but never experienced the military dominated governments, repressive conditions, and right-wing control that drove so many Thai students into the jungle. When I returned to Thailand in 1981, my friends were back from the jungle, out of jail, or studying overseas. The absence was long enough for my memories about Thai life in the early 1970s to solidify into case studies, yet for someone whose first experience of Thailand was during the regime of Prime Minister Thanom Kittikachorn (1963–1973), the early 1980s did not seem unusually repressive.

By demographic good fortune, I escaped the witchhunt in American anthropology experienced by anthropologists a few years senior to me. During the 1960s, American anthropologists had access to research funds for 'planned development' connected circuitously to the American Defence Department and ultimately, to efforts to 'contain communism' in Southeast Asia (cf Wakin 1992). As a Canadian CUSO volunteer and later, a graduate student in Bangkok on minimal research funding, I was oblivious to the battles raging in the American Anthropological Association over the ethics of Thai research, and consuming in the process the reputations of several outstanding researchers of Thai society. Although we received a letter and survey questionnaire from Margaret Mead in 1971, Canadian citizenship and transparent, minimal funding from sources unrelated to American foreign or military policy removed us from further scrutiny by the ethics committee of the

American Anthropological Association.

From 1981 to 1984, I visited Thailand regularly to work on a multi-disciplinary, multi-country study of the determinants of infant feeding among the urban poor. This required shifting to a new literature and new texts on Thailand, and introduced me to the skilled technocrats who managed research and development programmes and policy in Thailand. Survival strategies included scrambling to learn the language of public health and nutrition, and detaching myself from the 'Thai culture' I had been constructing and studying for the past decade. Indigenous Thai knowledge and practice was less relevant in the infant feeding study where meaning was shaped by comparisons among four countries.[7] In fact, cultural knowledge was an albatross around my neck, reduced to residual indicators in epidemiological accounting. I knew too much about Thailand to state the obvious clichés, but not enough to place bureaucratic culture into my construction of Thai society. Gone from this applied work was the need for interpretation of the meaning of indigenous texts. Instead, new objectives, new stakeholders, new players came together for purposes of managing money. In the early 1980s, I had not yet recognized the civil service, development agencies and research institutes as controlling structures worthy of ethnographic study. I ran in place to keep up with a new problematic about development and became a source for others less familiar with Thailand who selected at will pieces of my Thai experiences now reified as anecdotes, and placed them in new contexts – the placement of which I often disagreed with. Occasionally, I was paid for this task, reciting examples of Thai behaviour for groups of Canadian businessmen who wanted to be able to do more business with the Thai and show their sensitivity to Thai culture.

While I was involved with these applied projects, I began research on Thai food, a subject critically important to Thai identity within and increasingly outside of Thailand (P. Van Esterik, 1986, 1992a). Food can be approached archaeologically, ethnographically, scientifically, religiously, linguistically, medically, and from an advocacy perspective. Knowledge of food is gendered knowledge – less so than in many societies, but gendered none the less. It is a knowledge that is so basic, so close to daily lived experience, and so identified with women that it is not highly valued in Thai studies, and certainly not a topic for scholarly debate that would change the shape of Thai studies, comparable to politics or ethnicity. But it drew me back to gender concerns.

Following a summer of packaging development for consumption by thirty Canadian students attending the World University Service of

Canada (WUSC) Seminar in Thailand, I learned to speak development discourse well enough to fund an Institutional Linkage Program through the Canadian International Development Agency (CIDA). CIDA shaped this development discourse, and, guided by new documents on women in development (WID), I undertook to link York University and Thammasat University for the purpose of strengthening women's studies and WID projects in Thailand. This was a difficult experience, since I was required to be both financially responsible for funds used at both universities, and academically responsible for the Thai students who were expected to study at York University and return to develop women's studies in Thailand. Nevertheless, WIDCIT (Women in Development Consortium in Thailand) has been viewed as a successful model for institutional linkages (cf. P. Van Esterik 1991, 1995).

During the years of the linkage, I slipped easily into the world of Thai activist women because of my ease with the basic tenets of feminism that we shared but never articulated – that 'the personal is political' and that it is futile to separate theory from practice. My other academic and applied work concerned breastfeeding and the exploitative practices of infant formula companies (P. Van Esterik 1985b, 1989). Thus, I knew the rhetorical style and the rules of advocacy discourse even as it crossed cultural and substantive boundaries. Through this process, I began being treated as a WID expert on Thailand. I heard myself outlining WID agendas, answering endless questions about why so many Thai women become prostitutes, defending Thai Buddhism as an egalitarian rather than a patriarchal religion, reviewing the shortcomings and accomplishments of Thai NGOs, and giving my version of Thai feminism.

The position of expert on Thai women and gender issues arose uninvited. It began with the recognition that there was very little material available for teaching about Southeast Asian women – that there was a gap in the literature. To address this, and solve the problem of a missing course textbook, I prepared an edited book on women in Southeast Asia (1982). While I have tried to justify why I came to try and fill that gap, third-world feminists assume when white women try to 'fill the gap' they are appropriating the struggles of third-world women (cf. Mohanty 1991). I could not appropriate much because as I first began studying and teaching about women in Southeast Asia, I had not yet internalized feminist epistemology. In fact, it was work on Thai women's issues that raised my consciousness about feminist theory. I did not bring Western feminist theory to Thai women; they brought their versions of it to me.

The discovery of this personal feminism began from the comfort of working in Thailand; from the pleasure of getting to know Thai women; and from being treated by both Thai men and women as if I were competent, whether or not I brought any level of competence to the task at hand or to Thai studies. I sometimes felt more comfortable in Thailand than in Canada – senses more alert; more ready to test out new ideas; less constrained by my academic persona – and more aware of how cultural rules operate with regard to gender.

As a reminder of past research, I can look back over my collection of Thai cloth and clothes, acquired over many years of visits. The faded *phaasin* (tube-like skirt) from days as a volunteer and graduate student; the simple shifts of local cotton, casually stitched shapeless bags that appeal because of their comfort and colour; the horrible mistakes – a frilly Thai silk blouse in lime green, fuchsia and pinks purchased in blind confidence that this would brighten up a bleak Canadian winter (instead, a fluorescent nightmare that I can neither wear nor discard); later, the Thai national dress made from a gift of silk given in return for editing a Thai friend's book; and more recently, the popular *ikat* silk ready-to-wear jackets that now grace world runways, having been popularized by Queen Sirikit. I am just beginning to consider the changes in the systems of production and reproduction, and representation of Thai identity that underlie this closet collection (P. Van Esterik 1994). The indigenous knowledge of textiles – like food – is in the hands and heads of women. Although textile studies are not yet in the mainstream of Thai studies, at least I can be clothed in the research remnants and comforted by the beauty of Thai stuff.

At a recent Asian studies meeting, I presented a paper on gender and Thai prostitution, and a colleague asked me how I could justify my symbolic and interpretive work on gender in the face of the great need for more practical work on sexuality and HIV/AIDS. In response, I developed a futures research project positing HIV/AIDS as an agent of change in Thailand. I dropped the project after a Thai doctor criticized the concept, saying that it was inappropriate to speculate about the future when there was so much that needed to be known about the present. Now that my unpublished 'futures' have become unpublished 'pasts', I regret not pursuing these speculative interviews more publicly.

A key moment in motivating this book was my response to a plenary speech by Craig Reynolds to the International Thai studies conference in London, July 1993. While in perfect agreement with the tone, the intention, and the scholarship of his argument on the absence of gender analysis in Thai studies, I was unpredictably upset by the event. My usual response to conference papers is frankly exploitative. I sit, pen in hand, listening, not only to gain a better understanding of the speaker's subject matter, but amoeba-like to surround, assimilate, and absorb an insight that will help me work my way out of impasses in my own thinking. Hearing Reynolds' presentation, I felt frustrated that although I had chewed for many years around the edges of gender questions, I had been unable to produce the grand narrative of the Thai gender system that he called for. As is not uncommon in women academics, I blamed myself for not having completed such a synthesis. Sometimes I doubted that there was one to write, that I was inventing a creature only to produce an interpretation of it. But such discouraging, reflexive thoughts usually follow a particularly unproductive day.

The problem for me is that over the years, Thailand has become more familiar but less comprehensible. After three decades in Thai studies, the initial contrasts through which Thailand took shape are becoming more difficult to see; I see shades of gray where I used to see black and white. My experiences of Thailand have been slipping out of their provinces of meaning with alarming frequency recently. And I am at a loss to explain why these slippages occur so much more rapidly when gender is at stake. I think it is because I have begun to listen to the silences. When you speak about what is best left unspoken, you meet opposition and polite antagonism from Thai colleagues – both men and women. First, the Thai colleagues who say, with disappointment, 'We thought you understood Thai society.' And second, your friends get sick, with nerves stretched too thin, headaches from thinking too much, and stomach problems (*pen lom*). For Thai women to speak of male double sexual standards when married to or working with Thai males is painful and inevitably confrontational. Western analysts just go home after researching their pieces, leaving Thai colleagues to face accusations of being man-hating Western feminists.

The longer I work in Thailand, the more I realize the depth of my ignorance and the shallowness of my earlier understanding of Thai reality – particularly when I spoke about Thai women or of gender relations. But my earlier shallow versions – both empirical and speculative – were better received by my Thai colleagues because I was treading on the surface where I belonged, where others had gone before to define the conceptual terrain. When writing of gender, the comfort of tolerance and familiar terrain is gone. Off that terrain, I now feel like an intruder – a voyeur – where I have never had that feeling before. Perhaps that is why my most recent fieldwork was in Lao PDR, passing through Bangkok to obtain a visa to enter another, very different Tai space.

Thailand, Thai studies and anthropology have changed over the past quarter century and, as glimpsed in my reflections of fieldwork in Thailand, so have I. The changes in my personal circumstances – from volunteer and graduate student to professor and consultant – influenced the way I have been treated, the access I have had to informants, and the way I observed gender relations. I am not alone in observing that my relationship with informants and my views on gender have changed over time. Caplan has documented the changing nature of her relationship with her informants over her years of field research in Tanzania (1989). Circumstances alter the questions brought to research. And circumstances alter how situations are written about.

Locality, discipline and experience in and of Thailand converge in the writing of texts. The different points of view developed above elaborate the same experiences but all have been reduced to text. I would like to have been able to broaden the sensorium, to move beyond the gaze which has been so central to interpreting Thai culture. Knowledge of Thailand is lodged in my senses – smell, taste, touch and sight – and my motor memory: the knowledge of when and how low to *wai*, to bend hands or body when greeting others,[8] for example. I literally developed a feel for Thailand, and can only imperfectly translate to words and text, a dilemma that is commonplace in anthropology. I try not to privilege text over senses as the only legitimate way of knowing about Thailand and gender. The challenge is to ensure that data of the senses can be linked directly to material conditions and the lived experience of Thai. In the case of smell you would have to imagine a 'scratch and sniff' insert offering the smell of incense, jasmine, open sewers and chillies hitting hot oil. Fieldwork is in fact the work of processing tactile, visual, olfactory and acoustic-verbal matter (Fabian 1991:104).

The task of reducing experience to text has not been easy. Body and mind resisted. Fabian comforts with his discussion of writing and 'non-writing' following his research in Zaire, commenting on his unwillingness or inability to 'write up' a particularly careful and productive long-term project. Perhaps my difficulty in turning this project into a single text was also

a sign of liberation from scientism and from a conception of writing as a sort of production line, running from 'raw data' through theoretical processing, to final monographic assembly . . . (Fabian 1991:221)

At least, I am not alone.

Locating Thailand in Southeast Asia

To speak of the high status of Southeast Asian women or gender complementarity requires comparison within the region and between regions. This comparison has not been done because most gender research in Southeast Asia has focussed on the islands rather than the mainland. War explains some of the disparities between the amount of gender research in mainland and island Southeast Asia. Lao PDR, Cambodia, Vietnam and to a lesser extent, Burma have been otherwise engaged in the last twenty years and expended what little resources that could be spared for foreign and domestic research to more applied projects. Bowen extends this argument to Thailand where he attributes the lack of symbolic emphasis in Thai studies to the need for applied work, '. . . due in part to the greater devastation wrought there by war and AIDS' (1995:1050). Nevertheless, this work assumes that Thai gender systems are variants of larger Southeast Asian patterns. Placing Thailand within this regional context helps avoid the Thai except-ionalism so prevalent in Thai studies. Below I suggest some possible relations between the Thai patterns and other regional patterns in Southeast Asia for future comparative research to explore.

Mainland and island Southeast Asia both saw the rise of Indic states in what are now the nations of Burma, Cambodia, Thailand and Indonesia; and all display remnants of a glorious Hindu Buddhist past for domestic and foreign tourists (Pagan in Burma; Angkor Wat in Cambodia; Borobudur in Indonesia, for example). More significant for understanding gender, future research might explore how the process of Indianization reconfigured gender relations in different localities. Perhaps, as O'Connor (1989) suggests, Indianization began the process of establishing unifying hierarchically organized courts that eclipsed local communities and values that were beneficial to women.

Thailand may usefully be compared to other Theravada Buddhist societies in the region: Burma, Lao PDR, and Cambodia. While general comparisons between practices and temple organization exist (Ling 1993, O'Connor 1993), gender differences have not been considered. Yet all share the same Buddhist principles, and valuable comparisons could be made on how these play out in the different Theravada societies of the mainland. Contrasts with Islam and Christianity in the archipelago are of less importance for understanding gender relations in Buddhist Southeast Asia or in Thailand. But the task of identifying layers of Islamic and Dutch colonial rule overlaying Indonesian gender ideology, layers of Christian missionizing and Spanish and American colonial rule overlaying Philippine gender ideology, and layers of Islamic and British colonial rule overlaying gender ideology in Malaysia is daunting. Once that task is accomplished, it will be possible to speak with more authority about the significance of Thailand's non-colonized status. Despite the differences between 'French assimilationist rhetoric, Dutch tolerance of intermarriage, and Britain's overtly segregationist stance' (Stoler 1991:90), colonized Southeast Asia developed different sets of racial and sexual categories than Thailand. In gender relations, as in other domains, Thailand had no colonial elite to set fashions but rather borrowed selectively for her own purposes, and not as part of an agenda of colonial powers. We have, then, no tradition of colonial scholarship on Thailand that examines gender relations comparable to the rest of Southeast Asia.

Figure 1 Honouring Mother Rice (*Mae Prasob*) with cosmetics and gifts fit for a pregnant woman, Suphanburi Province

A more valuable dimension of comparison concerns rice – a crop that feeds bodies and minds in both island and mainland communities. O'Connor (1995b) has proposed a model of agricultural change and ethnic succession in Southeast Asia that could be expanded to include gender relations. Everywhere, O'Connor argues, growing rice evokes gender. Women work in the fields to produce rice. In rice cropping systems, rice is feminine – a woman who nurtures and must be nurtured (J. Hanks 1964, Josselin de Jong 1965). When humans try to dominate and control Mother Rice, they fail; in fact humans and rice are inter-dependent, as are men and women. This complementarity underlies patterns of social organization, women's involvement in economic pursuits and gender relations in Thailand and elsewhere in Southeast Asia. For example, the dominant, lowland populations of the islands and mainland combined bilateral kinship with matrilocal residence, giving women access to subsistence and social resources, and often direct inheritance by youngest daughter.

Women's 'relatively high status' in Southeast Asia glosses autonomy in the home and economic control of resources. (H. Geertz 1961, Keeler 1987); wives often manage household finances (even among patrilineal Lisu in northern Thailand, Hutheesing 1990) and dominate retail trade (in Java, Brenner 1995:24; in Philippines, Milgram 1998). Other potent-ially valuable comparisons include the impact of the American military on the growth of prostitution in Thailand, Vietnam (Eisen 1984) and the Philippines (Sturdevant and Stoltzfus 1992), and the place of trans-vestite beauty contests in shaping the construction of femininity and masculinity in Thailand, Philippines (Johnson 1997), and Java (Oetomo 1996).

Mainland and island Southeast Asia have deep historical connections (cf. Coedes 1964, Wolters 1982), since both contain speakers of Auston-esian and Austroasiatic languages and both developed comparable agro-cultural complexes. However, work on gender models in island Southeast Asia has not been widely applied to the mainland. While island Southeast Asia opposed male and female in great cosmic dualisms and set clear boundaries between male and female domains, mainland Indianized states built more on models of gender hierarchy than gender complementarity. Nevertheless, Reid's suggestion that in Southeast Asia '. . . it was not thought necessary to create artificial markers of gender through dress, hairstyle, or speech patterns, none of which stressed the male-female distinction' (1988:162) applies as well to mainland as to island Southeast Asia. Across vast differences of geography, we find assumptions that males and females are essentially alike or easily transgendered.

Atkinson and Errington's important book, *Power and Difference: Gender and Power in Island Southeast Asia* (1990) opened with a quote from my book on *Women of Southeast Asia* (1982) on the high status of women from that area, a statement that I take much further in this book. Their book focussed only on Malaysia, Indonesia and the Philippines, and contrasted the 'Centrist Archipelago' (Malay Peninsula,[9] Borneo, Sulawesi, Philippines, Java and Bali) where gender is eclipsed by relative age and spiritual power as principles of social hierarchy, and the dualistically inclined Exchange Archipelago of Eastern Indonesia and Sumatra where male-female oppositions form a synthesis (Atkinson and Errington 1990:viii). The Centrist preoccupation with unity contrasts with the Eastern emphasis on duality and matched pairs. Both contrast with mainland tensions between local gender complementarity and state-imposed gender hierarchies. But comparison does not mean remaking the mainland to fit the island experience. This is particularly important for gender studies since more overarching theory has been developed for the islands.

Mulder has most consistently argued for the necessity of comparison and ultimately the shared principles that unite island and mainland Southeast Asia. His work in Thailand, Indonesia and the Philippines (1992) demonstrates the similarity of basic concepts that inform every-day life, including the pre-eminence of order legitimated by reference to the past, disorder as moral decay, submission to superiors (based on age, rank, or power), moral hierarchies, assumptions about the basic inequality of individuals, the importance of reputation (face), avoidance of interpersonal conflict, and power as something tangible and access-ible. He writes: 'Morally good is to behave according to station and place, true is the awareness of what creates harmony, in opposition to what is false, dissonant, and unwise. This results in the beauty of a smooth arrangement, a calm composition expressed in affable manners and the absence of stir' (Mulder 1996:45). These themes, so basic to understanding gender in Thailand, apply to all three areas.

Ong and Peletz's edited book, *Bewitching Women and Pious Men* (1995) included one paper on Thailand and one on Singapore along with studies from the islands. The papers explored the relation between symbolic meaning and specific historical, political and economic forces, including globalization. Ong and Peletz argue that previous works on this subject '. . . tend to map gender formations onto divisions of Southeast Asia into "mainland" versus "insular" regions, "upland" versus "lowland" groups, "matrilineal" versus "bilateral" systems of kinship, or "inner" versus "outer" islands' (1995:8). These oppositions dominated earlier work on Southeast Asia, and while they are not the only significant dimensions of contrast, they could still be usefully explored for gender implications. For example, very little work has been done following up on Leach's observations concerning hill/valley contrasts. In the hills, women have positions within lineage systems and create linkages between groups. In valley systems, women have individual statuses as separate individuals (elite commodities, perhaps because of their beauty) or as chattels. 'A Valley Prince receives women as tribute; a Hill chiefdom gives them out as pledges of economic co-operation' (Leach 1961:66). This contrast between customary and tyrannical authority keeps hill and valley separate but related. Leach did not explore the part that gender plays in this system of differences, but it remains an important contrast particularly for future research on gender in upland areas of mainland Southeast Asia (cf. Hutheesing 1990, Eberhardt 1988).

Whether the differences between mainland and island gender systems may be attributed to the nature of state systems, and to the expansion of the male role in statecraft and formal religion as Reid suggests (1988:163), or to differences in the basic subsistence crops as O'Connor proposes (1993), Thai gender studies have an important place in on-going research on Southeast Asian gender systems.

Limitations

Scharfstein writes:

> To understand a culture as fully as possible, we must be willing to sacrifice some of the intricacy, acknowledge the vagueness that we can never think away or research to the end . . . (Scharfstein 1989:168).

In this book I have sacrificed some of the complexities of class and ethnicity. Considerations of Thai gender are presented from the centre, by the centre rather than from the margins. While I am concerned with gender, my focal question concerns women and representation. Peletz reminds us that contemporary feminist anthropology focuses on women not gender, with the result that '. . . a singular focus on the voices or experiences of women – especially one that fails to examine how these voices and experiences articulate with those of men and with encompassing structures of power and prestige – runs the risk of essentializing "woman", and otherwise hindering the realization of feminists' intellectual and political agendas' (1995:79).

To the extent that my research succeeds in communicating something of the Thai condition, I would like the information to be potentially useful to people working to change the position and condition of women and others in Thai society, and to address significant economic and health problems. For Thai specialists, it provides another perspective to react to and critique. It is one of a possible set of theories about contemporary Thai gender, not *the* theory.

To attempt to make sense of the cultural context of gender in Thailand is a tall order, and one that I undertake with humility and trepidation. Thailand made me the anthropologist I am today. In return for the privilege of using Thai experiences in this way, I want to see Thai studies engage more directly in the making of anthropology. My analyses of the Thai gender system are those of an outsider and an academic, a privileged position in that I do not have to take the consequences of my writing as a Thai woman or a Thai citizen. While I have tried to recognize indigenous Thai scholarship and hope to avoid doing injustice, I claim the right as an anthropologist to add another perspective, to test my interpretations and critiques of Thai culture. I hope I will be able to translate something of Thai experiences to readers without guilt, appropriation, or pride.

> If, despite the possible advantages in studying alien traditions, we decide not to enter into the intellectual, religious, or esthetic lives that others have created, we make what is in effect a moral decision to go it alone. In declaring the lives and thoughts of some group of humans to be irrelevant to our own, to have so different a context that nothing intellectually useful can be recovered from them, we declare ourselves to be incorrigible strangers. This declaration of estrangement is by human nature also an implicit declaration of superiority . . . (Scharfstein 1989: 191).

Notes

1. This book does not explore the pragmatics of Thai activism. I have participated in or observed the development of gender training courses, poll watch activities, union organizing of factory workers, HIV/AIDS activism and breastfeeding promotion. Activists have the practical knowledge of rape crisis

centres, HIV/AIDS hotlines, fax networks on the environment, demonstrations. Here is lodged the cultures of resistance that will play an important role in refiguring gender relations in Thailand. It is a particular challenge to insure that this experience and knowledge is integrated into gender research in the future.

2. Tai is an ethnolinguistic term referring to groups of related peoples including the Lao and the Shan who reside both inside and outside Thailand and who speak related Tai languages.

3. For visitors to the resort town of Pattaya in 1996, for example, the costs were particularly high. 'Some 45 foreign visitors have died in unexplained circumstances over the past year' (*Economist* 1997:32).

4. Reynolds argues that Southeast Asia as a field of study is 'a Western postcolonial project' (1995: 437). But Thai studies has never been framed by a single dominant Euro-American agenda, and had no tradition of colonial scholarship comparable to that developed by the French for Indochina and the Dutch for Indonesia; no foreign philology studies developed around the Thai language. On the other hand Thailand never experience what Stoler calls '. . . the strident misogyny of imperial thinkers' (1991:52)

5. A revitalized area studies might develop from a strong sense of 'travelling place' where locality is not essentialized. Particular markers of Thainess – foods and textiles, for example – are portable but still deeply contextualized. Little Thailands in Los Angeles, Chicago, or Vancouver refer back to Thai identity within the nation state. These exotic Thai elements are not relocalized on a global scale with global claims (cf. Vitebsky 1995:110) because the global is always reabsorbed into an expansive definition of Thai material culture – VCRs, FAX machines, sweetened condensed milk. This capacity to absorb new items of material culture and new practices and make them local and personal protects Bangkok (and increasingly Thailand) from becoming what Vitebsky calls '. . . a huge, cosmopolitan Benetton soup in which nothing is local any longer' (1995:109).

6. Thai studies may not have shaped anthropology, but it certainly shaped me. My story is a double discourse of which only one voice is audible to the reader; but the second person who shared many of these experiences – my husband, John – is either beside me, watching, commenting, correcting or silenced with difficulty because I will persist with my view of reality and not his. In writing my story, I am mindful of the unfinished 'book in a box' under my desk, entitled 'Double Discourse' where I had set out to explore the relations between the ethnographic texts produced by professional anthropologists married to each other – the Hanks' and the Potters' in Thailand the Geertz' in Java, the Nagatas' in Malaysia, Mead and Bateson in Bali, and many other coupled and uncoupled texts. But tensions became too disturbing, and what

began as an interesting theoretical and methodological point quickly became too personally disruptive to continue. And so the comparisons must be left for others to make between what is mine, what is his, what is ours.

7. Two of the study sites, Thailand and Indonesia present interesting contrasts. The Javanese research team argued every step of the way – budget, ethnographic method, sampling frame – and then did exactly what they agreed to do. The Thai research team agreed to both research and administrative conditions, and then did exactly what they wanted to do.

8. *Wai* is the graceful Thai gesture of greeting and showing respect by placing raised palms together and bowing the head.

9. Malaysia is considered part of the Centrist archipelago, interpreted as part of island Southeast Asia, not mainland Southeast Asia.

two

Ordering the Past: Representations of Thai Women

Woman as Icon: Greetings from the Past

In the early 1970s in Bangkok, you could not find a Thai greeting card for love or money. Dusty Hallmark cards and special-purpose Thai cards for funerals, weddings, birthday and New Year's greetings with designs that looked Euro-American could be found in some department stores. By the late 1980s, beautiful cards with greetings in Thai and English could be found in bookstores, often produced in limited numbers by charitable organizations. Cards selling for around $1.00 (US) each featured Thai women in traditional dress, in muted colours against idyllic rural backgrounds.

In 1996, on the outskirts of the night market at Hua Hin, a resort city in southern Thailand, tourists and Thais swarmed around vendors, selecting cards from among dozens of garish and elegant designs, bargaining for four or more cards for $1.00 (US). And the images! Thai classical dancers with their graceful upturned fingers, portions of old mural paintings showing women engaged in household tasks, beautiful children with topknots, women musicians in classical dress playing antique instruments, women carving fruit and vegetables into floral shapes, women wearing different versions of Thai dress – shoulders bared, one shoulder bared, modest high-necked jackets with long skirts, in all shades of sensuous looking silk with gold and gilt embellishments. A veritable feast of delectable commodities. Even women farmers transplanting rice in their conical hats looked graceful and full of joy. Flowers, jewels and silk – the gendered accoutrements of Thai beauty.

The visual appeal of Thailand attracts the eye and subverts the gaze from prostitution, pollution, poverty, and traffic jams. Thailand appeals to tourists but the public culture that appeals is constructed for and by Thai. The cards are a reminder of how that public culture exoticizes and reifies Thailand's image to enhance the country's international reputation and tourist appeal. This chapter explores how a sense of order is constructed through representations of Thai women, using two metaphors for time – one from Thai etiquette (*kalatesa*) and one from English literature (palimpsest). I then contrast this with the pragmatics of the Thai women's movement, showing how a sense of order underlies both representations of the past and contemporary feminist practice.

Kalatesa: Negotiating the Intersection of Time and Space

Kalatesa is a Thai noun that means proper, suitable or balanced according to dictionary definitions, and politeness, appropriateness, or context according to Thai informants. It explains how events and persons come together appropriately in time and space. Knowing *kalatesa* results in orderliness in social relations, *khwam riaproy*.

Kalatesa is a significant guiding metaphor throughout this book because it draws attention to the importance of understanding surfaces, appearance, face, masks and disguise as parts of important cultural strategies of interaction. It provides a way to give agency to the social cosmetic and elevate it into a significant social form, and to define Thai context in a culturally meaningful way. Context, then, is covering the moment in a particular way, social cosmetic writ large. *Kalatesa* is a Thai concept of great antiquity constructed from Pali and Sanskrit roots. *Kala* (*kan*, Thai) is the formal term for time in general – the quality of time particularly expressed as recurrent cycles – in contrast to *wela*, which refers to measurable time such as day, hour, minute. *Kala* means proper time, fate or destiny. *Kala* refers to the kind of time that fortune tellers are interested in. *Tesa* refers to space, or locality and is part of the word, *Prathet Thai*, Thailand.

Kalatesa is very much linked to language. Speaking properly demonstrates one's knowledge of *kalatesa*. To speak properly shows respect and manners, and shows one knows how to address people according to their rank – when to use royal language, polite language, and when to shift to words stressing social equality and politeness, such as thank you, pardon me, please. This is knowledge that must have been shared beyond the bounds of the Bangkok court and regional courts, or status hierarchies would not have been so effectively maintained in the hinterland. That is, whether or not the Sanskrit terms were known or the royal language used in rural communities, *kalatesa* would be understood, perhaps understood through other systems of knowledge such as traditional medicine or astrology.

Kalatesa appears in the fourth century AD Sanskrit medical treatise, the corpus of Susruta (*Susrutasamhita*) where it refers to the need to fit medicinal cures to the birth date and locality of the patient. The Thai medical treatise, the Pharmacopoeia of King Narai, written around 1659–1661, specifies that a physician must be aware of the balance of the body elements of a patient in addition to the place of birth and current residence, the season of onset of the disease, and the age of the patient (Ratarasarn 1989:115). Time and space intersect to affect both diseases and cures, and to maintain health.

Intersections of time and space – co-occurrences – are also communicated in performative terms through ritual, or mythopraxis, where cosmology meets pragmatics at a critical historical conjuncture (Ohnuki-Tierney 1990:9). Rural farmers' sense of temporality is more in tune with seasonal changes, and soil and water conditions than court systems of etiquette. Nevertheless, the interdependence between rural and royal is enacted in ritual. The royal ploughing ceremony in Bangkok which brought together the forces of Brahmanical power to mark the moment for first ploughing was discontinued after the revolutionary coup of 1932 and only reinstated in 1960. In a conversation in the 1970s, a successful farmer in a village near Uthong, Suphanburi Province, attributed his dependable rice crops to the royal ploughing ceremony which he assumed had been continuing during the period in question. To him, the success of his local ritual propitiating the guardian spirit of his rice field depended on the successful enactment of the royal ritual in Bangkok. As Hanks noted for Bang Chan:

> . . . this simple ceremony without the preceding royal ploughing ritual at the capital may well be ineffectual. The king . . . addresses higher beings in the hierarchy of gods and angels . . . With word passed down from on high, the many local guardians are prepared to assist in every valley and backwater. (1972:78)

There are thus many routes for interpreting *kalatesa* outside the royal centres.

Kalatesa is embedded in a complex astrological tradition operating in court and village settings for hundreds of years, although today interest in astrology is considered to be highest among educated, urban middle class and lowest among farmers and the urban poor (Cook

1991:237). Knowing what is ahead allows graceful acceptance of fate. Astrology is another way to characterize the relation between past, present, and future. Cook writes that 'destiny is identity manifested over time' (1991:234). History demonstrates the destiny of a nation, just as individual horoscopes provide a basis for individual identity.

Details about the quality of time, the intersections of personal time calculated from moment of birth, and planetary configurations are not limited to ritual specialists in royal or village contexts. Knowledge of conjunctures in time is not inaccessible esoteric knowledge but widely shared among literate villagers through easily accessible books such as *Promelikit Chabap Luang* (Brahma's 'destiny', royal style). The widespread distribution of knowledge of such 'level-one calendrical expertise motivates the need for elite calendrical experts to provide authoritative advice on avoiding mistakes' (Gell 1992:77). Thus, literary skills have not eliminated the need for astrologers.[1]

Children are taught from birth to recognize *kalatesa*, lest they *phit kalastesa* (make an error in *kalatesa*). But in my experience the concept is rarely talked about or written about, except to correct children. It is so deeply taken for granted among Thais that I knew the concept years before I learned the word. In the 1980s, a popular song called *kalatesa* reminded teenaged listeners about what they should say, how they should behave '. . . life is about learning right and wrong, understanding *kalatesa.*'[2] But now Thai friends complain that fewer young people know *kalatesa* and so there have to be books written about it. Thai high school textbooks identify the abandonment of foundations of morality and good manners as sources of Thai social problems. Mulder found that up to 75 percent of school time goes to the teaching of morality, good manners and conduct, and state ideology (1996:56), in addition to hygiene classes that teach elegant and graceful comportment (1999:306). Similarly, Phibun Songkhram, Prime Minister from 1938–1944 and from 1948–1957, made use of social etiquette and external appearances as the basis for his new definition of Thainess, one that conformed to his understanding of what Euro-Americans defined as civilized, modern, progressive yet distinctively Thai, and one that would strengthen Thai nationalism. As Phibun explained to the Minister of Education in 1942, 'The exhibition of high culture by the people is one sure way of maintaining the sovereignty of the nation' (Suwannathat-Pian 1995:111). This desirable form of culture could be achieved by cultivating 'proper social etiquette and mannerisms' so that 'Thai etiquette' would be renowned and respected worldwide (Suwannathat-Pian 1995:112, 117). He explicitly acknowledged the importance of both interior and exterior or surface appearances as aspects of Thainess. Phibun's manipulation of these surface appearances to create a sense of order draws attention to the chaos and disorder raging in Thailand following the 1932 coup. His passion for order is discussed in more detail in Chapter 4.

Kalatesa is very much concerned with surfaces, with appearances, but in Thai society these surfaces matter. Knowledge of *kalatesa* is expressed through dress, language, and manner. Certain choices are appropriate, like wearing bright clothes at weddings but modest black clothes at funerals. Guidelines for appropriate behavior at funerals, weddings, and official functions were specified by the Phibun government in announcements and regulations (Suwannathat-Pian 1995:117). Topics of conversation must also suit the time and place, such as appropriate conversation topics for meals, for mixed company. One must not talk about things that will upset others. If you overhear a personal conversation you should withdraw. You were in the wrong space and time. Surely this is equally true in polite Canadian settings. 'Yes', said my Thai friend, 'but in Thailand the lapses (*phit kalatesa*) matter more.' Someone who violates *kalatesa* loses face and respect (*barami*). A person could be open and friendly in conversation, but still have to consider *kalatesa*. Knowledge of *kalatesa* stops a young professor from arguing with a senior professor. *Krengchai*, the feeling of embarrassment in the presence of powerful people, is the feeling that arises when you have violated *kalatesa*. If you have knowledge of *kalatesa* and a full understanding of context, including knowledge about the people you will be interacting with, then you will not feel embarrassment or discomfort, will not feel *krengchai*, and will be less likely to *phit kalatesa*. Yet many occasions for these mistakes concern foreigners because the status of foreigners within Thai social organization was and is ambiguous.[3]

Thais socialize themselves, their children and their visitors to develop contextual sensitivity; that is, what a person knows about the world plus the context within which this knowledge is to be elicited (Gell 1992:109). Like a child, a newcomer or a tourist is not expected to know *kalatesa* beyond rules defined by the state such as dress codes for entering temples. Hence, the acceptability of and tolerance for the newcomer, the tourist, over the more experienced person who is expected to know *kalatesa* and whose violations are noted with disapproval. But even after many years in Thailand, one seldom knows when boundaries are crossed, when one has *phit kalatesa*, only that the coming together of time and space and relationships is not quite right, that either the knowledge of contexts or persons was incomplete or inaccurate. (Or you refuse to operate within the system of *kalatesa*, refuse to test your understandings, and take refuge in being an ignorant foreigner; or for Thai nationals, leave the country.)

Kalatesa is not identical to the English meaning of context (although several Thai informants translated *kalatesa* as context) as it does not refer to a broad, static framing for text or practice, but to the coming together of immediate circumstances in time and space in a certain fashion. As when looking through a kaleidoscope, certain things come into a relation all at once, or not at all, relations in such delicate juxtaposition that a slight shift in time or space alters the experience. The quality of the moment has changed. Geertz (1966) captured this quality in his discussions of time and person in Bali, although his formulations have been critiqued for understating the practical, political uses of time measurement and overstating the rule-governed ritual uses (Gell 1992).

Time and space come together to order appropriate social interaction in varying contexts depending on the social position of the actors and on their individual characteristics – *kalatesa*. But time and space also come together to govern another set of activities – festivals (*tesakan*, space/time). Here, time and space are specially marked in celebration – as a cultural time out – another way to understand context, but one not explored here.

Kalatesa in the sense of articulating formal written rules for correct behavior is probably quite recent and court based. It may have been an important means of social control. For example, rural peasants and urban poor would have to exhibit knowledge of *kalatesa* in order to interact effectively with government officials. While the very poor and the nobility might have opportunities to resist *kalatesa*, the middle class and Sino-Thai had more to gain from cultivating *kalatesa*. *Kalatesa* is now part of a middle-class Bangkok expression of order (*riaproy*), a middle-class imitation of royal style.[4] It must also vary by ethnicity and region; what is *phit kalatesa* in one area of the country might be acceptable in another. Thus *kalatesa* highlights regional, ethnic and class differences as well as gender.

Kalatesa is not in itself gendered, and acts to control the behavior of males as well as females. But it appears more relevant to females as it was communicated through the elite expectations of court women. Why are women held to different standards of *kalatesa*? The Western answer might be the subordination of women. The Thai answer might be that it takes skill, knowledge, talent and ability to use *kalatesa* rules appropriately, and women have that knowledge. Further, women have a greater stake in using rules well. But *kalatesa* operated to ensure that women had few means of escaping from the structural constraints of Thai society. Women were less able to 'escape to the forest', find refuge in a monastery, or practise other patterns of withdrawal, avoidance and escape that characterized Thai individualism.

Men have to conform to *kalatesa* as well in order to fit into a social hierarchy. They, too, are judged on appearance, and rely on patrons; but they also have other means to assert their identities, including access to the *nakleng* (thug) role. It is possible that Thai women's knowledge of *kalatesa* has been mistaken for subordination, particularly by Euro-American analysts.

Kalatesa may be thought of as a court-based model of gender relations layered over the more egalitarian gender system operating at the village level where women's efficiency, efficacy and power counted for more than her adherence to gender-based etiquette. But these are questions to be answered by ethnographic fieldwork on the relation between various Tai systems of gender and the royal style of how to be male or female – questions which will be opened up by working with the Thai concept of *kalatesa* in conjunction with historical frameworks.

Palimpsests: Unfolding the Past

In Southeast Asia, ideologies and meanings of each new age are always engaged in a dialogue with earlier ideologies, before the process of legitimation is complete (McKinley 1979:307, 308). Past ideologies reoccur and influence later ideologies by adding layers of new meanings, new interpretations which then become commentaries on these changes. So, too, with material objects (cf. P. Van Esterik 1984) and represent-ations, both visual and textual. Images of women of the past reappear in the present. I refer to these layers of images and meanings as palimp-sests. The term palimpsest refers to parchment or slate from which old writing has been erased to make room for new writing. The act of writing over an earlier draft version of something that has been wiped out suggests that the original version has disappeared. But palimpsests are never completely erased. Consideration of the long, narrow Thai palmleaf manuscripts and the illustrated manuscripts made of one continuous sheet of paper folded or fastened accordion-style suggests a further elaboration about what was written before, what underlies the most recent version. Beneath the stylized painted figures can the faint outlines of the earlier draft still be discerned? Faint images from the past may be read as distortions when viewed in contrast to more recent versions. I find this image intriguing because it suggests layers of representations from the past that have never been completely erased – inscriptions and representations that can be read, however faintly and incompletely, even in the latest, most contemporary versions. Palimpsest captures both embeddedness and the idea of the 'unfolding' of social time, the synchronicity of past and present. Literally 'thick descriptions' of the past leach into the present.

Folded palmleaf manuscripts provide two visual metaphors for this layering. The first refers to the unfolding of the manuscript in such a way that a viewer can see portions from all the leaves at the same time, like a fan incompletely opened. The second, the palimpsest proper, refers to the actual and potential drafts that have been incompletely erased in inscribing each new leaf. The first meaning evokes simultaneous representations and a plurality of images within an essentially unitary, connected construction presupposing some widely understood fundamental axioms which may be either accepted or resisted (or both). Palimpsests allow us to see '. . . cracks through which the past creeps up on modern society' (Fabian 1991:223).

To explore the second meaning, consider that the pages of palmleaf manuscripts contain both writings and drawings. Palimpsest manuscripts might reveal past inscriptions in a number of ways. First, letters, words or small pieces of the earlier version might be clearly visible, incompletely erased by later inscribers. Second, the background colour might have been so strong in earlier versions that it permeates the new text. Third, some letters, lines or features might have been copied over and over again so often that their imprints in the new version become stronger through time. Fourth, earlier representations may have been completely erased, so totally rubbed out that their absence and vigorous erasure is notable in later versions. This second approach to layering may reinforce the first, more holistic meaning of layering by confirming the consistent style of representation over time, by 'fanning' through the overwritten, the erasures, the new drafts and the later corrections. These underlying images predispose one reading over another. Conditions of society at any one time are products of conditions and meanings that have gone before, and predispose one reading over another, relegating other meanings to background.

Palimpsest is the textual equivalent of the art historian's pentimento. When painters change their minds and alter something in their pictures, the old form may begin to show through in a ghostly way. The 'ghost' suggests to some that the painting must be an original, since it shows artists changing their minds and painting over a prior image.

Murals on Thai temples are also painted over, a reminder of the impermanence and deterioration of all material things. As in Wyatt's study of a temple in Nan (1994), what is painted on a wall complements what is written in a text. Thus, past voices and images are heard but not necessarily in the chronological order in which they were spoken/ inscribed. Instead we selectively attend to what we wish to hear and see of the past. Many past representations contradict official history, official texts, official voices. But this does not necessarily mean that they become voices of resistance. Only that their power to sway is context sensitive, context dependent. Further, people's own experience guides them to what models of the past should be validated and represented in the present moment.

Palimpsest and pentimento are visual reminders to consider the potential for reverse or alternative representations. The metaphorical use of objects like palm leaf manuscripts and temple paintings is consistent with Thai modelling of the past in concrete and visible forms, as will be discussed further in Chapter 4.

Historical Representations of Thai Women

The metaphors of palimpsest and *kalatesa* help explicate gender representations of Thai women. Much of the recent writing on Thai women - my own included - reads like a collage of perpetual presents, overlaid by occasional references to figures of the past. How can these remnants of meaning that surface and resurface in discussions of Thai women be used without constructing gender as pastiche, romanticizing the past or idealizing mythical heroines?

Representations of contemporary Thai women reflect selected and invented historical and literary pasts. What strikes visitors to Thailand from the first foreigners recording their impressions of the kingdom in the seventeenth century to the diaries of current tourists is the visibility of Thai women. De La Loubère writes of Ayutthaya, ' the wives of the people, managing all the trade, do enjoy perfect liberty' (1697/ 1969:76). These observations and oft told myths from Thai history reinforce the assumption that 'women in Thai society are better off than in many other societies' (Vichit-Vadakan 1994:519). Historical overviews on Thai women stress that women and men were legally equal in the Kingdom of Sukhothai (Boonsue 1998:6). Nang Noppamat, alleged consort of King Ramkamheng, the warrior-king of thirteenth-century Sukhothai, is credited with developing rituals such as *Loy Krathong* which glorify women's beauty and desirability. Gender equality is a valued part of the myth of the golden age of Sukhothai to be discussed further in Chapter 5. In this view, feudal Ayutthaya destroyed the traditional rights of Thai women by codifying Khmer hierarchical laws and imposing them over Sukhothai egalitarianism. Other models downplay the existence and extent of both gender subordination and slavery in the Ayutthaya period and earlier. Bowie (1994) has critiqued casual approaches to slavery such as the following: 'For centuries, Thai peasantry enjoyed a relatively free and easy life in social interaction, although they suffered from poverty and slavery' (Tantiwiramanond and Pandey 1991:15), arguing that slavery and gender inequities did not fit well with Thai romantic views of their past. Examples of cultural intimacy such as prostration, polygamy, prostitution and slavery were all sources of external embarassment that might draw the disapproval of powerful outsiders (cf. Herzfeld 1997).

Among the images of women in Thailand's past as war captives, tribute wives or concubines, are the warriors: Queen Srisuriyothai of Ayutthaya (1548–1569) who fought against the Burmese; Khunying (Lady) Muk and Khunying Jan (1785) who also fought against the Burmese; Khunying Mo who saved Nakhon Ratchatchasima from the Lao army during the reign of King Rama III; Queen Chamadevi of Lanna who counted menstrual blood among her weapons (cf. Morris 1994a). Feats of bravery by individual women – especially royal women – stimulated the incorporation of these stories of powerful, militarily dominant women into Thailand's official historical narrative.

While the stories of powerful Thai women reveal something about the building of the narrative of national identity, they can also reveal the state's 'deepest paranoias of sovereignty and control' (Appadurai 1996:190). For example, the Thai woman historian who dared to suggest that the commemorative statue of Khunying Mo might be as much about confirming the locality's loyalty to the state following an abortive coup as glorifying a local heroine was accused of treason. Keyes locates the conflict in the attempts to situate Khunying Mo in two distinct and conflicting national narratives, Lao and Thai (1996).

Both heroines from the past – Khunying Mo and Queen Chamadevi – reappear in the present through their mediums, transcending their positions in time and space and collapsing the palimpsest or folding it back on itself. As spirits, these historical figures can intervene in the lives of contemporary men and women. It is overwhelmingly women, or men who appropriate femaleness through transgenderism (Morris 1994a:52) who access the power of the past through mediumship.

Metaphors move thoughts in a particular direction and are often captured in proverbs and songs. Images of powerful women from the past are perpetuated in proverbs about women's ability to wield a sword as well as rock a cradle. But they coexist with a more commonly cited proverb: 'Men are the front legs of the elephant: women are the hind legs of the elephant', cited to demonstrate Thai women's subordinate position or the complementarity of men and women, depending on the feminist politics of the speaker. But, as Srisambhand and Gordon (1987:14) point out, the elephant's hind legs are the first to move.

Another proverb often cited to demonstrate the position of women in Thailand – 'Man is human, woman is buffalo' – certainly looks bad for the buffalo/woman. On questioning Thai specialists on the meaning of this proverb, it was pointed out that while humans are open to illusion, buffaloes are hardworking and reliable. Key to interpreting meaning, however, requires more analysis of context, how and why the proverbs are cited.

Literary and Artistic Discourses

The dominant artistic and literary discourses on Thai women are both illuminating and paradoxical. Gender representation in the arts is not isomorphic with women's participation in society or to gender relations in everyday life. However, there are powerful linkages between artistic and literary images of women and the uses to which gendered images are put. In fact, the arts are where gender boundaries are most often questioned, and in the case of Thailand, blurred or reversed. In the Thai visual and dramatic arts, the feminine is glorified and not devalued; male robustness is not as aesthetically central as it is in Euro-American arts.

According to a leading Thai literary critic (Nagavajara 1994a), Thai literature expresses feelings as well as ideas, and requires synaesthetic appreciation to an extent that renders it inaccessible to all but the most skilled foreigners who know how to listen and imagine 'in Thai'. Literature has the capacity to delight, but this delight is heightened by sharing. Thus, the conviviality of performance is a critically important part of the oral tradition. Performers and audiences must come together in time and space, sharing interaction time.

Many Thai literary works were burned in the fall of Ayutthaya to the Burmese in 1767. Restoration was made through oral literature and memory (Nagavajara 1994a:32). While the early Bangkok kings tried to replenish the stock by composing and commissioning new literary works, they also selected and revised to suit the political task of cultural consolidation. Thus, current accounts of historical Thai literature reflect the biases of the elite males who salvaged the past, not the historical moments of creation and performance. The palimpsest of Thai literature reveals these biases as they permeate subsequent layers to reach contemporary viewers/readers.

Thailand's classical literary tradition was very much an elite discourse, extolling the virtues of the good, dutiful woman who exemplified grace, beauty and self control. Perfect control and order in the palace reinforces the image that the court rules over a peaceful, legitimate and properly constituted Buddhist polity. Thai dance-dramas, narrative poetry, puppet shows and other performative and literary expressions emphasize the oppositions between refined centre and coarse periphery, beauty and beast, royalty and commoner, divine and demonic. (The democracy protests of 1992 also pitted 'angels' against 'devils', and I elaborate on this opposition in Chapter 5). Interest in such oppositions is maintained through the endless plays on disguise and deception of surface appearances. Women very much participate in this play, representing both the refined and the coarse, and all stages of appearances between. The theme of transformation and disguise reverberates through Thai artistic representations. An ogress queen, ugly, with long teeth is transformed by a magic bath into a beautiful girl of seventeen – the only fitting wife of a king (Jumsai 1973). Women mimic the golden court image of the palace in contemporary performances such as *lakhon chatri* (dance-drama), where appearances' deceptions may be played out complete with fake Rolex watches (Grow 1996).

Classical Thai literature also services the Buddhist *dhamma* and is didactic in form. Representations of women in literature and theatre exemplify obedient sacrifice: do good, maintain morality, uphold truth. This didactic literature defines expectations for women in Thai society – the expectation that women should remain virgins until marriage, serve their husbands faithfully, keep house, and work longer and harder than their husbands. In the literary and artistic traditions can be found one source of the oppositional thinking dominating gender debates in Thailand today, the opposition between women as beautiful temptresses and women as dutiful wives and mothers.

Literary discourses reveal glimpses of *kalatesa* in the *rabiab* (neat) consciousness emerging from the court tradition of Bangkok. Elite women were trained through literature and drama to be as virtuous as Sita, Rama's wife in the Ramayana epic. Patriarchal controls emanating from courts and palaces and replicated in popular genres such as *lakhon chatri* and *lakhon chakchak wongwong* (televised folktales) glorified women's subservience. The Thai court trained women in the palace to crouch, crawl, sit, stand and walk appropriately, to be good, tidy women, 'flowers for bees to suck honey from', and co-incidentally to be polite, obedient servants for the rich and powerful.

Suphasit Son Ying (Words of Wisdom for Women) was written around 1837–1840 by the poet, Sunthon Phu, in the reign of Rama III, and was used for decades as a school text for Thai students. Pongsapich points out that the writings of Sunthon Phu '. . . reflect not only the world view of the writer at the time he was writing, but also a world view he unintentionally contributed to shaping' (1986:24). This text provides advice to young women on the wifely virtues. The values of virginity and 'composing' one's appearance are discussed in the sections on marriage and beauty in later chapters. While Sunthorn Phu's poetic advice to women sounds quaintly achronistic and irrelevant to the lives of modern Thai women, in 1968 a Bangkok women's club called the Safety Pin Club laid down ten oaths for women, including the second that admonished women to 'try as much as possible to be gentle, sweet and beautiful' (Rutnin 1988:103). The palimpsest has been incompletely erased.

Similarly, Javanese didactic literature from the mid-1800s written in 'intimidating male voices' instructs elite women on the wifely virtues of how to be pleasing and submissive to their husbands (Florida 1996: 210). As in Thailand, this male fantasy contradicts the prevailing gender relations in nineteenth-century Java.

Novelists of this century continued the didactic tradition, writing about women's lives as exemplars of virtue and sacrifice. Rutnin identifies Kunjara Debyasuvan who wrote under the pen-name, *Dok Mai Sot* (fresh flower), as the first influential Thai woman writer. Writing in the late 1920s, she stressed sexual equality, the professional competence of Thai women, and their special commitments to a sense of excellence, while her older half sister, Boonlua glorified the gentle, obedient *phuu dii* (people of quality, dignity, and propriety) whose lives exemplified knowledge of *kalatesa*. *Dok Mai Sot* criticized polygamy in her writings, pointing out that while the rich can afford two wives, poor men can live off two wives. It falls to middle-class Thai men, 'who are either too morality-conscious or unable to support more than one wife, or westernized in this aspect', to develop a model of Thai monogamous marriage (Rutnin 1988:113). *Dok Mai Sot* develops strong, well-educated women characters who experience conflict with the Thai system (Rutnin 1988:32). Men with many wives and mistresses are presented in novels as demonstrating power (*barami*), a theme reverberating through contemporary defenses of polygamy and prostitution.

After the Second World War, the lessons taught through the arts included those of social justice and equality. Literature emerged as radical discourse in the work of Jit Phumisak (1930–1966) and others. His work interpreted Thai literature as a product of a corrupt and oppressive autocratic ruling class, and critiqued the 'incurable sexual obsessions' of elite men (Nagavajara 1985:70). For this reason, Jit and other radical writers argued against the use of classical Thai texts in schools because of their outdated feudal content and lack of relevance to the lives of young people (Harrison 1994:28).

Harrison (1994) points out that the literary oppositions of good and evil in classical Thai literature are reproduced in the 'literature for life' fiction of the 1970s where evil capitalists face virtuous peasants. The 'literature for life' fiction expressed more socially progressive ideas. Thai women writers seeking 'social equality and freedom' strove to liberate women 'from the framework of tradition' (Rutnin 1988:114). Yet Thai 'tradition', particularly regional traditions, contains powerful female figures, in addition to the delicate flowers of the palace.

Women characters are often strong and complex in the classical Thai literature, unlike the characters in more contemporary fiction where women are portrayed as vain and dumb, as in the stories in *In the Mirror* (Anderson and Mendiones 1985). Female figures in classical narrative poetry are heroines representing the ideal woman who may be forced by circumstances to act against their ideal nature. Yet many are depicted as men's equals, actively involved in the complexities of life and plot. The heroine, Wanthong in the popular epic poem, *Khun Chang, Khun Phaen* is the prototype of the fickle woman, powerless to determine her fate, commanded by men. Yet elements of Wanthong's life are visible palimpsests in contemporary films and television shows. These elements include: '1) a woman's consciousness of the misery she experiences and feels as the natural and inescapable result of being born female; 2) her desire to please everyone she loves, often to her own detriment; and 3) her frank acceptance of her own beauty and of its negative effects on her life' (Kepner 1996:7).

The literary images of women expressed in classical Thai literature represent elite, *phuu dii* images of women applicable to the cities and royal courts, and not to the traditions of the periphery which sustained an oral tradition filled with feisty, powerful women who were men's equals. For example, one of the most striking forms of oral performances in rural areas of northeast Thailand were the poetry 'contests' as courting dialogue between men and women. Compton writes that the work of the oral poets or *mohlam* in northeast Thailand and Laos '. . . is a cultural group's way of playing with sound and presenting feelings and ideas in language that is attractive to the listener's ears or the reader's eyes' (Compton 1992:231). Both men and women were adept at improvisation, verbal play and punning, often with racy content. The mural paintings from northeast Thailand surveyed by Pairote Samosorn (1989) confirm this eroticism, as paintings from pages 218 to 223 illustrate copulating elephants and monkeys and birds displaying womanly breasts and genitals; seductions 'in broad daylight'; women with skirts open to their upper thighs; and a grinning couple described as 'courting', with his hands on her breasts and her hands holding his erect penis. So much for the demure *phuu dii* and didactic moral tales of the palaces.

Representations of women emanating from the court and propagated by the *phuu dii* of the last century are not the only representations of women flooding the newsstands and television channels today. In addition to advertisements and Western situation comedies dubbed in Thai (including 'Bewitched' and 'Leave it to Beaver'), Thai folktales remain popular on television, as generations of children and adults in both rural and urban communities are exposed to the adventures of polygynous princes and their wily wives. These televised folktales emphasize the conflict between co-wives, and between father-in-law and son-in-law. A common but totally unrealistic theme is the compassionate co-wife who keeps the two quarrelsome co-wives in line. Wajuppa notes that some Thai women themselves still indulge in the world of traditional fairy tales (1992:13). Current television programming refers back to these classical images, the glorious, golden romantic era somewhere between the ancient kingdom of Ayutthaya and nothing that ever existed on Thai soil. These historical soap operas represent nostalgia for an idealized past, the way things ought to be, palimpsests of extraordinary tenacity, providing glimpses of significant gender imagery persisting in the discourses of the contemporary Thai women's movement.

The Thai Women's Movement

Gender categories, representations and metaphors are not the stuff of Thai women's praxis, nor do they motivate the Thai women's movement. Women's groups address problems such as prostitution, sex tourism and HIV/AIDS. In Thailand, there is no strong tradition of women's protests or nationalist struggles for independence. Early efforts to form women's groups and raise women's issues (1855–1935), resulted primarily in welfare activities (Pongsapich 1986:1), elite women giving charity to their less fortunate sisters. Before the end of the absolute monarchy in 1932, elite Bangkok women carried out voluntary activities to promote national security and welfare under the sponsorship of the Queen, as groups like the Thai Red Cross do today. For a brief period before 1932, there was a flurry of demands from well-educated middle-class women who called for equality and educational opportunities for women, criticized patriarchy and polygamy, and argued their case in a series of women's magazines and newspapers including, *Kulsatri* (1906), *Satri Niphon* (1914), *Satrisap* (1922), and *Ying Thai* (1932) (Barmé 1995). These women activists formed the first private voluntary women's organization, the Thai Women's Association of Thailand, still existing today (Tantiwiramanond and Pandey 1991:27). While there was discursive space for these women's voices, they were not heard over the nationalist appeals of the 1932 coup when the needs of the country for constitutional democracy outweighed the needs of Thai women for equality.

The current wave of interest in 'women's problems' emerged as part of the democratic movement of the mid-1970s (1973–6). During this period, the Women's Status Promotion Group was formed. However, the democracy movement was by no means an outpouring of support for women or a recognition of gender imbalances in Thai society. Student activism was stronger than gender activism. In the student protests of 1973 and later protests, women students often lead the marches carrying pictures of the royal family. They took part in student demonstrations and suffered the consequences – death, imprisonment, and assault. But they did not bring gender activism to the forefront of radical politics.

In the climate of political reform between 1973 and 1976, women's studies and gender issues became more prominent.[5] Women's issues were therefore included in the fourth five-year development plan as part of human resource development (1977–81), but it was not until the fifth and sixth plans (1982–91) that specific groups of women were targeted to be beneficiaries of government services, partly in recognition of the UN Decade for Women (1975–85). Both the fifth plan and the twenty-year Long Term Women's Development Plan (1982–2001) drew attention to poor women in the country's poorest provinces, particularly those in agriculture, and also targeted groups such as Buddhist nuns and women in prisons. By the sixth plan (1987–91), women were no longer considered as a separate target group although attention returned to population control. The seventh plan (1992–7) includes women's issues as an annex based on existing long-term development plans for women, and adds a focus on women and development (Tantiwiram-anond and Pandey 1991, Boonsue 1992).

Thai women and indeed the Thai Women's Movement embraced the linkages between women and development, and later gender and development with enthusiasm. But in this embrace lie the seeds of co-optation and comfort with management logic. Ferguson reminds us about a problem with adopting gender and development language and concepts: '. . . to be firmly located in the public realm . . . is to be embedded within bureaucratic discourse' (1984:23). Her work contrasts feminist discourse with bureaucratic discourse. With the involvement of large-scale development assistance projects, Thai women's groups have been drawn into this bureaucratic discourse, developing projects, training courses, and gender analysis seminars with the assistance of foreign aid money, much of it Canadian.

Thai grass roots women's groups are often at a disadvantage in international forums because English is irrelevant for most rural Thai women. Standards of English teaching in the rural areas are low because the language is used only by those few who have direct need to interact with English speakers. Generally, one or two women who have acquired these skills are chosen to represent all rural Thai women. Even with some knowledge of English or interpreters, rural women may have difficulty participating in international forums because of their dis-comfort with Western-style argumentation. While urban women's groups diversified and proliferated, traditional collective action by rural women has been declining (Tantiwiramanond and Pandey 1991:31), a reminder of the importance of urban/rural differences as well as class and gender in understanding women's collective action.

Progressive women's NGOs were not developed until the 1980s. Friends of Women (1980), Women's Information Center (1984), and EMPOWER (1986) were all influenced by the international feminist movement (Tantiwiramanond and Pandey 1991:31), although they address Thai concerns and operate according to Thai standards of practice. NGOs, including women's groups are viewed as threatening by the government and must be registered. Groups like EMPOWER that form around specific concerns such as prostitution tend to keep their mandates narrow and select their venues of confrontation with care. Yet they have the flexibility to respond to new issues such as HIV/AIDS. Thai women's groups are considered more Western than other NGOs because of their presumed relation with Western feminism.

Thai Women's groups have participated in international women's organizations with enthusiasm, participating in Thai branches of Zonta (1971), Soroptimist (1974), Business and Professional Women's Association (1964), and Promoting Business for Women Association (1974), sending Thai delegates to UN women's conferences, and participating actively in field trips within Asia and elsewhere, particularly those connected with business and commerce. Their diplomatic and courteous demeanours make Thai leaders of women's groups – particularly elite women's groups – ideal candidates for participating in international forums. The head of the Asia/Pacific Regional planning committee for the Conference for Women in Beijing and the head of the NGO forum were both Thai women.

Women's Studies emerged out of women's movements as feminism's 'academic arm'. In Thailand, women's studies as an academic discipline is in its infancy, and exactly how women's studies will fit into the Thai university curricula is far from clear. It is difficult to develop the content for undergraduate courses on women's studies when only a few professors see the need for the subject matter. In the absence of student demand or supportive administrations, changes in the curriculum will be accomplished only very slowly. Nevertheless, Chulalongkorn University, Thammasat University, Khon Kaen University, Chiang Mai University, and Prince of Songkla University, among others, have research, teaching or outreach programs on gender or women's issues. While English language materials on feminist theory, and topics such as women's health, women and the environment, women's work and violence against women are available in the various university resource centres around the country, they are seldom used by Thai academics, and are of little use for addressing the pragmatic concerns of Thai women's groups. Instead, women's groups are always trying to mobilize funds and obtain office space, computers, telephones, fax machines and photocopiers, non-trivial resources when considered against academic or civil service salaries. However, the impact of Thai women's groups on skills training for women and on increasing public awareness of women's problems is considerably greater than their limited numbers would suggest.

.From the perspective of an outsider who had occasion to participate in many meetings with women's groups in the late 1980s and early 1990s,[6] groups appear to be strongly divided by class, yet deeply interconnected by personal linkages. One woman may wear many different hats as academic, activist, government consultant, with several different women's groups. Their effectiveness is enhanced by the density of activist networks, and the personal interconnections between activists, academics, researchers and particular individuals in government.

The avoidance of conflict is of primary importance in women's groups; if conflict develops, then new groups form around the factions, multiplying the number of groups and agendas. *Kalatesa* provides the code for smoothing over differences across class, ethnicity, age and interests. Mechanisms for the smooth functioning of groups are well developed and important parts of the Thai cultural repertoire. In the context of seminars, workshops, evaluation meetings, and even budget negotiations, the needs of individuals are adjusted to meet the needs of the group, with adherence to superficial form and appearance more important than content. Through almost ritualized behavior – opening and closing ceremonies with high-ranking guests, positioning the symbols of national identity (usually a Buddha image, flag and photographs of the royal family), the placement of documents, tastefully served snacks, the fluidity of social interaction is guaranteed, and participants surrender to the immediate context shaped by the objectives of the meeting. How strange it felt to sit in a seminar discussing the possible class implications of urban occupations for women while university servants crouched low beside the professors' chairs distributing cups of tea and snacks. The sloppy eating of foreigners damages the conduct of group work as much as the failure to address contradictions in gender policies. This I learned when I overheard others mention my participation in the meeting, and found my awkward attempts to fish excessive sugar out of my coffee made a more lasting impression than the issues I tried to raise about class differences and gender.

A range of Thai women's groups work together by virtue of the fact that they do not present a single unified critique, theoretical stance, or model of gender relations in Thai society. The contradictions between different views of women, gender, feminism and development may well be seen by the more astute academics, but they are not considered important. Social injustice and gender inequity were deeply felt by younger women, and these interests coincided with those of external donors and the UN women's agenda.

If different women's groups tried to produce a single model of Thai gender relations, their different objectives, assumptions, and working style would become obvious, preventing productive cooperation. Instead, groups and individuals sit together in formal seminars, and work on related development tasks to improve the status of Thai women, assuming they share the same understandings of 'improve' and 'status' and 'development'. They work hard to establish consensus in order to cooperate on long-term strategies. But, when younger women speak of abstractions such as rights and justice and the praxis of women's roles in labour unions, older elite women often prefer a charity model and shy away from these 'leftist' concerns – concerns that in their pasts were defined as unThai, and by extension, dangerous, subversive, and destabilizing. Meetings end, donors run out of funds, but the work of negotiating personal relations between older and younger, males and females, in male-dominated institutions is ongoing and all-engrossing.

The most activist of the Thai women's groups have chosen for pragmatic reasons to focus attention on exceptional groups such as prostitutes and victims of rape rather than on gender analysis of the life experiences of ordinary women. These women's groups tackle practical, immediate problems rather than develop indigenous feminist theory. As a result, their analyses of specific issues such as prostitution or environmental issues are seldom applied to gender relations in Thai society generally.

Most groups do not openly express a great deal of resistance to the dominant power structures within the country. One activist, when asked for an example of women's resistance, commented on a woman model who posed nude for advertisements, and later posed for an ad fully dressed, gazing directly at a man's trousers. She commended this as a very strong act of resistance. Other examples she gave of resistance included women who 'start the flirting'. But other stories circulated through the media provide greater challenges to Thai gender relations. Mentioning that 'the ducks are hungry' is enough to remind Thai men of the stories of women who cut off the penises of their philandering husbands and fed them to the ducks, or found some other prominent way to display them.

Some of the founders of women's NGOs are academics who teach women's studies courses and also work on women's development projects. Several women with a long history of involvement with different aspects of the women's movement in Thailand offered advice to me with regard to the use of the word, feminism, and the use of Western feminist theory in Thailand. Below I present a few of their voices, based on fieldnotes taken during or after gender workshops held in Bangkok in the early 1990s. I present them anonymously, because I fear my understandings of their arguments may not do them justice, and thus could upset the delicate balance between women who strive to keep their differences hidden from each other as well as from outsiders.

Following her feminist training in Europe, Lek began to look for exploitation and domination among rural Thai women. When the structures of domination were not revealed or stated by rural women, she attributed this to false consciousness. Instead she turned to an examination of the sexual division of labour in rural Thailand. In technical production tasks, she saw that rural men tended to carry out the hard, short tasks and women, the lighter, longer tasks. A saying reflecting this balance suggests that men start tasks while women finish them. This complementarity extends to the value of the tasks done by men and women in agricultural work, but breaks down under cond- itions of industrial work. In the past, women of strength were favoured over women of beauty, reflecting a more balanced view of women. As strength became less important, beauty became a more important criteria in rural communities. Beauty, she acknowledged, was probably always a significant criteria in elite culture. The shift in preference from strength to beauty encouraged the shift from balanced complementarity to gender hierarchy. Popular culture and mass media continues to divert attention from class, hierarchy, and feudal ideology. In her view, Thai leftists never paid sufficient attention to ideological systems, culture, gender and religion.

While the Bangkok-based royal elite model of gender relations speaks of the fore and hind legs of the elephant, the rural egalitarian model stresses the two wheels of the cart that must go together for progress to be made. A valuable approach for Thai feminism, she argues, would be to build on this complementarity and flexibility, this overlap in male and female values, and to stress Thai women's sources of power, their potential, and their effective female way of working. There has been too much emphasis on Thai women as victims, and not enough on women's resistance. This may be because middle-class women lack the confidence to participate in feminist work. Or in a less generous assessment, she hints that middle-class businesswomen who join women's groups only work for causes that benefit themselves directly, with little concern for Thai women generally.

A second leading activist, born to a Sino-Thai merchant family, began questioning the accepted position and expected behavior of Thai women when she was very young. Nong was punished for asking why her clothes – particularly her underwear – could not be washed with those of her father and brother. 'Jesus and Buddha came from women's vaginas, so what's the problem with washing my clothes with those of the rest of the family?' she asked her mother. She saw herself as an existentialist with no religious beliefs, but more recently she has reclaimed her Buddhist spirituality. According to core Buddhist principles, focus must be on our existence as human beings – genderless, gender free with our differences irrelevant to our shared experiences of *gert*, *to*, *jeb*, *tai* (birth, aging, illness, death). She cannot and will not accept unfair differences in treatment between men and women, and has been an activist for over a decade. The sexual double standard she finds particularly hard to take. For example, she asked a man who 'played around' if he would go out with a woman who also 'played around'. No, he said, horrified; it would be like using someone else's toothbrush. She said that was how women felt – they didn't like to use other people's toothbrushes either. Her attempt to develop these parallel arguments for men and women was greeted by her male colleagues with disbelief, anger, and incredulity.

Nong first heard the term, feminism, in 1986, and associated it with bra-burning Americans. She did not read feminist books until 1990 when she participated in a brief women's studies course in the Philippines. Yet in the 1980s, she led a progressive women's group in a protest against sex tourism aimed at the Japanese Prime Minister. Many Thai reporters were angry about the protest, and accused the women of following Western feminism, being man haters, and demonstrating angry, confrontational behavior. Her activism was all accomplished without awareness of the term, feminism, or of the content of Western feminist literature. Now she admires South Asian feminists and sees their feminism as relevant to the Thai experience.

Daeng, an activist with substantial experience in gender and development projects, is critical of the Thai women's movement, inferring that Thai feminists have not really thought through gender analysis or a Thai perspective on feminism. For example, she objected to them always repeating old arguments – about beauty contests, or the universal subordination of women – without considering local experiences that question those assumptions. I expressed my opinion that as a Canadian and an outsider to Thai society, I was struck by the fact that Thai women were considered competent by both women and men. She responded that most Thai feminists would not agree with me, but that Thai women who did not consider themselves feminists would agree. She saw this difference in interpretation as a clear example of the emphasis in Thai feminism of defining Thai women as victims and not as active agents in the construction of their own situations. To label oneself as a Thai feminist meant denying women's power and stressing the overwhelming constraints of patriarchal structures.

A leading academic who teaches Women's Studies at a Bangkok

university is much less activist than the others discussed. Malee is obsessed with the importance of non-confrontational, non-oppositional approaches to women's issues. She does not view Thai men as hindering women's progress, nor blocking the opportunities of women who are well educated, well prepared. She would like to see non-confrontational language used by Thai feminists. She argues that women should not 'attack' men, or show them how they oppress women and discriminate against them, or men will feel badly and not support the women's movement. At first, she saw Thai feminists imitating Western feminists, but later saw them take a more discriminating stance and examine women's issues in a broader perspective, as, for example, through ecofeminism. She agrees with elite older women leaders, that Thai women's characteristics should be viewed positively and valued, not changed or devalued.

Noi, a much respected academic, publishes widely on Thai women. Before a seminar on Buddhism and women, several Thai feminists spoke about beauty, fashion, make-up and feminism. They noted that Thai feminist activists tended to dress very simply in jeans and T-shirts and wear no make-up. As Noi was becoming more comfortable with a feminist label and identity, she wondered if she offended the activists by dressing up and wearing make-up. Was she making a statement that she didn't want to be making? She felt that in certain contexts, it was appropriate to 'dress up' as long as one did not 'cling' to it. The decision not to dress up or to use make-up could also be seen as a political statement against consumerism. But by continuing to 'dress up' and wear make-up, she feared supporting the idea that women have to dress up to please males. Although women may say they dress to please themselves women who are 'dressed up' all look the same from the outside, even if they have different intentions inside. These lifestyle issues run deeper than concern to be politically correct, for they reflect on gendered presentations of self and cut to the core of *kalatesa*.

The F-Word in Thai Gender Studies

These sketches suggest the diversity of personal experiences and inter-pretations motivating participation in the Thai women's movement. They reflect differences in class, age, ethnicity and sexual orientation. And yet the women all participate regularly in the same women's seminars and projects. Their practice and logic reveals the discomfort that many Thai women have with the word, feminism. Nevertheless, they all manage to work together and support each others' efforts when it is in their interests to do so. The conversations reveal a wide range of variation in what they understand to be the content of the term, feminism. Yet I identify their work as feminist.

Thai use of and resistance to the term, feminism, raises questions concerning the interpretation of Thai feminism. Are women's advocacy groups in Thailand feminist? Is feminism a viable concept in the women's movement in Thailand? Or are these questions misguided, a misrepresentation of Thai women's concerns. In a comprehensive review of Thai NGOs addressing women's issues, Tantiwiramanond and Pandey hint at their discomfort with the English term and its Western content:

> In western society the word 'feminism' sometimes connotes a strong 'anti-male' attitude. It often gets confused with lesbianism. Because of this impression of confrontation (male-hatred), or individual pursuits (often related to 'bra-burning', free sex), the word 'feminist' is often disliked (frowned upon) or explained differently in the Third World specifically in Thailand. There is no feminist movement in Thailand as a unified theory. Those using it assign levels of meaning to it: welfare, autonomy, choice, and justice. (1991:10)

Rejection of the label, feminist (either in Thai or English) occurs for many different reasons.[7] According to one Thai activist, many supporters of the Thai women's movement are not feminists, and view feminism as irrelevant to their goals and activities. They reject strategies of direct confrontation which they view as an implicit part of feminism. Even the most progressive women's groups avoid referring to themselves as feminist on the assumption that feminist groups are by definition confrontational. In the words of a member of a progressive Thai women's group:

> Sometimes if the approach is aggressive, . . . it creates weariness and withdrawal . . . The common ground is to make everyone see the importance, and need not to suffer. Militancy does not have to alienate others. Also, we must remember that women's work requires patience. (Tantiwiramanond and Pandey 1991:104)

Other activists argue that there is no such thing as a distinctively Thai feminism. Feminism is intrinsically and extrinsically foreign. They reject the term and the concept because it is considered Western and inappropriate for analyzing the position and condition of Thai women.

Pongsapich criticized Thai analysts who use Western feminist theories uncritically: 'Concepts and theories related to women have been presented as translations and interpretations of western theories' (1986:34). These theories 'reflect the pattern of male-female relations in western countries where there are different socio-political contexts' (Tingsabadh and Tanchainan 1986:77). There is no consensus on the definition of a distinctively Thai feminism, beyond the shared awareness of women's oppression and exploitation.

This argument parallels the discomfort many Thai women activists express in discussing patriarchal oppression. A report on why feminism has not 'taken off' in Thailand argues that middle-class urban women prefer to deny that male domination exists and prefer to consider Thai society as male-guided rather than male-dominated (Tantiwiramanond and Pandey 1991:60). Such hair-splitting is useless to activist groups addressing the problems of violence against women, HIV/AIDS and sex tourism.

Feminism as a term and a concept is translated into Thai only with difficulty. Most often, the English term is used, perhaps to stress the lack of conceptual equivalence in Thai. The term *satri niyom* is often used to translate feminism. This phrase could translate back as 'woman-ism', implying a reverse discrimination. A more accurate literal translation is even more ambiguous - popularizing women, or favouring women. In an awkward double meaning, the term might just as likely be used to refer to a man who is a 'womanizer'.

It is equally difficult to translate the idea of gender and gender analysis.[8] A literal translation of gender, the relationship between men and women, is often assumed to refer to sexual relations, and not gender. The Thai term for women's studies is less problematic, combining the concepts of women and expert knowledge: *satrisiksa*. Several Thai feminists refer to themselves as *naksatrisiksa*, experts on knowledge about women, rather than as feminists. But the term *satrisiksa* does not presume gender analysis per se, nor in fact, imply any critique of the social system or the Thai system of gender relations.

Before considering these definitions further, we must recognize that we are mapping a Western sexist language (English) onto a less sexist language (Thai), where parts of speech are not identified as masculine or feminine, and the fact of existence in human form (*phuu*) is prior to the transitory states of maleness and femaleness from the perspective of Buddhist logic.

Some of the discomfort with the term feminism builds from the longstanding assumption among middle-class, urban Thai men and women that feminism in its meaning as women's liberation is irrelevant in Thailand. '(Thai women) have never heard of women's liberation but they (have) already achieved it' (Tantiwiramanond and Pandey 1991:23). This sentence from an oft-quoted letter reflects a strong middle-class bias, and is probably the most common position I heard expressed by Thai males. Male technocrats on a study tour of Canadian universities grumbled about Thai women 'ruling the roost' and having too much influence in household decision making. This context made it difficult for me to raise gender issues in the meeting. How often have North American women been silenced by having Southeast Asian males boast of the high status of women in Southeast Asia, thus reminding us of our role in transmitting an alien and unwelcome ideology? How much more difficult it must be for Thai women to raise gender issues in male-dominated policy meetings.

A male head of a Christian NGO who works with women activists dismissed feminism as being irrelevant and inappropriate for the analysis of Thai society. He said the word is always spoken in English, is not widely understood, and is usually negatively received. It is equated with first-wave American 'women's liberation' which he defines as denial of biological sex differences and a desire to reverse the division of labour 'so that men have to cook for women'. His version of indigenous Thai feminism starts from the assumption that women are powerful, citing words based on *mae* (mother), such as *mae thup* (general), *mae nam* (river), *mae phim* (teacher, one who 'prints' the student) and women's management of finances. He views rampant capitalism and consumerism as destroying more egalitarian Thai gender relations based on rural matricentred values.

Feminine power is well represented in the Thai world view where it is grounded in the spirits of earth, water and rice – all basic to subsistence and survival. Jane Hanks identified this as the power to nurture in her paper on 'The Ontology of Rice' (1964). But feminine power also destroys male potency in the form of menstrual blood which can reduce women to a 'polluted and morally degraded entity' (Tanabe 1991:188). Discomfort with the ambiguities of feminine power may also underlie Thai men's and women's discomfort with the word, feminism.

Conclusions

Being born Thais we were taught to be proud of our independent country and even so being Thai women, we are proud to learn of our better position than that of our foreign sisters. This is because we had neither foot binding which occurred in China nor sati or widow-burning which happened in India. Thai women have played important roles both within and outside the household, especially rural women. They have worked side by side together with men in the fields, managed marketing systems and have contributed to decision making within the family. Thai women are respected as mothers and wives fulfilling their roles and duties in childrearing and taking responsibility for the well-being of the family. (Tanchainan 1987:4)

Sucheela Tanchainan, along with other Thai writers, recognizes the high status of Thai women as a trope, illusionary, acknowledging, however, the contradictions resulting from the existence of positive images alongside representations of Thai women as victims. These words, written by a Thai women's rights activist, capture the character of the official representation of the position and condition of Thai women, as espoused by several elite women's groups including the National Council of Women of Thailand. The quote stresses the complementarities between Thai men and women, rather than the inequalities between them. Assessments of 'the status of Thai women' present the contradictory arguments that Thai women in the past had power and high status but lost both in the process of modernization, and arguments that the origins of women's oppression lies in the past (Pongsapich 1986, Boonsue 1989, Gardiner and Gardiner 1991, L. and J. Hanks 1963). Another discourse pits women against men. 'Part of women's gaining equality would be the relative deterioration in the power and economic situation of men' (Srisambhand and Gordon 1987:8). This view of gender relations as a zero sum game contributes to the negative feelings generated towards feminism and feminists in Thailand.

From the range of images of Thai women, analysts select heroines and feminine qualities to meet their needs. Most striking is the fact that conflicting representations of strong, competent women exist alongside the obvious evidence of inequalities and discrimination against women, without cancelling each other out or engendering undue conflict. Representations are not easily separated by region or class, but reflect something of the palimpsests of Thai women, past and present, throughout the country. We are left with images not of uniformity but of diversity – of multiple contested gender statuses and ideologies not of a single hegemonic system. Even central Thai cannot be figured as a homogeneous system, as differences in class and ethnicity are articulated in different localities and different contexts.

One context assumed to be consistent is that of Theravada Buddhism. It is regularly evoked to account for the position and condition of Thai women. As a dominant ideological system, it requires a more detailed exploration, and is the subject of the next chapter.

Notes

1. Ten Brummelhuis attributes the Thai ability to adapt to their cosmological environment by choosing the right time and place, by knowing *kalatesa*, to hierarchic individualism (1984:50).

2. I am grateful to Parissara Liewkeat for pointing this out to me and providing me with the Thai lyrics to the song.

3. Early accounts of travellers to Thailand confirm that at certain times outsiders have been welcomed, invited into inner circles of power, and permitted to flaunt rules of behaviour. At other times, violations would be punished, and foreigners would be closely controlled.

4. Richard O'Connor cites Nithi Aewsriwong on this point. *Kalatesa* may have a structural role in preserving order among competing models. Sino-Thai middle class adopt royal models and construct identity through *kalatesa* and the accumulation of modern goods. In this sense, the middle class is best defined as not royal, not poor (O'Connor 1995a:43).

5. The first two development plans (1961-71) stressed rapid economic growth through import substitution, with no focus on women in spite of their growing importance in the labor force. Women figured in the third plan as a target group for family planning.

6. My observations of these networks ended in the early 1990s. However I have kept up with their activities through newsletters and student research. I suspect the avoidance of conflict is becoming more difficult as resources become scarcer and more Thai women observe how other women's groups conduct themselves.

7. Being a feminist but avoiding the label is not uncommon in North America, often based on assumptions that feminists are pushy, extreme, radical, and concerned with petty matters far removed from women's everyday concerns. It is not only Thai or Asian women who hesitate to use the term, feminist, particularly with reference to themselves. Many young Western women dread the word and reject its use. A film on the lives of five sixteen-

year-old girls in Toronto captured their image of feminism. None of them knew anything about feminists beyond the fact that they did not want to be one. One thought it meant lesbian, another, that males and females should not be equal because it 'twists biological things' and was wrong. Many women and men have an emotional as opposed to a rational, instrumental response to the word; willingness to call oneself feminist may not reflect one's attitudes toward gender roles but a whole host of other concerns. Research reflects this discomfort with the word, with various surveys from 1986 to 1991 showing a high of 56 percent and a low of 25 percent of women accepting the self labelling of themselves as feminist (Mansbridge 1993:8–9). Many women are not at home with the word. It is for others to continue the task of explaining how feminism, a powerful and useful body of theory and practice, become a pejorative term, conceptually linked to mythical events like 'bra-burning'.

8. The concept of gender itself is difficult to translate into Thai. Even after the gender training workshops conducted in NGOs and universities throughout the country, participants have had difficulty understanding the concept of gender. As a Thai male participant explained after participating in a three-day gender analysis workshop, he understood everything in the workshop (which was presented in Thai) except for one word. That word was gender, inserted in English into Thai speech throughout the workshop. The problems of translation are immense and underappreciated, resulting in the use of the English word, gender, in place of Thai glosses or circumlocutions. The problems are non-trivial, as Donna Haraway (1991) discovered when she was asked to define 'gender' for a Marxist dictionary that would be translated into German, Chinese, French, Russian, and Spanish. Even closely related Indo-European languages differed as to whether they distinguished between sex and gender, a distinction that is critically important to feminist theory. Actions translate more easily than words across these differences. Jackson raises similar problems with translating *phet*; a term which is used to refer to sex, gender and sexuality.

Buddhism and Gender Ideology

Thailand is a Theravada Buddhist country. To be Thai is to be Buddhist. These truisms persist despite the fact not all Thai are Buddhist; not all Buddhists by birth are Buddhist by practice; and Buddhist practice varies by class, region and ethnicity. But neither middle-class urban nor rural Thai are opting out of religion. Rather, they are selecting from wider options such as lay meditation, the asceticism of groups like Santi Asoke, or prosperity cults such as Dhammakaya. Buddhism must be front and center in a book about Thai gender because Buddhism matters to Thai people in many different ways, and is a key component of Thai identity. It has a profound impact not only because of its texts and rituals, but also because of the paradoxes emerging from the gaps between doctrine and everyday life. Gender is enmeshed in these paradoxical gaps.

Buddhism and the Interpretation of Thai Society

There is no Buddhism that exists outside of local expressions of Buddhist practice, no texts except those produced by people – usually men – in particular times and places. Vitebsky reminds us that a knowledge which is timeless and spaceless is also useless (1993:109). Buddhist knowledge, because it is experientially based is not easily separated from context and locality. These assumptions separate ethnographic work on Buddhist societies from history of religions and theological perspectives on Buddhism. Thailand has a long tradition of anthropological work that deals directly with the problem of linking text-based practices with local interpretations of these practices (cf. Tambiah 1970, 1976, 1984; Keyes 1984, 1989; Kirsch 1982, 1985; Terweil 1975; O'Connor 1993; Tiyavanich 1997; J. Van Esterik 1977; P. Van Esterik 1982, 1986). But

65

critics point out that Buddhism has been overused, inappropriately used, and its explanatory power overextended (Tannenbaum 1995; Basham 1989) as if everyone in the country were devoted practitioners reading Pali texts by the hour instead of breaking precepts, shopping and watching television. But Theravada Buddhism provides many Thai with a way of viewing the world, a sense of reality, moral standards, and shared language and metaphors for analyzing their existing life situation. As a living tradition, these morals and metaphors are constantly changing.

One approaches religious traditions with care, walking the line between the dangers of reducing Buddhism to a determinant, the explanation of all things Thai, and ignoring its ideological force because of the difficulty in identifying belief, pinning down meaning. Religion as a fixed and immutable 'cultural given' becomes out of bounds for discussions of development, gender or political action. Religion may be consciously avoided as a dangerous direction of inquiry. Identifying something as religious, traditional or cultural removes it from critical scrutiny and provides an excuse for inaction. As Lazreg (1988) has argued, religion is often privileged in explanations of gender, and assumed to be the bedrock of the cultural system. Buddhism has been used to explain many aspects of Thai society from individual personality to development strategies. Thai personality, psychological orientations, and values have been attributed to changes in Buddhist belief and practice by both Thai and foreign analysts. Psychologist, Komin, criticizes these blanket approaches, such as using the Buddhist emphasis on working towards one's own salvation to account for personality traits like individualism. She critiques arguments that the Thai are non-committal, indifferent, smiling and emotionless because of the Buddhist emphasis on detachment, and calls for more empirical work, more consideration of behaviour incongruent with Buddhist values such as status orientation, extravagance, aggressiveness, competitiveness, and violence (Komin 1990:11, 12). Buddhism is credited with orienting Thai personalities toward permissiveness, tolerance, non-involvement in the affairs of others, and non-violence. These traits are confirmed in the mask of placidity and pleasantry that falls into place in social situations, particularly when foreigners are around. But Thailand also has the second highest murder rate in the world, and vicious gossip is a basic means of social control in both urban and rural settings; neither reflects Buddhist values.

Buddhism and Women

When Buddhism is evoked in discussions of gender or women in Thailand, it is usually attacked as a patriarchal institution that oppresses women. Khin Thitsa, in addition to many Thai feminists, blames Buddhism for the subordination of Thai women, and locates textual support for the oppression and subordination of women: 'Buddhism provides a moral framework for man's hierarchical precedence over women, inasmuch as it sanctions polygyny and all beliefs and practices which devalue the female sex' (Thitsa 1980:7). She states that '. . . Buddhists believe that birth as a woman indicates bad *karma* or demerit (*baap*) from past lives' (1983:24). Rebirth as a human indicates insufficient *karma* to end the cycle of rebirths, but enough to be born on the human plane where opportunities exist for making merit.

Two commonly cited references to support the argument that Buddhism oppresses women include King Mongkut's defence of polygamy (Reynolds 1977), and women's desire for rebirth as men, expressed both in texts and conversations, past and present. For example, in 1399, a Thai Queen of Sukhothai prayed that through her merit, she might be reborn as a male (Reid 1988:163). Is this evidence of her recognition of women's oppression under Buddhism or of the fact that she would have access to more political power had she been born a male? Women's preference for male rebirth could well follow from the common sense observation that Thai men often have more power and resources than Thai women.[1]

Thai feminist, Sukanya Huntrakul, argues that religion puts women in a lower moral status, leaving them with less education than men and fewer opportunities to improve their socio-economic status. She argues that Buddhism determines implicitly if not explicitly the religious/moral inferiority of women, and has left women with concrete socio-economic disadvantages (Hantrakul 1988). Does this imply that women of high socio-economic status with successful businesses are not religious? Not Buddhist? How were they able to escape the influence of their religion? Or is it only poor women who are oppressed by Buddhist institutions and logic? Thai feminists are clearly faced with some exceptionally challenging analytical problems when they try to link material conditions with moral status based on Buddhist ideology, particularly if they depend on Buddhist texts to do so.

Use of Buddhist Texts

How is gender framed in Buddhist texts? Identification of gender bias in ancient texts and current religious institutions and practices requires careful distinction between Buddhist institutions and Buddhist logic; Buddhist practice and Buddhist beliefs; and popular Buddhist texts and canonical Buddhist texts. To date, researchers have concentrated most attention on popular Buddhist texts and Buddhist institutions, such as the monkhood which excludes women from the most valued roles within the ordination tradition.

Anthropologists are wary of equating universal religious texts with current local practice or assuming that texts determine behavior. Local reinterpretation of texts fits with the Buddhist argument that texts should always be tested and challenged by experience. However, monks encourage the belief that unenlightened individuals may not be able to trust their own experience and so must support the monkhood and accept monastic interpretations of texts. Nevertheless, reinterpretation of text and testing through experience is to be expected within Buddhism.

Greater attention to reinterpreting the primary canonical texts from a Thai feminist perspective might open up a new way of conceptualizing the relation between Buddhism and gender ideology. One potential for reinterpretation lies in the recognition that texts reflect social conditions at the time the texts were written, including the biases of their male interpreters. Rita Gross has identified some of the formidable obstacles facing anyone undertaking a feminist reinterpretation of Buddhist texts. Working through multiple levels of androcentrism requires recognizing the biases in selecting what documents to preserve in the historical record and what texts to ignore. The biases in the textual record are compounded by androcentric biases in Western scholarship on Buddhism and androcentric biases in contemporary Buddhist practice (Gross 1993:18). Others have also been searching the texts for a usable past for a Buddhist feminism (Murcott 1991; Bartholemeusz 1992; Cabezon 1992, Kabilsingh 1991).

In 1992, I attended a lecture by a well-known monk who taught at Wat Mahathat in Bangkok, in order to learn more about the interpretation of Buddhist texts. After two hours of extraordinarily dry recitation of the names of each of the books, sections, and chapters of the *Tipitaka*,[2] he noticed the dazed, bored look on the Thai and foreign, monk and lay faces in the audience. He apologized briefly, explaining that texts do not matter in Buddhism, that one did not need to know or understand them, that the Buddha cautioned against trusting texts and words without understanding and knowing oneself. He explained that the teaching exists on two levels, the mundane (*lokiya*) and the supramundane (*lokutara*), and it is difficult for a lay person to understand texts. Knowledge of texts, he said, is not necessary for happiness. It is only necessary for monks who teach. This is the argument that monks give to encourage attendance at sermons. But most monks know very little about Buddhist texts beyond what they recite in services. Monks who know the texts well, do not usually question them. While many laymen and laywomen may know a great deal about Buddhist texts, men claim more right to question the authority of the monks simply because they are men and have the potential for being ordained. Accepting the authority of the monks as representatives of the *Sangha* is very different from accepting their knowledge of the texts. Nevertheless, the attitude that it is sinful (*baap*) to question the authority of monks is widespread in Thailand, alongside the attitude held by many that monks are quite lazy and not very knowledgable.

This does not mean that Buddhism does not shape the consciousness of most rural and urban Thai who identify themselves as Buddhist. Texts and stories may provide a reference system for guiding everyday life decisions, a source of metaphor or a stock of memorized stanzas, as, for example, magical verses or *katha*. To suggest that the four Noble Truths are alien and esoteric concepts to most Thai (as Truong does, 1990:132) trivializes the knowledge and understanding of Thai laity, and imparts an unnecessarily privileged position to monks who may not have great knowledge of metaphysical principles. It is a mistake to assume that a great gap of knowledge exists between laity and monks, and between popular and textual Buddhism. The gap between men and women lies more in legitimized authority than in knowledge, particularly now that women have increasing opportunities for acquiring knowledge of Buddhism. In addition, women's knowledge of Buddhism may well lie in domains other than texts. I have argued that Thai women's knowledge of Buddhism may also be expressed through food and commensality, an important part of Buddhist rituals (P. Van Esterik 1986). Even esoteric and paradoxical knowledge can be coded through everyday practices, providing alternative frameworks for interpretation.

Feminists writing on Thailand often make use of Buddhist texts to make their arguments about the subordination of women. Often single stories are cited as if textual evidence were equivalent to contemporary practice or belief. The questions of Queen Mallika on obtaining beauty and wealth (from the *Anguttara-Nikaya*), or the Buddha's reluctance to ordain women (from the *Culla-Vagga*), are cited as evidence for the subordination of women under Buddhism. The story of Mara sending his daughters, Lust, Hate, and Desire, to tempt the Buddha, is cited as textual evidence of misogyny and the subordination of women. But Mara also took the form of a beautiful young man to seduce nuns (Murcott 1991:145), a reminder that men's bodies can be equally distracting to women bent on spiritual quest. Popular Buddhist treatises such as the *Trai Phum Phra Ruang*[3] provide examples of dutiful wives, subordinated to their husbands. In fact, the Brahmanic ideal of absolute wifely devotion to her husband became the Buddhist cultural ideal as well (Murcott 1991:95).

The feminist case against Buddhism has not been without its critics. Sivaraksa argues that 'if feminists could be more careful in their analysis and study their subject more thoroughly, especially those dealing with spiritual traditions, their criticism would be much more convincing' (1988:63). Nevertheless, he acknowledges that 'we need to study the position of some feminists in condemning Buddhism for exploiting women in Asia' (1988:59).

The *Jataka* stories, popular Buddhist texts best known to Thai villagers through sermons, wall paintings, and oral narratives, recount the former lives of the Buddha, and are considered to be misogynist (Gross 1993:42). Suwanna Satha-Anand (1996) provides an excellent example of the popular Vessantara-Jataka tale where Prince Vessantara becomes a Buddha in his next life for his generous act of giving away his wife and children, while Madsi, his wife receives neither attention nor credit for her devotion and selfless acts.

The identification of texts that fuel feminist fires is always selective, for the ambiguity and paradox of the canonical tradition also provides materials that support rather than degrade women. Both canonical and popular Buddhist texts are rich and complex sources of paradox – available for interpretation and reinterpretation from different perspectives. Buddhist texts give contradictory images of women. Keyes (1984), for example, discusses images of women as mothers and mistresses in popular and canonical religious texts. One lesson from this fact is that there are lots of stories, and no one story has the truth; there are hundreds of stories and hundreds of truths, because particular acts lead to particular consequences in individuals' lives. This is the basis of the core concept of dependent origination, *paticca samuppada*. It is an error of understanding to assume that particular acts of individual men and women have general consequences for all women or all men, a fact better understood by Thai Buddhists than by many of their analysts.

Divergent and contradictory images of women may come from very distinct strands in the texts. We hear not a single uncertain, wavering voice, but a multiplicity of voices with very different views of women and the feminine. Sponberg (1992) identifies four strands within Buddhist texts, each entailing distinct beliefs and actions. These strands are neither historically nor regionally exclusive, although Sponberg does suggest some chronology. The existence of these distinct strands encourages selective interpretations that further individual and collective interests. Sorting out these strands may provide a basis for reconciling divergent views about gender, women and femininity.

The first theme is soteriological inclusiveness, which confirms that sex or gender is no barrier to enlightenment, that the path is open to women. However, 'inclusiveness asserts neither sameness nor a lack of hierarchical differentiation' (Sponberg 1992:12). The second theme, institutional androcentrism refers to the view that women can only pursue a religious career within a regulated institutional structure that preserves male authority and female subordination (Sponberg 1992:13). Ascetic misogyny is the third strand of hostile, vituperative attitudes toward women; it probably has roots in a pre-Buddhist set of beliefs associating women with dangerous, uncontrolled sexuality, and polluting bodily fluids. The fourth strand, soteriological androgyny offers most promise for the development of a Buddhist feminism. This considers Buddhist practice as a dynamic state of nondualistic androgynous integration, revalorizing the feminine, but stressing that all beings manifest the full range of characteristics conventionally identified as gender specific (Sponberg 1992:25). To fit this conceptual model to the Thai case, future research might add to this framework concepts like matricentric grounding reflecting notions of feminine power still strong in rural Thailand, to offset to some degree South Asian ascetic misogyny, and patriarchal structuration which serves to reinforce institutional androcentrism, and links the ideological system more directly into the hegemonic discourse of the Thai nation state.

Soteriological Inclusiveness

Popular and canonical Buddhism confirm that the path to enlightenment is open to women, in spite of discourses that perpetuate the oversimplified notion that women cannot achieve high spiritual status unless they are first reborn as men (Truong 1990:137). There is substantial textual evidence, particularly in the Psalms of the Sisters (*Therigatha*), to support the argument that women can attain *Nirvana* without rebirth as males first. These sixth-century BC psalms provide evidence of the capacity of women to attain spiritual wisdom. This text, first translated into English and published in 1909, does not figure prominently in Western scholarly literature on Buddhism. Nor is it used extensively by Thai feminists who gravitate to the more andro-centric texts to demonstrate sexist bias in Buddhism.

One group of poems are by Siddhartha Gautama's concubines whom he left, along with his wife and son, when he took up the homeless life. Seven of these *rajorodha* or royal concubines left verses recorded in the *Therigatha*:

Tissa, practice the practice.
Don't let attachments overwhelm you.
Free from ties
Live in a world without obsessions.

(Murcott 1991:25)

Sunari-Nanda (beautiful Nanda) was taught by the Buddha to medit-ate on the foulness of the diseased, impure rotten body of a lovely woman, stinking of decay. Nanda wrote:

So day and night
Without letting up,
I looked at it this way,
And by my own wisdom,
I perceived it fully,
I saw.

Watching carefully,
I plumbed to the very origin
And saw this body as it really is,
Inside and out.

Deep inside myself,
I have lost interest in passion.
I am careful, quenched,
Calm, and free.

(Murcott 1991:27)

In the *Therigatha*, prostitutes reach enlightenment on hearing the words of the Buddha. The multifaceted lives of courtesans provide important models of and for the complexity of women's lives, and a reminder of the futility of Judeo-Christian efforts to pin down and place prostitution on one side or another of a moral fence.

Early Buddhist texts and Thai popular texts affirm, yet do not celebrate, the fact that women are humans with the characteristics associated with full humanity. In spite of the frequently cited Thai saying 'men are human; women are buffalo', there is no Buddhist questioning of women's humanity. In the *Samyutta Nikaya*, when King Pasenadi of Kosala expressed disappointment at the birth of a daughter, the Buddha is reported to have told him, 'A woman child, O Lord of men, may prove even a better offspring than a male'. Women's inclusion in the soteriological goals of the religion requires some explication of the concept of Buddhist personhood and *karma*.

The conditioned sequences of cause and effect is the driving force behind any consideration of rebirth as human male or female. This process is best understood in Thailand by a consideration of rebirths and *karma* (*kam*), a more familiar idiom than philosophical discussions in the *abhidhamma* on dependent origination for many Thai. Knowledge of rebirth emphasizes the transitory nature of present identities as humans with male or female features. For every rebirth may be experienced as a male or female (or in fact an animal, or spirit). But the Buddha never took female form in the *Jataka* tales. According to the *abhidhamma* texts of Theravada Buddhism, among the material qualities which make up a living organism are twenty-four derived qualities, including the qualities of the femininity-faculty and the masculinity-faculty. These faculties are not internal to the person, but external and subtle or difficult to perceive. Buddhaghosa, an important fifth-century analyst, ascribes the different interests and inclinations of men and women to either the power of femininity (*itthindriya*) or the power of masculinity (*purisindriya*), neither of which has any inherent connection with the possession of a particular set of sexual organs (Zwilling 1992:206).

Unlike the Judeo-Christian tradition where identity as male and female is fixed for eternity, Thai men and women have the possibility of experiencing existence as male or female every rebirth (and recall this is only 'a subtle difference, difficult to perceive'). In fact, it is only the very last moment before birth that the femininity-faculty or masculinity-faculty is adjusted to produce a male or female infant (Rajadhon 1961: 127). In other Buddhist traditions, a person is born in the form of either sex because of the final clinging of the mind to that form before taking a new birth.

The concept of *karma* is regularly used to explicate gender differences. Yet *karma* as a technical term in Buddhism never signifies anything but moral or immoral action. It '. . . never means the result of action, as often wrongly conceived by western authors' (Nyanatiloka 1972:130). This use of the term *karma* to signify the result of actions and the fate of humans (or even whole nations) is a misconception spread in the West through the influence of Theosophy (Nyanatiloka 1972:77). However, the idea of rebirth as a woman as a result of misdeeds in past lives is widespread in Thailand, perpetuated more through popular Buddhism than through examination of philosophical texts such as the *abhidhamma*. One source of this argument is the story of the adulterous husband who went to Hell for five hundred lives, was reborn a woman for five hundred lives, a *kathoey* (male transvestite) for five hundred lives, a castrated animal for five hundred lives, and later was reborn as a man. Sathien Koset includes this story in a Thai publication on Thai culture (1962: 111–12), and it has since been cited by authors demonstrating the negative evaluation of women within Buddhism (see, for example, Srisambhand and Gordon 1987:12).

However, if *karma* is identified as a key Buddhist concept underlying gender ideology, then feminist research must examine the concept in all its complexity. Nyanatiloka cautions against trivial interpretations of *karma*, and argues that a real, and in the ultimate sense, true understanding of Buddhist *karma* doctrine is possible only through a deep insight into the impersonality and conditionality of all phenomena of existence (1972:79). The statement that bad *karma* determines rebirth as a woman makes no sense within Buddhist logic. A deeper understanding of *karma* requires understanding how volition or will conditions bodily actions (including unlawful sexual intercourse), verbal actions, and mental actions leading to consequences in this life, the next life, and future rebirths.[4] Separating these components might discourage oversimplification of the relation between *karma*-result and gender determination. Such an exploration might also provide productive concepts for understanding the complexity of gender relations in Thailand today, and stimulate the development of a more informed Buddhist feminism. Soteriological androgyny, discussed below, provides space for such a construct.

Institutional Androcentrism

In spite of the historically longstanding doctrinal position in Buddhism that women should not be discriminated against, there is ample evidence in the Thai tradition that women are denied access to the most valued Buddhist resources in the country, and face an androcentric monastic order (*Sangha*) unsympathetic to their concerns whether they

Figure 2 Lay women in white prepare to attend temple service, Suphanburi Province

be improving the condition of nuns, pressing for ordination for women, or pursuing charges against sexually active monks.

Women do much of the work of Buddhism. If you counted only those who serve as fields of merit for others, and who administer temple finances, the work of Buddhism would be accomplished overwhelmingly by men. If you counted the work necessary to maintain and reproduce Buddhist institutions, much of the work of Buddhism would be seen as women's work, not only in the practical provision of services for monks and novices, but also in the monitoring of morality in the *Sangha*. Much of this work is undervalued and unrecognized, because of the structure of the monastic system in Thailand.

In Thailand, as in other Theravada Buddhist countries, the *Sangha* does not permit ordination of women as monks. However, women were ordained during the time of the Buddha, and the order of ordained women (*bhikkhuni*) survived into the eleventh century in Sri Lanka, with some reports of *bhikkuni* in Burma. However, the order was never established in Thailand. Ordained women followed 311 *Vinaya* rules, more than the 227 *Vinaya* rules of the monks, in addition to an extra set of eight rules (*Gurudhamma*) guiding the relations between ordained males and females in such a way as to ensure the superiority of *bhikkhu* over *bhikkhuni*. These eight rules imposed by the Buddha on the order of nuns might well have been later insertions by those biased against the ordination of women. Who inserted the words and for what immediate purpose may never be known. Who decides what words reflect the true intentions of the Buddha, and what words were the later insertions of the unenlightened, the biased?

Thai *mae chii* or 'lay women in white' are not equivalent to *bhikkhuni* although they also meditate, teach, and provide ritual services for laity, in addition to providing domestic services to monks. I use the term nun to refer to these pious women who wear white, shave their heads, and observe five or eight precepts, and retain the Pali term, *bhikkhuni* to refer to women who are ordained and follow the *bhikkuni patimokkha* (the rules of the order).

One problem faced by *mae chii* is that they are not considered fields of merit for laity because they are not ordained (cf. P. Van Esterik 1982). Yet Thai women speak as if gifts to nuns including alms rounds are meritorious and can achieve good. There is no textual evidence that only monks can be fields of merit. In Sri Lanka, donors do not consider women as formal fields of merit, but Bartholomeusz argues that they serve as 'attenuated' ones, symbolizing the *dhamma* (1992:52).

The lack of respect accorded to Thai nuns is attributed to assumptions about their lack of knowledge of Buddhism, and their demeanour, including sleeping during services and begging in the streets of Bangkok. Most nuns live on the outskirts of temple compounds and spend their time cooking, cleaning, and otherwise assisting monks in addition to services and study. They work so hard that they may fall asleep during services, further reinforcing their image among the laity as being less worthy than monks. In fact, many nuns may live in a state of semi-starvation because they may not have food offered to them for days. I regularly visited a small temple on the outskirts of Thonburi with a middle-class Thai woman who used to bring food to her elderly nanny who had taken up the white robes of a nun. She shared the food we brought with a tiny wizened, crippled woman who became a *mae chii* after years as a court dancer in the palace of Rama VI (1910–1925). She said no one brought her food anymore and she was too crippled to walk to the communal kitchen for her meals.

Until recently, nuns had very little time to study, meditate or practice, unless they were fortunate enough to reside in one of the few well-supported nunneries in Thailand (e.g. Wat Pak Nam in Thonburi; Mae

Chii Institute, Bangkok; Paktho Institute, Ratchaburi Province; Tham-glaeb, Petburi Province). Currently, they have access to *dhamma* study similar to that given to monks, in addition to special Pali studies, *abhidhamma* examinations, and training in meditation. While monks may also be uneducated and have little knowledge of Buddhist texts (although they have more opportunities to study), they appear to be unwilling to share privileges, resources and power with ordained women.

According to the *Vinaya*, b h i KK*h*uni were prohibited from serving monks. Out of compassion for the *bhikkhuni*, the Buddha set down a rule to protect them from being used by monks, after '. . . he came to know that certain *bhikkus* made the *bhikkhunis* clean and dye rugs for them and by so doing deprive them of their time for putting more effort towards spiritual development' (Kabilsingh 1984:167). This rule was included in the rules for women (*bhikkhuni patimokkha*) but not the rules for men (*bhikkhu patimokkha*). If nuns were ordained as *bhikkhuni* according to the *bhikkuni patimokkha*, who would provide these free services to monks? *Mae chii* can do work that is forbidden to monks by the *Vinaya* rules. It is therefore in monks' interests to dis-courage any changes to women's ordination status which would restrict them from serving monks.

Why would Thai nuns not object to serving monks in this way? With no feminist re-evaluation of their spiritual worth, some nuns are eager to acquire merit to improve their chances of rebirth as men, and see this as an excellent opportunity to do so. Not all Thai *mae chii* feel oppressed. Many want enough support to be able to pursue *dhamma* practice. Similarly, not all Buddhist women are pressing for the re-establishment of the *bhikkhuni* ordination tradition for women. For one reason, the *Vinaya* rules would place them in a subordinate and dependent relationship with monks. A Western Buddhist nun residing in England explained in answer to a question about full ordination for women that if women are seeking *bhikkhuni* ordination for status, then they should disrobe. The spiritual life is about letting the ego die. If full ordination for women comes, it must come not because it is sought after. In her opinion, pressure for ordination comes from status seeking, not from real *dhamma* practice. Few feminists would agree with her assumptions about how to advocate for change, but her sentiments are echoed by monks who prefer the status quo. As the Dalai Lama has said with regard to women's rights: 'It is correct to struggle for one's rights, not with pride or jealousy, but with a view toward taking on one's share of responsibility in the critical task of improving the quality of human society' (Fitz-Gerald 1992:8).

The re-establishment of the *bhikkhuni* order under Theravada *Sangha* approval is not a high priority in Thailand except among a small number of devoted women followers of Voramai Kabilsingh, a Thai woman who received the *bhikkhuni* ordination according to the Mahayana tradition in Taiwan in 1970 and heads a woman-focused temple on the outskirts of Bangkok. The obstacles to ordination facing this route to increasing spiritual options for women have demonstrated the divisions among women and men, *mae chii*, and monks. Those who favour reviving the ordination tradition face criticism and contempt for their efforts. A safer route has been efforts to improve the position and condition of *mae chii* through providing more educational opportunities and financial support for separate nunneries. This more conservative route is necessary because of the well-entrenched androcentrism within Thai monastic institutions, and the attitudes they have imparted to the laity.

In spite of the undeniable institutional androcentrism of the Thai *sangha*, or perhaps because of it, lay meditation was open to laywomen, and many excelled as meditation teachers, bypassing the *sangha* altogether. In the regional traditions, female ascetics were admired and supported by the laity (Tiyavanich 1997: 281).

Ascetic Misogyny

Misogyny, the hatred or fear of women and feminine, is not widespread in Buddhist texts, according to Gross (1993:22). Falsely linked to Buddhism, but deriving from non-canonical meaning systems are beliefs and practices related to women and pollution or defilement. Fearing women's power to pollute and defile, restrictions were placed on women so that men and sacred objects charged with protective power do not lose that power through contact with women's bodies. According to Kabilsingh (1988:10–11), the low value attached to female bodies, and the assumption that female bodily processes are polluting and destructive of male power, emerges from Brahmanism, not Buddhism. The impurity associated with menstruation, for example, is in no way derived from Buddhist teaching. The source of these ideas on pollution is the Brahmanic beliefs and practices of the Ayutthaya period (1351–1767), when Brahman rituals were used to produce magical charms and amulets to protect soldiers during battle. Magical charms became ineffective when in contact with menstrual blood or menstruating women. Buddhist texts do not stigmatize menstruation, but rather note in a matter-of-fact way the canonical rules requiring *bhikkhuni* to wash their menstrual cloths and hand them over to the *bhikkuni sangha* for distribution to the next women needing them (Kabilsingh 1984: 106).

Women's lower garments are also used to represent weakness and unmanly behavior. During the 1992 democracy protests in Bangkok, a man donned a woman's skirt to protest 'unmanly reporting by state controlled media' (*Bangkok Post* 12 May 1992). A woman's skirt was considered something dirty and polluted, taboo for men to touch (Reynolds 1987:57). Nevertheless, women's garments have also been conceptualized as powerful, possessing the capacity to destroy male power. Recall the legend of Queen Chamadevi, the Mon leader of the Lamphun area, Northern Thailand, confirming the power of women's polluted lower garments. To avoid marriage and loss of her kingdom, she wove fabric from her lower garments into her suitor's hat, rendering him unable to hurl his spear and claim her hand and kingdom (Morris 1994a).

In addition to linking women's bodily processes to pollution, ascetic misogyny perpetuates the fear of the power of women to undermine celibacy. Fears about women seducing men and monks could well be linked to the difficulty that celibate monks faced in trying to repress thoughts of sexual intimacy (Murcott 1991:100). The image of women as impure temptresses may also be cited as evidence of ascetic misogyny. Murcott claims that 'under the Buddhist system, a woman, regardless of her role, was considered to belong to an intermediate plane between animals and men' (1991:78). This statement is unsupported and inaccurate. As Gross repeatedly demonstrates, Buddhism is one world religion whose teachings do not support misogymous questioning of women's humanity.

Soteriological Androgyny

Soteriological inclusiveness confirmed women's ability to attain higher spiritual goals; soteriological androgyny furthers the task of breaking down the relevance of gender categories. Attachment and clinging are more significant problems than self and sexuality in the ideology and practice of Theravada Buddhism. Buddhist concepts of male and female are weakly developed in the canonical literature. In the logic of Theravada Buddhism, we come to realize that we hold the false belief that there are male and female humans with separate identities and selves. The concept of person is the conventional truth of the unenlightened (Collins 1982: 179). It is an error of understanding, an instance of thinking on the ordinary level and not the *karmic* level, to think that there are fixed entities such as men and women. This is illusion and unreality. In Theravada Buddhist *dhamma* language, the ultimate truth (*paranamattha sacca*) is that there is no person or self but rather a succession of moments of awareness, constantly dying and being reborn, that cluster in the bodies of individuals (Tobias 1973:59).

Core Buddhist teachings build from the concepts of non-self (*anatta*), impermanence (*anicca*), and dependent origination (*paticcasamuppada*). In this framework, the individual has no ultimately fixed or determinant nature (Sponberg 1992:10). From the concept of *anatta* comes the disposition to understand that there are no personality traits attributed to men or women. Such a personality belief is a '. . . theoretical error caused by seeing a relation, of one sort or another, between "self" and the *khanda*' (aggregate, mass, or heap) (Collins 1982:133). This false personality belief is called *sakkavaditthi*.

Non-self (*anatta*) is explored in abstract philosophical *abhidhamma* texts and made meaningful with difficulty in everyday life in rural Thai communities. As a monk scholar explained, not that there is no self whatsoever, but that the self exists solely in relationship to other beings, past, present, and future. The Burmans of central Mynmar (Spiro 1970), Shan in northern Thailand (Tannenbaum 1995) and central Thai rural farmers in Suphanburi Province link non-self or *anatta* to lack of control of mind. The mind is like a monkey, moving around, unable to settle down and concentrate, until it is controlled through meditation. This metaphor of mind as monkey is widespread in Thailand. You do not have to be an *abhidhamma* scholar to understand the uncontrolled mind as a monkey, when monkeys can be seen flipping from the branches of trees outside temples. Thai Buddhists listen to sermons on the subject and see monkeys on temple paintings on a regular basis. This interpretation of non-self is a realistic way of making sense of an important Buddhist soteriological concept. Other opinions on *anatta* expressed by male farmers in Suphanburi linked it to death and the coming apart of the body, the spreading of *metta* or loving kindness, and a sense of selflessness (J. Van Esterik 1977).

The concept of impermanence (*anicca*) also underlies the Buddhist approach to male and female identities. The karmic conditioned sequences of cause and effect are what motivates and explains behaviour, not any attribute of self such as masculinity or femininity. Just as in the Judeo-Christian tradition, it makes sense that man is created in the image of God, so in Theravada Buddhism it makes sense that humans do not have permanent fixed characteristics for eternity (Tobias 1973:55).[5]

At the higher levels of consciousness, there is no male, no female. *Nirvana*, the cessation of rebirths, is beyond any consideration of masculinity and femininity, and to argue that both males and females can reach this level is an error of understanding, and a distortion of Buddhist logic concerning gender. Enlightenment is simply not embodied, and therefore could not be embodied in either gender.

Invoking Buddhism

In the following four chapters, I invoke Buddhism as one of many strands of interpretation that strengthens the hand of the state in developing national identity (Chapter 4), renders beauty meaningful (Chapter 5), rationalizes prostitution (Chapter 6) and trivializes gender (Chapter 7).

Buddhism and the State

Thailand has 'developed' at a rapid rate recently, with the fastest growing GNP in the world in the late 1980s. But vast problems have resulted from the unequal distribution of new wealth, and the effects of rapid industrialization. Non-governmental organizations (NGOs) have been critically important in providing programs that attempt to bridge this gap. For many of these groups, their slogan, *NIC pen narok* (to be a NIC – newly industrialized country – is to be in Hell), reflects their recognition of the problems caused by rapid changes in the country. The logic that underdevelopment is caused by a decay in Buddhist morality is also used by Thai Marxists to explain the corruption of the capitalist era.

Prawet Wasi, a well-known Thai Buddhist activist, has made explicit what he proposes should be the role of Buddhism in development – a development that must be strongly moral and ethical. He argues that pure Buddhism promotes morals and ethics through *sila* (morality) which he links to a low level of consumption and a decrease in materialism, *samadhi* (a peaceful mind for improving one's behaviour), and *panya* (understanding the nature of things), and is necessary for perfect development. Buddhism becomes the guardian of the community's harmony, a way to unite its members and resist state exploitation and capitalism (Nartsupha 1991:125). Although Prawet Wasi sees this as reinterpreting Buddhism, in fact he has brought a middle-class, urban, and philosophical bias to the indigenous rural Thai concept of a moral community. Prawet Wasi professes equality between men and women in all domains including religion, but he cautions against reviving Buddhist ordination for women. He sees such efforts as an uphill battle that would waste energy and opportunity, and raise conflict.

Since, the 1960s, the monkhood has been involved in community development work in rural areas, first on government orders to combat the threat of communism and later as socially engaged monks seeking alternative models of development (Tiyavanich 1997:274). Since monks were generally more trusted than government officials, the Thai government wanted to make use of monks to legitimize their development work; however, local monks also became critics of that work. Monks' involvement in development work could be justified as an expression of concern for all sentient beings. Development monks also aimed to restructure lay merit-making activities around support for development projects, a subject of particular relevance to women who are the most active merit makers in rural Thailand. Meeting basic human needs must also be seen as a prerequisite for spiritual development. This argument is conveniently forgotten by critics of the merit-making activities of prostitutes who are seldom able to meet their basic needs.

Buddhism has also been interpreted as a hegemonic discourse, serving a conservative agenda by providing those subordinated by it with a commonsense, taken-for-granted world view that supports the political interests of the ruling elite. The notion of hegemony[6] is one means of addressing the problem of how to relate the material conditions impinging on women's lives such as tax structures, maternity leaves, wage differentials, and marriage laws, with ideologies such as Buddhism, and competing ideologies like Marxism, capitalism, development and consumerism. Yet the explanatory potential of Buddhist hegemony has seldom been applied to gender relations.

In the absence of an agreed upon indigenous Thai feminist theory, Marxist analysis has taken on considerable analytical importance in explaining 'cultural factors' and the relations between Buddhism and gender. Both Thai Marxists and Thai feminists searched for the essence of a 'pure' Buddhism devoid of cultural trappings, an impossible task. Radical critiques of feudal Thailand were seldom concerned with gender or men's oppression of women. As one radical wrote: 'The richness of Thailand ensures that there will never be starvation. But the way that men treat each other in this happy land is disgusting' (Wedel 1987:72). There is, however, no mention of the way men treat women. Radical views from male intellectual Marxists were not always flattering to women. From Jit Poumisak's speech in 1952: 'As a consequence the Thai woman is ignorant, incapable and automatically subjected to being "the rear feet of the elephant" following Thai tradition' (Wedel 1987: 99).

Radical writer Jit Poumisak's 1957 analysis of Buddhism and his brief references to women were translated and discussed by Reynolds (1987) and Wedel (1987). In *The Real Face of Thai Sakdina Today*, Jit argues that Buddhism is a feudal remnant, an instrument of rule rather than a source of spiritual and social security (Reynolds 1987:12). Under these conditions, women were treated contemptuously, oppressed as human beings inferior to men and reduced to sexual objects. The feudal laws of the Ayutthaya period (1351–1767) clearly defined women as chattels of husband or father who could be sold into slavery; men retained these rights over women until 1867 (Wedel 1987:99). History does not tell us how these laws were enforced. The Three Seals Law of 1805 compiled during the reign of Rama I continued to control women by confirming the husband's legal right to treat his women and wives as private property, bestowing punishment on them including execution and managing wives' money and land brought into the marriage as he saw fit. Assumptions about a man's right to sell his children resurfaces today in the parental sale of daughters as prostitutes to escape debt bondage.

Legal reforms of patriarchal laws that appear to improve the status of Thai women such as the Abolition of Slavery Act (1874), the Land Act (1901), and the Monogamy Act (1935) were part of the system of consolidating state power in the formative years of the Chakri dynasty. But neither the patriarchal laws nor their reformed versions should be considered Buddhist laws. Buddhist institutions and Buddhist principles are conflated in Jit's argument. Certainly, state religion supported feudal practices; but these practices can not be equated with Buddhism.

The institution of the monkhood (*Sangha*) has been criticized by pro-democracy groups and grass-roots development workers. They argue that Buddhist institutions have been recast by the ruling class to use as a means of oppressing women and other subordinate groups. This concern with recasting ideologies invites Thai analysts to seek ways to integrate Buddhism and Marxism. Wedel (1987) explains how Thai Marxists disagreed with Marx in the area of religion and tried to re-fashion both Buddhism and Marxism to make the two compatible. In this interpretation, Buddhism itself is not viewed as oppressive; rather Buddhist institutions were distorted by the ruling class as a means of oppression (1987:213). Even the radicals were deeply Buddhist, and stressed the potential of 'pure' Buddhism to transform society in ways compatible with Marx, although they differed as to the means of achieving these ends – violent revolution or individual morality and meditation.

Buddhism and Beauty

Buddhism should be totally irrelevant to practices such as beauty contests that commodify women's bodies and create the illusion of beauty on the surface of those bodies. In fact, canonical and popular Buddhist texts provide images of beauty that re-emerge in popular practice. Buddhist rationale for appreciation of beauty includes the idea that physical beauty reflects merit store, good deeds in past or present lives, and moral purity. Clarity of complexion, grace and serenity were reflections of moral goodness, one guide to knowing merit store. Ugliness, unfortunately, conveyed the opposite, although since all acts have *karmic* consequences, both evil and goodness may have to be worked out in each individual's life, on each individual's face.

In the Pali texts containing the discourses of the Buddha, the questions of Queen Mallika to the Buddha, and his answers, expand on this point. She asks:

> Reverend Sir, what is the reason, and what is the cause, when a woman is ugly, of a bad figure and horrible to look at, and rich, wealthy, affluent, and high in the social scale? ... Reverend Sir, what is the reason, and what is the cause, when a woman is beautiful, attractive, pleasing, and possessed of surpassing loveliness, and indigent, poor, needy, and low in the social scale? (Warren 1969:228–9)

The Buddha links these conditions to the woman's behaviour in former lives; perhaps she manifested no hatred or anger, but at the same time gave no alms to monks. By this paradigm, beauty is the result of moral goodness (practising *sila* or Buddhist morality), and not feeling anger, spite, or envy in former lives, while social status is more affected by giving, *dana*. But the questions of Queen Mallika acknowledge paradox and contradictions in the life experiences of women. It is not difficult to account for a poor, ugly woman, or a rich, beautiful woman, on the basis of assumptions about good and bad behavior in former lives. Buddhist logic leaves potential for a beautiful person to become ugly, an ugly person to become beautiful, or an ugly person to be morally good. Thus it is possible to account for beautiful, poor women, and rich ugly women within this Buddhist logic. The

Buddha's explanations reinforce theories of dependent origination, that all actions have consequences that must be worked out in the future. Contradictions affirm rather than challenge *karmic* status. For example, a beautiful prostitute is understandable since in her present life, she is working out both good and evil.

'The perception of beauty arises depending upon a large number of factors including past *karma*, present life, family, education, and surroundings' (Khantipalo 1990:18). Modern Thai monks tell us we can appreciate beauty as long as it is done with detachment. 'Beauty as an abstract quality does not decay, but what perceives it does, as well as the object of beauty' (Khantipalo 1990:20). The grisly pictures of skeletal and rotting beauty queens frequently displayed in temples and featured in the Buddhist Promotion Week displays, are meant to remind people about the impermanence of bodies and the fading of beauty.[7] Buddhism teaches detachment from the body through emphasis on the decay and impermanence of its physical form. The body is illusion, appearance only. Contemplation on surface appearance fuels fascination with form and beauty, as discussed further in Chapter 5.

Buddhism and Prostitution

Feminist critiques of Buddhism usually relate directly or indirectly to prostitution. In fact, analysis of Thai prostitution has often substituted for analysis of gender relations in Thailand, as if explaining Thai prostitution were adequate for understanding the position and condition of Thai women. There is great danger in using prostitution as a proxy measure of women's status in Thailand. There is even greater danger in separating out prostitution as a social problem or a health problem, and isolating it from other gender issues. In Chapter 6, I discuss how several Thai analysts have evoked Buddhism to explain prostitution.

In her (1990) book, *Sex, Money and Morality*, Truong argues that prostitution has been consolidated by the biases inherent in Buddhism, although acknowledging that prostitution arose from social conditions external to Buddhism (1990:131). It is important to include in discussions of prostitution the ideological context provided by Buddhism, but without relevant knowledge of Buddhist texts, beliefs and practices, Truong's argument is dangerously ineffective, confirming analysts' assumptions that prostitution is a problem of poverty, a problem best left to economists to explain, without further consideration of cultural and ideological context.[8]

Troung raises the issue of prostitutes' merit making (Truong 1990: 137). Prostitutes can and do improve their *karmic* status in a wide range of ways – including donations to temples, feeding monks, supporting a *thot phaa paa* (ritual of giving monks' robes), and sponsoring ordinations. These forms of merit making are practiced by women and men throughout the country. Mattani Rutnin describes efforts to suppress a scene in her movie on prostitution in northern Thailand where a monk shows a seven-storey building paid for by donations from prostitutes (1984:4).

Figure 3 Giants depicting the fate of adulterers in hell, Wat Phairongwua, Suphanburi Province

Unchastity or unlawful sex breaks the third of the five precepts that laity undertake to observe. But the third precept is interpreted by many Thai men as a promise not to commit adultery – that is, not to have sex with someone else's wife, a very narrow definition of unlawful sex.[9] Buddhism – both popular and canonical – is in no way ambiguous about the punishment due adulterers, even to the point of specifying fixed penalties for specific acts. Let the punishment fit the crime. At Wat Phairongwua, a popular Buddhist temple and 'theme park' in Suphanburi Province, the classification of sexual acts and demeritorious consequences are represented in giant tableaux depicting in gruesome details the hells occupied by adulterers. According to the *Trai Phum Phra Ruang*, there are sixteen auxiliary hells located like satellites around eight large hells. Auxiliary hells number 13, 14 and 15 are reserved for men and women who commit adultery with other men's wives or women who betray their husbands. They each differ in the nature of their punishments: bodies stabbed with lances until they are torn into small pieces, blood and pus flowing out; bodies crushed by fiery red iron mountains, 'pressing their bodies many times in the same way that sugar cane is pressed'; bodies hung upside down into a pit, beaten with fiery red iron clubs; bodies chased up and down kapok trees, torn by flaming thorns (Reynolds and Reynolds 1982:78–9). In both canonical and popular Buddhism, the consequences for adultery are specified, painful and not ambiguous; but they are also not deterrents.

Unlawful or inappropriate sex is more often identified as *akusala* or unwholesome rather than as sinful. Indeed, unlawful sex would need to be defined for each situation, each context. It certainly could not be circumscribed by definitions provided in early Buddhist texts. To invoke Buddhism to 'explain' prostitution is to confuse absolutes with social definitions of *karmic* consequences.

Buddhism and the Thai Sex-gender System

Theravada Buddhism does not have a great deal to say about sexuality; sex is simply irrelevant to Buddhism except as it refers to monastic celibacy. In Buddhism, sex is not a sin; sex, like eating, is considered simply another form of bodily attachment. 'Buddhist texts take a consistently negative stance to all expressions of sexuality as being impediments to spiritual progress' (Zwilling 1992:210). Homosexual and heterosexual acts carry the same moral significance (or insignificance) from the perspective of textual traditions within Buddhism (Cabezon 1992). Homosexuality is a problem when it causes suffering, but it is viewed as suffering or bad luck rather than as evil (Jackson 1989:60). Understanding of gender differences may begin with the distinction between sexually active (householder) and sexually inactive (celibate monks and other religious). Marriage, of lay persons, for example, is not the business of Thai monks. Communal rituals surrounding marriage and other household celebrations are irrelevant to Buddhism, and are thus derived from other ritual traditions in Theravada countries, in Thailand, the Brahmanic and guardian spirit complexes.

Truong refers to a Buddhist discourse on sexuality which

> distinguishes the male and female body socially through the inclusion and exclusion of specific qualities as part of their biological functions (potency and receptivity, purity and pollution, creativity and functionality). This differentiation has imparted different definitions of sexual needs, desire and significance to men and women. (Truong 1990:195)

Social conditions in Thailand support men's expression of their sexual desires – expressed homosexually or heterosexually – rather than women's expression of their sexual desires, a point discussed more in Chapter 7. Nevertheless, women are blamed for being the objects of male desire. If men cling to their craving for sex or for women's bodies, then the problem lies in their clinging, not in their objects of desire (Sponberg 1992:23). Of course, male bodies are also objects of sexual desire, and if women cling to their craving for male bodies, they are equally burdened. Men, then, are equally an enemy to the purity of women, a text conveniently forgotten by Thai monks (Kabilsingh 1995:4).

Buddhist Feminism

Buddhism is widely celebrated for its tolerance. It is therefore surprising that more work has not been done on how Buddhist logic can be used for strengthening women's struggles for equality, and shifting gender assumptions in a direction more favourable to women, in Thailand and elsewhere. I have identified how selected Buddhist texts and practices will be used in the following chapters. But some ideas persist and have been more fruitful than others: 'the attitude that there is something wrong with female birth has been far more popular and widespread than the idea that gender is irrelevant and women are not to be denigrated' (Gross 1993:116). While both Thai and Western feminists point to aspects of Buddhism that are patriarchal, androcentric, or misogynist, Buddhist feminists stress the compatibility of Buddhism and feminism, and strive to develop the potential of soteriological androgyny. Androgyny affirms both male and female. A sex-neutral model denies both male and female[10](Gross 1993:222).

Rita Gross' *Buddhism after Patriarchy* (1993) has articulated the most complete feminist revalorization of Buddhism, and concludes that no Buddhist teachings support gender inequity or gender hierarchy, although the concept of *karma* was reinterpreted to justify male dominance (1993:209–10). Buddhism is androcentric but not misogynist (1993: 119). She takes the position that Buddhism in general is essentially egalitarian and liberating for all beings (1993:127), and Thai Buddhism does not contradict that position; neither does it elaborate on it.

While feminist potential exists within Thai Buddhism, Thai women have not had access to sufficient power to bring out the androgynous potential within Buddhism. However, the potential is there in the core teachings of Buddhism and does not need to be imported from Western feminism or Western Buddhism. Apologists for Buddhism assure us that since Buddhism provides freedom to women, that hysterical 'women's lib' is an unwanted Western import . While Buddhism is less sexist than many world religions, it does not have a clean bill of health. 'Not even noticing that women are being discriminated against is a more dangerous form of opposition to gender equality than outright opposition to egalitarian reforms' (Gross 1993:117). This is particularly true when the practice of Buddhism is examined in specific localities such as Thailand.

Buddhism and feminism share many features; both Buddhism and feminism begin with experience, stress experiential understandings, and move from experience to theory. Commitment to experience encourages 'going against the grain', holding to unconventional insights. Finally, both explore how the mind operates, and how habitual ego patterns block basic well-being (Gross 1986:47–9). I argue in Chapter 7 that both also question the idea of fixed, transcendental gender identities, a critical point for examining gender relations. However, Buddhism provides only one part of the context of gender relations.

Increasingly over the last few decades in Thailand there are new religious practices that support women and new religious roles for women, including women meditation teachers who instruct monks as well as laity (J. Van Esterik 1982). Where practice and belief appear to subordinate women, there are new initiatives by women to remove these obstacles to their full participation in Buddhist life. This optimism (expressed by an outsider and a non-Thai) in no way negates the importance of understanding Buddhism as a hegemonic force in Thai society today nor the need to remove all obstacles to women's equity. There is clearly a problem in the real world for women who are discriminated against to argue that at the upper levels of cosmological space, there is no male, no female.

The existence of Buddhism as a dominant ideology does not preclude regional, ethnic and class variations in the interpretations of that ideology, tensions concerning its transmission, or active resistance to it. However, Buddhism may have the potential to inspire a vision of a non-oppressive utopia where sex and gender are less relevant, and a number of different gender positions can co-exist. Buddhism offers yet another way to deconstruct person and gender. Since Buddhist concepts of self (and non-self) differ so fundamentally from Western concepts of the individual, a Buddhist feminism may be able to integrate class and moral action into its ideology more successfully than has Western feminism.

But ideologies, exist in the material world, where they are manipulated for political ends. Just as Marxists have re-interpreted Buddhist philosophy in a way consistent with their theories, so feminist theorists are re-examining Buddhism to see the extent to which Buddhist wisdom is compatible with feminist wisdom. Modern state Buddhism with its stress on control through correctness of ordination rituals resists changes that would benefit women. Efforts to understand how gender fits within modern state Buddhism also require examination of Thai nationalist ideology and public culture, the subject of the next chapter.

Notes

1. Several villagers in Suphanburi Province interviewed in the early 1970s answered a direct question about desired rebirth state by saying that they should not desire rebirth as either male or female, lest they be reborn of indeterminate sex or not as humans (J. Van Esterik 1977).

2. The *Tipitaka* refers to the three baskets of the Pali canon, consisting of the *Vinaya Pitaka* (monastic rules), *Sutta Pitaka* (sermons of the Buddha) and the *Abhidhamma* (commentaries and philosophical discourses). Thai transcriptions and translations of Pali are also available.

3. The *Trai Phum Phra Ruang* is a cosmological text attributed to Phya Lithai, heir to the Sukhothai throne, written around 1345. The cosmology is familiar to urban and rural Thai through stories and paintings.

4. Under some conditions, merit can be transferred to deceased relatives to improve their chances of rebirth. This is clearly seen in the simple but powerful ritual of *kluat nam*, where merit made is shared with all sentient beings or specified relatives by pouring water during the monks' recitation of a powerful text. In Kukrit Pramot's famous novel *Si Phaendin* (Four Reigns), the heroine Ploi, transfers merit to her parents in this way.

5. On a more pragmatic level, politicians have made use of *anicca* to justify changes in government power structures. After former Prime Minister Pridi Panomyong failed to regain power in the 1950s, he went into exile in southern China and wrote about the integration of Buddhist and Marxist approaches to change using the concept of impermanence (*anicca*) (Wedel 1987:110).

6. Hegemony refers to a lived set of ideas and meanings which present an ideological order of political and cultural domination expressing the needs of a dominant class as if it were the natural order of things.

7. Popular magazines such as *191* displayed in full colour photographs of gruesome deaths including decapitated bodies, decomposing corpses, and dismembered corpses (Hamilton 1991: 369).

8. Truong argues that in Thailand, the Buddhist religion '. . . provides the people with a worldview, shapes their consciousness, and acts as a subjective form of power which provides legitimacy to social relations' (1990:131). Yet she also assumes that knowledge of metaphysical issues is restricted to monks, and that lay people are taught through parable and folk tales, with the result that '. . . the Four Noble Truths or the Eight-fold Path remains alien and esoteric to the majority of Buddhism's followers' (1990:132). Truong assumes that Buddhism is not cognitively salient to Thai Buddhists, yet looks to Buddhism to explain the status of Thai women and the existence of prostitution.

9. A Thai man who identified himself as a moral Buddhist said he always asked prostitutes if they were married, and chose another if they replied that they were married. A socially engaged Buddhist would consider that having sexual relations outside the context of love, responsibility, and respect breaks precepts, whether or not such behaviour is proscribed in the texts.

10. There is danger in developing a model of androgyny that denies sexuality, particularly in the face of HIV/AIDS.

Part II

Representations

Representing Thai Culture

Culture and Representation

In the last chapter, I argued that Buddhism is important for understanding gender relations. While Thai individuals differ with respect
to the importance of Buddhism as an influence in their lives, there is
no doubt about the importance of Buddhism as a fundamental part of
Thai national identity, expressed as respect for nation, religion and
monarch. This chapter does not examine Buddhism and politics, but
looks instead at the links between the representation of women, and
the representation of the Thai nation state. Exploring these relations
takes us further behind the scenes at Thai provincial fairs, into shopping
malls, and through the many heritage sites preserved by the Thai Fine
Arts Department. At many of these sites, we are joined by tourists –
both domestic and foreign. And many ask the same questions we ask
here: are these authentic Thai experiences in authentic Thai localities?

Thai elite have been playing with historical palimpsests to define
and redefine national identity throughout the last century, juxtaposing
representations and texts to find the essence of Thainess (*khwampen
Thai*). Mulder identifies Thai as an archetypal presentational society
(1992:159), one that resonates with Featherstone's definition of postmodern. He defines postmodernism in the arts as:

> the effacement of the boundary between art and everyday life; the collapse
> of the distinction between high and mass/popular culture; a stylistic
> promiscuity favouring eclecticism and the mixing of codes: parody,
> pastiche, irony, playfulness and the celebration of the surface 'depthless-
> ness' of culture; the decline of the originality/genius of the artistic
> producer; and the assumption that art can only be repetition. (1991:7)

In this sense, the Thai were postmodern before they were modern,
creating images of themselves based on their own 'Orientalism',[1] and

representing themselves to others with consummate skill. Thus national identity was constituted internationally from free-floating signifiers from Thailand's past, but responsive to global pressures and opportunities (see also Winichakul 1994, Tejapira 1996).

As individuals and as shapers of institutions, Thai shift between contexts easily and skilfully, influenced perhaps by Buddhist orientations to impermanence. Concern with a civilized face and image becomes a particularly prominent part of Thai national identity formation after contact with European colonizers active on their eastern, western, and southern borders.

Colonial Discourse, Nationalism and Heritage

Colonial rule shapes how the past is represented. Streckfuss argues that Thailand's narrative of nation is framed by colonialism – made conspicuous by its absence (1993:123). As the only Southeast Asian nation to remain free of direct European control, Thailand approaches representations of her past with an unselfconsciousness lacking in other Southeast Asian nations. Thailand has had no experience in dismantling colonial empires and institutions, and as a nation state, has been interpreted by historians as demonstrating a continuity of social, political, economic and cultural structures uniquely Thai. Thus nationalism must have a different rationale in Thailand, one based on avoiding colonialization rather than experiencing it. In fact, Bangkok itself colonized its periphery. As a non-colonized but 'informally colonized' nation, Thailand benefitted from not having to fight old enemies who were now under colonial rule (Burma, Malaysia, Laos, Cambodia and Vietnam). As Anderson says, their old enemies were too weak to fight and their new enemies, too strong (Anderson 1977:21). This allowed Thailand to be more selective and open to Western and European influence than her colonized neighbours whose exposure to the West was structured and controlled through colonial institutions.

As Mitchell describes for Egypt (1988), new methods of disciplinary power penetrate more effectively in areas colonized by European powers. For example, neither model development villages nor school discipline were as effective in Thailand as in colonies such as Egypt. Without national independence movements developed in opposition to colonial powers, the Thai governing elite had little need for mass nationalism or women's liberation movements which often accompanied independence movements. The legitimacy of the hegemonic Buddhist social organization and *sakdina*[2] social relations remained intact, delaying the break between the Thai elite and the masses (Sunthraraks 1986:76). Opposition between the elite and the masses took precedence over colonizer versus colonized. The myth of Thai identity promulgated by Prime Minister Phibun Songkhram discussed below argues that the Thai lacked a nationalist oriented character precisely because of their ability to adapt to external circumstances and select foreign innovations. In practical terms, this eased the adoption of things foreign and their redefinition as Thai. 'It is not enough to go to a foreign country to acquire specific skills, but that it is more desirable to be able to imbibe that foreign culture in all its aspects so that one can glean out what is good for one's own country' (Nagavajara 1994b: xxxii).

Concerns about nationalism and national identity proliferate when nations and national borders are threatened. But much about national identity can be learned from the construction of identity of nations and nationals at peace. Thailand is an excellent example. Its borders are essentially unchallenged, although the loss of land to Cambodia and Laos was a high price to pay for appeasing the French at the end of the nineteenth century and after the Second World War. Over the last 200 years, the country has been acutely sensitive to construction of national identity, or as Tongchai Winichakul (1994) has argued, the geo-body of the nation.

Tongchai Winichakul's masterful book *Siam Mapped* (1994) explores how the logic and technology of 'mapping' created the geo-body of the Thai nation. However, gender has no place in his account - the geo-body is unsexed or unmarked masculine. Women appear only as tributes or in marriage alliances with marginal vassals. Tongchai problematizes space but naturalizes gender. But he uses an interesting metaphor with regard to the geo-body. The trope of the nation as motherland is expressed as common soil or the great underworld serpent (*naga*), the goddess of the earth. By the end of the nineteenth century, the metaphor has become masculine, as the royal body of the divine king becomes the embodiment of the territorial space of the nation state (Winichakul 1994:133–4).

Studies of nationalism and national identity are often gender blind, as if nationalism, politics and economics were all the exclusive domains of men. Since state efforts to create nationalism are intimately connected to military service and electoral politics, the absence of women is not surprising. Citing the absence of women in Anderson's *Imagined Communities*, Pratt notes that, 'Women inhabitants of nations were neither imagined as nor invited to imagine themselves as part of the horizontal brotherhood . . . Gender hierarchy exists as a deep cleavage in the horizontal fraternity' (1994:30–1). Recently, Parker et al in their book on *Nationalisms and Sexualities* (1992:2) have explored the complex linkages between sexuality, and nationalism as a passionate need, legitimated through a national discourse of civil liberties. Since Anderson's pioneering work on nationalism as the 'deep horizontal comradeship' of imagined communities (1983), nationalism has been seen – like gender – as a relational term in a system of differences (Parker et al 1992:5, Jeffrey 1999).

Studies of Thai nationalism most often stressed the personal skills of the kings of the Chakri dynasty and their prime ministers as they negotiated with Western powers to protect Thai sovereignty, thus emphasizing the continuity and uniqueness of Thai kingship and culture. Anderson (1978a), and more recently Winichakul (1994) and Reynolds (1991) have challenged this picture, arguing for a more complex and less elitist view of the process. Nevertheless, it is useful to review this official version of the nationalism of Rama VI and Prime Minister Phibun Songkhram to examine how and where gender was relevant to their arguments.

The Nationalism of Rama VI (Vajiravudh – 1910–1925): King Vajiravudh came to the throne in 1910 after being educated in England. He viewed the monarchy as the key to nationhood. His official elite nationalism sought to impose 'a standardized, homogeneous, centrally sustained high culture (that is, Bangkok, central Thai culture) on its subjects (Barmé 1993:9). His writings admonish 'free-born *men* . . . not to forget our race and our faith . . . How could a *man* who respects himself remain idle?' (Vella 1978:91, emphasis mine).[3] In a frenzy of militaristic nationalism which excluded women, Vajiravudh drew around him young men who shared his interest in the performing arts and military rituals. His Wild Tiger Corps, a mass paramilitary group formed to promote national unity, bypassed the military and elevated commoners to positions of responsibility and intimacy with the royal person. The corps was modelled after the men who guarded the frontiers of ancient Thailand, men known for their ruggedness, loyalty, fearlessness and knowledge of nature and warfare. Although the Wild Tiger Corps ended with Rama VI's reign, the junior branch survived as the government-sponsored Boy Scouts (Support Foundation 1985:Vol. 6, 19). The infamous village scouts whose right-wing beliefs supported state repression in the 1970s and 1980s (Bowie 1997) may also be a more dubious descendant.

Vajiravudh's brand of elite nationalism was aimed at the bureaucrats

(Wilayasakpan 1992:63), primarily a male audience. Many innovations such as team sports owed much to his British private school experience of male bonding. His obvious preference for male friends and his reluctance to marry and reproduce cannot be judged by Western models of gender and royal propriety, as only the latter would be cause for concern within the Thai sex/gender system, as discussed in Chapter 7.

Vajiravudh's relations with women may have been strained, as his portrayal of them in literary and theatrical works was stereotypical and unflattering. Nevertheless, in the beautiful commemorative volumes celebrating each king of the Chakri dynasty published by the Royal Palace in 1985, Vajiravudh is pictured dressed as the heroine, Marie, in a play he directed, and as a Japanese beauty in Gilbert and Sullivan's the *Mikado* (Support Foundation 1985:Vol. 6,49, 51).

Vajiravudh, like Prime Minister Phibun discussed next, took it upon himself to 'raise the status' of Thai women, as he viewed the status of women as a symbol of the degree of civilization of the country (Vella 1978:152). While colonial discussions of Egyptian mentality linked Egypt's moral inferiority to the status of its women (Mitchell 1988: 111), Thai constructions of national identity were less misogynous. Vajiravudh's concern, like Phibun's, was for appearances: he writes, 'Please understand that others are taking our measure' (Vella 1978:153). And when appearances are manipulated, attention always turns to women.

Vajiravudh identified three major restrictions on Thai women: their limited freedom to socialize with men on equal terms, their limited access to education, and the practice of polygamy, which was viewed by Europeans as particularly barbaric. Minor problems concerned their appearance, including women's black teeth from betel chewing, their short 'brush-cut' hairstyles, and wearing *chongkraben*, the comfortable draped pants worn by men and women. Western travellers to Thailand, used to the extremes of gender opposition in European constructions of masculinity and femininity, were clearly confused by the similarity in appearance between Thai men and women – their clothing, hair-styles, and daily activities, for example (cf. Bradley 1981, Bowring 1857). Vajiravudh was particularly concerned because Westerners did not view elements of Thai dress simply as examples of cultural differences in fashions, but as deliberate strategies to keep women unattractive, and thus in bondage (Vella 1978:154). This attitude would be particularly anathema to Thai sensibilities because of the importance of aesthetic appearance underlying Thai gender constructions. The King encouraged his women friends and relatives to wear their hair long and wear the more stylish but restrictive skirt-like *phaasin* rather than the draped pants (*chongkraben*) worn by men and women in rural and court settings. Even hats were encouraged, and the new fashions were widely imitated among urban elite.

Thai women were advised to put devotion to nation ahead of devotion to spouse, but show devotion to nation by looking after their husbands and instilling nationalistic values in their children. Vajiravudh sought to break down the separation of the sexes in public by encouraging women to accompany their husbands to public events such as theatre parties. But women had no direct role in advancing the cause of nationalism beyond the changes in their appearance and leisure activities. In fact, changes in women's roles and appearance introduced Western elements of femininity rather than reinforcing Thai femininity. Vajiravudh relied on voluntarism, exhortation, and propaganda to accomplish his nationalist goals (Vella 1978:270), in sharp contrast to Prime Minister Phibun Songkhram who attempted to use force and enact legislation to carry out his ideas about civilizing Thai women and Thai culture.

Prime Minister Phibun Songkhram (1938-44, 1948-57): Prime Minister Phibun tried to impose modern concepts of the state and leadership on Thai society in an attempt to establish a new relation of hegemony not based on the monarchy. Nevertheless, the *sakdina* system with its notions of hierarchy based on royal power persisted after the 1932 coup abolishing the absolute monarchy, and has been slow to change. Sunthraraks identifies the persistence of *sakdina* mentality as a '. . . passive acceptance of authority, conformity to existing views of conduct, and a belief that the world and life are governed by the Buddhist law of Karma' (1986:43). Phibun aimed to change this through the use of art, literature and culture. After the 1932 coup, a series of government offices operated to formulate and propagate the government's version of Thai national identity. Part of Phibun's nation-building strategy was to develop 'Thai-ness' and impose a 'Thai Great Tradition' to demonstrate the strength and unity of the Thai nation. Ironically, this official version of Thai culture was based on Western models and created by the suppression of a number of local traditions, most notably, the Lao of the northeast and Lanna of the north, both of which had distinctive scripts, literature, and artistic traditions that were all but destroyed in the efforts to build a Thai national identity.

The National Cultural Development Act passed in 1942 defined culture (*wathanatham*) as showing flourishing development, good order, harmonious progress of the nation and good public morals. Culture,

by the Royal Institute's official definition, refers to characteristics that
denote growth, orderliness, national unity and progress, and good
public morality. It was considered the duty of Thai people to comply
with national culture by preserving what was good in traditional
culture. Prime Minister Phibun and other builders of Thai nationalism
assumed that culture could protect Thailand against undesirable foreign
influence, just as it would protect her from communism in the 1960s
and 1970s. These optimistic assumptions about the power of culture
would not have been made in a country overcoming direct colonial
rule. Cultural nationalism was a project of the state not a direct response
to Westerners, although early nationalist strategies may well have been
a response to colonial threats and the need to regulate the national
image abroad.

The National Cultural Development Act of 1942 established the
framework for the task of cultural construction and nation building.
According to Phibun, the National Culture Council was established to
prevent the spread of Japanese culture into Thailand (Numnonda
1978:242). The National Culture Council begun in 1943, was divided
into five offices – culture through the mind (Bureau of Spiritual Culture),
through customs (Bureau of Customary Culture), through art (Bureau
of Artistic Culture), through literature (Bureau of Literary Culture) and
through women (Bureau of Women's Culture) (Numnonda 1977:203,
Wilayasakpan 1992:117). It drew real and invented provincial and
regional 'little traditions' into the Thai nation state in a construction
of Pan-Thaiism as manifest destiny. Yet the classical court traditions of
music, literature, and dance were neither fostered nor promoted as part
of this new Thai identity, but simply preserved as part of Thailand's
cultural heritage (Wilayasakpan 1992:131). In fact, both court and
regional traditions were more or less ignored in preference for Western
invented traditions – rather like the Thai preference for building a
new temple instead of restoring an old one. Phibun's nationalism
was intended to erode the traditional hegemony of the monarchy
(Sunthraraks 1986:120), and thus it is not surprising that he should
not look to the court traditions for unifying cultural symbols.

A series of twelve Cultural Mandates or National Conventions
(*ratniyom*) were issued by the government between 1939 and 1942 to
demonstrate to the outside world how modern and civilized Thailand
was. They were modelled after the royal practice of issuing royal
prescriptions to set cultural standards (Reynolds 1991:5). These mandates attempted to encourage mass rather than elite nationalism.

This superficial approach to nation-building through cultural reconstruction was given some legitimacy by the association of Thai scholars such as Phya Anuman Rajadhon and Luang Wichit Watakan and others whose research and writing on Thailand have made a significant contribution to the representation of Thainess both internally and externally during this period of nationalist ideological mobilization (1938-1944). But as far back as 1931, government critics called on the government to stop trying to create a civilized veneer and start devising solutions for the nation's problems (Copeland 1993:166). These Cultural Mandates shaped the dominant discourse of modernity in Thailand (and in Thai studies) even after the rules themselves were withdrawn.

On 3 November 1939, Phibun issued a law requiring people to eat Thai food, wear Thai clothes, purchase Thai products and support public activities to build Thai national identity. The first of Phibun's economic Conventions called on the public to 'buy Thai' – to purchase local products and support Thai enterprises. While the Thai elite were well attuned to international shopping in Europe or Hong Kong for luxury goods unavailable in Thailand, lower income urban Thai could now 'buy Thai' at state-run Thai product stores. Under Phibun's Bureau of Customary Culture, Thais were encouraged to develop 'materialistic culture' as a deterrent to communism (Wilayasakpan 1992:120). Even culinary habits were affected as noodle carts were built and recipes supplied to the public to encourage 'noodles for lunch' (Numnonda 1977:204). The public were taught good dietary habits and were encouraged to eat more meat, vegetables and eggs instead of rice, *nam prik* (chilli paste), leaves and salt and 'unmentionable creepy crawlies' (Suwannathat-Pian 1995:126, Numnonda 1977:206). Ironically, Thailand's low-cost and high-quality diet that Phibun was disparaging probably contributed to the country's successful economic transformation.

Other more benign inventions of Thai tradition included promotion of the greeting *sawatdee* for use on an analogy with English 'hello' (formerly it was only used in written texts of poetry or religion), and the dance form, *ramwong*, transformed from a northeastern folk dance tradition, danced to songs composed by Phibun's wife Laiad (Suwannathat-Pian 1995:127).

Efforts to reshape the national image physically included dress. One of the Thai national characteristics defined in 1944 included: 'The Thais are a well-dressed nation' (Suwannathat-Pian 1995:124). The new dress code permitted wearing uniforms, Western clothing (properly worn), or traditional Thai clothing (properly worn). Thai beauty contests (discussed in the next chapter) displayed how to wear Western and

Thai clothing 'properly', and were developed as part of Phibun's nation-building strategy. Women received particular attention for the implementation of these dress codes. Far from being invisible, women were the public embodiment of Thai culture, and the state made use of women's bodies in a number of ways. Many of the innovations in the construction of Thai identity concerned women, their dress, appearance, and demeanour. Phibun's speeches and journals suggest that Phibun felt that Thai women needed to be upgraded in appearance as well as in substance. Like Vajiravudh, he wanted them to dress, and wear their hair and make-up in a manner that would appear modern and Western to foreigners. Particularly during the Second World War women were encouraged to dress in European style to remind the Japanese and the Europeans that Thai were like Westerners, not like Japanese. Women were required to wear hats ('Wear a hat for your country', 'Hats will lead Thailand to Greatness'), stockings, and *phaasin* rather than *chongkraben*. In recent years, Queen Sirikit has promoted Thai national dress for women based on old court styles – *Thai Boromp-iman, Thai Chakri, Thai Chakrapat, Thai Ruen Ton*, and *Thai Chitrlada*. Like the 'archaeological dances' celebrating Thai kingdoms of the past performed at the National Museum[4] and other tourist sites since the 1970s, these gender performances celebrate women as icons of Thainess.

Rural and poor urban Thais who did not have funds to adopt the dress code would make hats out of bamboo, coconut fronds, and palm leaves, and borrow clothing from neighbours (Wilayasakpan 1992). Women wore *chongkraben* under their skirts. Older women – particularly in rural areas – could not change their clothing style, but they were denied government services if they did not appear in Western dress (Kamphibol 1987:255). 'Old women who were found wearing *chongkraben* were forced to restyle their wraparound skirt to *phaasin* on the spot' (Wilayasakpan 1992: 151). Ploi, the heroines of Kukrit Pramoj's widely read novel, *Si Phaendin* (Four Reigns), is advised by her husband, Prem, to stop wearing *chongkraben* and begin to wear *phaasin* which she considered the dress style of northern women. She complained that she wouldn't know how to walk in a *phaasin* (Pramoj 1981:140). Women could be arrested for going without a hat – for 'breaching culture' (Numnonda 1977:211). Wilayasakpan notes the case of a woman who was stopped on her way to the market because she was not wearing a hat, whereupon she put her market basket over her head (1992:151). While these stories may reflect the actions of authoritarian officials with little understanding of Phibun's intentions, most anecdotes refer to women as victims of these arbitrary regulations. There were signs of resistance. Thai women who overdressed in unsuitable Western fashions were referred to as *mam kapi*, smelly Western women (Rutnin 1988:6). Even royalty objected. Queen Srisavarinthira when asked to put on a hat for a photograph snapped 'No! If you really want me to put on a hat then cut my head off and put the hat on it yourself' (1988:239).

Representations of women as part of Thai cultural identity focus not on their status or their abilities but on their appearance. Phibun expressed pride that the Thai now looked good:

> I have seen in our society today, [something] which has made me happy
> . . . proper dress and correct manner are no different from other civilized
> countries . . . In the past, it was seldom that one heard the remark 'I saw
> a well-dressed lady.' One only heard 'I saw a beautiful [face] lady' But
> now, men remark after coming back from any social affair that 'I was
> lucky today because I met a lady who wore a **skirt** and **hat** . . . and
> gorgeous **shoes.** She was as beautiful as any lady from any other country.'
> (Chaloemtiarana 1979:143)

Phibun's policies were meant to upgrade Thai women to the status of women in Western countries. No one seems to have suggested the possibility that although the position and condition of Thai women differed substantially from that of European women, it was not always inferior. He intended to upgrade their status by promoting their education, guaranteeing their rights, and setting up women's groups and cultural clubs to oversee welfare and charity events (Kamphibol 1987). This latter innovation preserved *sakdina* hierarchy as elite women would 'up-grade' common women by holding bazaars and fairs for charitable fundraising, as elite women's groups still do today in Bangkok. Much of this upgrading work was accomplished by Lady Laiad, Phibun's wife, who chaired the Women's Bureau of the Office of Cultural Affairs under the National Culture Council. The Bureau also commissioned songs to celebrate the virtues of Thai women (Nagavajara 1994:xxvi). There were other concrete initiatives in Bangkok to encourage women to do some of what men did – the establishment of an all-female orchestra, a military unit of women, along with the short-lived Women's Cadet Academy.

Perhaps Phibun's most unrealistic expectations concerned the regulation of marriage, not only by legal means – laws that required the registration of only one marriage – but also by specifying the nature of marriage itself. This much ridiculed regulation admonished men not to commit adultery, gamble, or drink – a difficult task, as all three remain the basis of Thai masculinity. Men should give women control in the house; give them jewellery; take them to fairs; carry their parcels; learn about their feelings; eat, sit and walk with them; and kiss them when returning to and leaving the house. Husbands should admire their wives and treat them as friends, and society as a whole should treat women as the mothers of the nation, the flowers of the nation, and the will-power of the nation (Kamphibol 1987:67–9). Kukrit Pramoj's novel, *Si Phaendin* (Four Reigns) ridicules Phibun's instructions: 'This morning . . . my very own "flower of the nation" assaulted me as I was leaving the house. I sweetly told her to blow me a kiss and she gave me a blow instead. My poor f. of n. has no *wattanattam* (culture)' (1981:411). Putting this ideology into practice, Phibun declared a national mother's day and as we will see in the next chapter, put the 'flowers of the nation' on display in national beauty contests.

Women activists use the metaphor of the flowers of the nation as a point of resistance. In the poem 'Assertion of the Flowers', Chiranan writes that flowers have thorns, too.

The flower has sharp thorns
It must not bloom to await praises from others
Rather, it blooms to accumulate
Great fertility for the Earth.

(Translated by Wajuppa Tossa 1992)

The development of national beauty contests in the 1940s are linked to Phibun's attempt to transform *sakdina* mentality and develop the concept of democracy. Copeland illustrates a political cartoon showing Miss Democracy as a beautiful young woman (1993:157). But beauty contests support more than challenge this *sakdina* mentality and have no direct links to democracy unless one includes the recent efforts of beauty agents to scout out poor rural beauties and enter them in regional contests. There was certainly no consciousness of gender equality evident in Phibun's use of women, only a continuation of a cultural pattern stressing the appearance of women as a measure of their worth.

Since women were both the transmitters of culture and signifiers of Thai culture in the new object-oriented Cultural Mandates, and since their behaviour was even more stringently controlled through the Mandates, are we to conclude that Thai women were considered more civilized than Thai men? Elite women in Bangkok may well make such a self-assured but unconscious interpretation; such an interpretation would be unthinkable and inarticulatable in the public military discourse of the state. Fortunately, the Thai elite are not prone to the

logical machinations of gender analysis, nor the resolving of contradictions. And so the appearance of women continues to be used to
represent tradition and modernity simultaneously.

The decision to change the name of the country from Siam to the
ethnically exclusive name Thailand in 1939 was debated in parliament.
In a narrow translation, Thai means free, but it has been used 'to refer
to long-standing, culturally similar groupings of individuals who,
through their military capacity and social cohesion, were able to maintain
their independence in the face of more powerful and expansive groups'
(Barmé 1993: 27). Hence the longstanding association of Thainess with
freedom, independence and adaptability. Thainess – *khwam pen Thai* –
is in essence preserved from the past and constructed and reconstructed
as is useful in the present.

Rather than adopt the word, *Tai*, and claim members of ethnic groups
residing outside Thailand's national borders, a decision was reached to
use the word, Thai. The reason reveals yet another connection between
national identity and women:

> Thai with an H is like a sophisticated girl with her hair set, her lips
> touched with lipstick and her brow arched with eyebrow pencil while
> Tai without the H is like a girl who is naturally attractive but without
> any added beautification. (cited in Numnonda 1977:202)

Thus, even the public presentation of the word, Thai, was not unconnected to the public presentation of Thai women. The analogy of a
beautiful woman takes on even greater significance considering the
state sponsorship of beauty contests.

Concern for a civilized appearance continued under Prime Minister
Sarit Thanarat (1959–1963), whose idea of national well-being was
defined in terms of 'wholesomeness, dignity, properness and resource-
fulness' (Chaloemtiarana 1979:168). Cleanliness and order (*khwam
riaproy*) were basic to his version of Thainess. These traits, he expressed
in his own lifestyle. He was described as 'a person who valued beauty,
who dressed in clean and well-pressed clothes, washed his face many
times a day, had his hair always combed, and acted with social properness (*riaproy*)' (Chaloemtiarana 1979:189). His mistresses did not detract
from this image because he chose beautiful women. In fact, he was
admired for his ability to acquire movie stars, beauty queens, night
club hostesses, even young students as mistresses. His 'lady-killer' image
enhanced his power, his magical virility, and conformed to a dominant
model of Thai masculinity (Chaloemtiarana 1979:339), whereby the

acquisition of beautiful women conferred status. Nevertheless, prostitution must have offended his sense of order and cleanliness because
he passed laws against the practice in 1960, sending a few unfortunate
women to rehabilitation institutions where they could become clean-
living women.

More recently, the National Identity Board and the National Culture
Commission were created to support Thai culture and promote Thai
publications such as *Thai Life* and *Thai Culture*. These initiatives were
intended to preserve Thai culture and to encourage the adaptation of
authentic Thai traditions. Thai creativity was also recognized as an
important part of authentic Thai culture, permitting the invention of
new elements of Thainess.

In the 1980s, the National Culture Commission launched a spiritual
development project that identified twelve undesirable Thai values.
These included: 1) immorality, 2) materialism, 3) weak work ethic, 4)
lack of national sacrifice, 5) lack of Thai nationalism, 6) preferring
individual gain to group benefit, 7) spending beyond income, 8)
consumerism, 9) acting big or tough, 10) living beyond one's economic
status (eat well, live well *kin dii*, *juu dii*), 11) fatalism and belief in magic,
and 12) abandoning rural ways of life. These undesirable characteristics
were to be replaced by the five desirable values: 1) self-reliance, diligence
and responsibility, 2) frugal spending and saving, 3) discipline and
abiding by the law, 4) religious ethics, and 5) following the slogan:
nation, religion, monarchy (Pongsapich 1990:9). This campaign perpetuates Phibun's assumption that state decrees can shape the attitudes
and practices of its citizens. The values themselves stress the importance
of hard work and diligence, as expressed in the writings of Luang Wichit
Watakan (cf. Barmé 1993), and are reiterated throughout the school
curriculum (Mulder 1999).

The writings of Luang Wichit Watakan featured women who overcome adversity and succeed against all odds. They serve as role models
by displaying strong will and determination to overcome misfortunes
and sacrifice for the nation. In the words of one heroine, 'For women,
death is definitely better than the selling of their bodies. I cannot
imagine anything lower than prostitution' (Sunthraraks 1986:166).
Nevertheless, Sunthraraks concludes from a review of these works, that
the Thais willingly accepted the social inequalities around them (1986:
166), including the subordination of women.

Love of country and the assumption of its superiority over others is
not new in Thailand. Further, assumptions of national superiority can
exist even in the face of ignorance of the condition of other compatriots,

of regional lifestyles, and of other ways of expressing Thainess. Marcelo de Ribadeneyra, writing in 1601 (of events in 1582) observed that: 'The Siamese reportedly loved their country loyally and would do anything to prove that Siam was better than any other kingdom or nation' (cited in Cortes 1984:424).

The Thai state, past and present, is concerned about how Thainess is expressed within the country and represented outside the country. For Westerners who have never visited Thailand, their image of the country may well come from seeing *The King and I* on stage or screen. The play and film are roughly based on Margaret Landon's book *Anna and the King of Siam* (1944) which was based on Anna Leonowen's autobiographies recounting her experiences as governess in King Mongkut's court (*The English Governess at the Siamese Court*, 1870; *Siamese Harem Life*, 1873). The book, *Anna and the King of Siam*, was not banned in Thailand, in spite of its trivial and inaccurate picture of palace life, although the 1956 musical film version starring Yul Brynner and Deborah Kerr is still banned. These preposterous Western representations of royalty were not sufficiently relevant to have any impact on Thai life that would be considered treasonous. Charges of lèse majesté were reserved for treasonous actions such as speaking negatively about the right-wing state-sponsored Village Scout movement or writing criticisms considered subversive, such as those by Sulak Sivaraksa (cf. Bowie 1997:31, 279). The film, *Anna and the King of Siam* with Rex Harrison was not banned in 1946, and even the later musical version with Yul Brynner did not cause an uproar among elite Thai and royalty who reportedly were not offended by it. In fact, Queen Sirikit attended the musical in the United States in 1985 and met Yul Brynner who played King Mongkut (Peleggi 1994:58). Thailand was much more exotic and compelling than *The King and I* could possibly represent in a musical with a Western storyline. Ignorant foreigners were not a significant threat to national security or identity. But in November 1998, Thailand rejected the request by Twentieth Century Fox to film a remake of the version, *Anna and the King of Siam*, on location in Thailand, arguing the script still portrayed King Mongut as a 'brutal buffoon'. Allowing historical inaccuracies and distortions to persist would show disrespect to the monarchy and defame Thailand (*Bangkok Post*, 12 Nov. 1998).[5]

Political Uses of the Past: Models and Miniatures

Concern with image management, saving face and surface appearances all motivate representations of Thainess and explain why women carried such a significant symbolic load. Representations of Thainess are also located in miniature models of Thailand's historic heritage. Women and monuments are both constructed and controlled by hegemonic state power. Outsiders and insiders are encouraged to gaze on both, as both are reduced to proportions that can be totally encompassed at a glance.

Culture (*wathanatham*), custom (*prophaeni*), and heritage (*moradok*) are concepts most assuredly oriented to the past, but to pasts which are drawn close to the present through palimpsests deemed to be of use to the future. Fabian argues that culture, a notion oriented to the past, '. . . a nostalgic idea at best . . . a reactionary ideologeme at worst . . .' served anthropology as a short term for a 'theory of knowledge'. To Fabian, culture 'enshrines order as the negation of chaos' (1991:191–3). As such, the concept is ideally suited to the Thai case developed here. Fabian speaks of anthropology as the science of disappearance. Thai deal with the threatened disappearance of the so-called authentic Thai past by selecting pieces for retention, recollection, and adding them on to the palimpsest that is Thai culture. 'Traditionally, the problem with representations has been their "accuracy", the degree of fit between reality and its reproductions in the mind' (Fabian 1991:207). The representations discussed here are actively produced '. . . in the strong sense of transforming, fashioning, and creating' (Fabian 1991:209). Nostalgia for an imagined past guides these representations.

Susan Stewart (1984) has analyzed the relation between scale and significance in Euro-American representations. Her discussions of the miniature and the gigantic resonate with Thai historical reconstructions.[6] The miniature, linked to nostalgic versions of childhood and history, '. . . presents a diminutive and thereby manipulatable version of experience, a version which is domesticated and protected from contamination' (Stewart 1984:69). The production of these controlled representations of the past occur in Thailand as politically motivated heritage replicas making claims in the real world about past, present and future.

Culture construction has been an important political strategy in Thai nation building since the founding of Bangkok and the Chakri dynasty in 1782. Remnants of Thailand's past are excellent resources for building a politically useful heritage. With no colonial past to sweep away, both government and private citizens can find and display evidence of past greatness.

> Vestiges of the past can only survive through the selective and indeed political action of conferring the status of heritage on something and denying it to something else. (Peleggi 1994:8)

Recognizing the importance of the famous Cambodian temple Angkor Wat as an antecedent to modern Siam, King Mongkut had a model of the Khmer temple complex constructed in the Grand Palace in Bangkok some time in the 1860s. This model dates from the time when Thailand exercised sovereignty over Cambodia (1863). The temple model resembles the engraving of the principal facade of Angkor Wat from *Voyage d'exploration en Indo-chine* by Francis Garnier, 1873 (cf. Swaan 1976:138). The model was 'Thai-ized' by the substitution of Thai architectural features for Cambodian ones. While French academics claimed Angkor Wat as a measure of the past genius of Khmer civilization, a global treasure and 'wonder of the world' in true Orientalist fashion, the Thai made more political use of the temple and its replica. At a time when Thailand was balancing claims and counter claims against the French possessions in Indochina, it is the symbolic claim in the form of the miniature Angkor Wat that has stood the test of time, as it is still on display in the courtyard of the Temple of the Emerald Buddha in Bangkok. Ironically, pieces of Angkor Wat could also be purchased at the Thai border throughout the late 1970s and 1980s from Cambodian refugees, or ordered directly from albums in Bangkok antique shops where original carvings or more likely, fakes could be chosen for delivery. The looting continues; Thai police recently seized 117 sandstone images of Buddhas and Hindu gods from Angkor destined for Bangkok antique stores (*National Post* 7 January 1999).

Cambodia also displayed a 'mini' monument from Angkor Wat in 1968 to celebrate the fifteenth anniversary of Cambodia's independence (Anderson 1978b:307). The replica of the Bayon, like Mongkut's model of Angkor Wat, was already a 'mini' replica of the abode of the gods, the heavenly city reproduced as a microcosm of the macrocosm in many Indianized states in Southeast Asia (cf. Heine-Geldern 1956, Tambiah 1976).

Other 'real' Khmer temple complexes have been used to strengthen the link between the Thai monarchy and the Khmer Empire. The famous lintel from Phanom Rung, a Khmer temple in Buriram province dating from before AD 890, which was returned to Thailand in 1988 from the Art Institute of Chicago, was declared a 'cultural treasure' whose return was a 'point of national pride' (Keyes 1991b:271). At the opening of the Thai Arts and Craft Year (1988), Buriram Province decorated its stall as the Phanom Rung temple with the missing lintel indicated by a sign demanding its return in Thai and English (personal communication, E. Cohen 1988).

Along with many other archaeological objects, the lintel was stolen from the site sometime in the 1960s. Either before or after it was stolen, three copies were made. One is exhibited in Cologne, one in Geneva, and one in San Francisco. Presumably, each museum believes it has the original lintel from the thirteenth-century temple. The marketability of objects representing the Khmer heritage of Phanom Rung inspired artisans to produce these copies. The process of restoring old monuments and creating replicas of buildings and artifacts for aide memoirs or souvenirs (cf. P. Van Esterik 1985), develops and validates skills that can be utilized for other purposes. One such entrepreneur developed the Buriram Local Art Promotion Center to produce sandstone carvings that are '90% accurate' Khmer. He feels that these high-quality imitations will prevent the looting of ancient monuments. The sandstone he takes from the same source that was used to make the original monuments. With the opening of his center, local artisans could safely come 'out of the closet' and produce imitations without fear of being accused of plundering sites or of being part of the antique fraud market producing fakes (*Bangkok Post*, 7 June 1988). It would be naive to assume that the legitimate production of replicas precludes either selling instant antiques or looting sites. However, even art historians and government officials have suggested that the availability of fakes should help to protect the 'real' Thai heritage (Alexander 1984:108).

More devastating than the looting and faking of these Thai artifacts was the claim by art historian, Piriya Krairiksh in 1986 that the Ram Khamhaeng inscription of Sukhothai attributed to King Ram Khamhaeng dated around the 1292 enshrining acts central to Thai concepts of democratic rule was a deliberate historical fake that could not have been written before the fifteenth century. This attack on the inscription undercuts the foundation myth of the nation. The phrase in the inscription, *nai nam mi plaa, nai na mi khao* (in the water, there are fish; in the fields, there is rice), recited daily by Thai schoolchildren is a metaphor for prosperity under a righteous king (*dhammaraja*). Close to the heart of Thai national identity is Sukhothai, the 'Dawn of Happiness', 'Thailand's Camelot', evidence of Thailand's 'Golden Age'. Krairiksh argues that the inscription could not have been written in the thirteenth century, but was composed between 1850 and 1855 by King Mongkut (Rama IV) to link the Chakri dynasty more closely to Sukhothai, perhaps as exemplar for his new reforms while reaffirming traditional Thai values, or to impress European officials.

Her Royal Highness Princess Galyani Vadhana, in her role as Honorary President of the Siam Society, introduced Chamberlain's edited volume, *The Ram Khamhaeng Controversy* (1991) on the Sukhothai debates, acknowledging that the questioning of the authenticity of the Ram Khamhaeng Inscription amounts to a monumental challenge to Thai history. 'This is a serious matter in Thailand, for if the allegations against the inscription were proven to be true, we would certainly be forced to reinterpret the history of the Thai nation' (1991:ix). Most Thai and foreign scholars who have researched or wrestled with the linguistic and cultural analysis necessary to assess these claims conclude that they are false, that the inscription was written in the thirteenth century by the founder of Sukhothai. Yet the challenge to the authorship of the inscription is a reminder that if Mongkut had not had at hand evidence of royal greatness from the past to legitimate his patriarchal rule, he would have had to invent it (cf. O'Connor 1991:298).

Sukhothai Historical Park with 193 restored monuments arranged in a pleasant, well-landscaped park opened in 1988 with funding from UNESCO, the Japanese government, the Thai government, and private donors. But the restorations were criticized for '. . . the alteration of archaeological evidence through arbitrary reconstruction of monuments in order to suit the interests of the tourism industry' (Peleggi 1994:85). Answering criticisms about the accuracy of their reconstructions, a Fine Arts Department deputy director-general appealed to the need to satisfy the local people who appreciated the site for its religious significance rather than its accurate replication of history (Peleggi 1994:36). Indeed, the historical park appeals both to Thai and foreign tourists. Following in the 'Wonders of the World' Orientalist strategy, UNESCO added Sukhothai and the neighbouring towns of Sri Satchanalai and Kamphaeng Phet to the World Heritage list in 1991 (Peleggi 1994:20).

Bang Pa In was founded in the seventeenth century as a summer residence for the kings of the Ayutthaya dynasty. In the latter half of the nineteenth century, King Mongkut (Rama IV) and King Chulalongkorn (Rama V) built livable showcases symbolizing 'all that is most characteristic of Thai architecture' (Clarac and Smithies 1972:166). Anderson refers to this complex as 'an incoherent jumble of miniature replicas of "typically Thai" palaces and garish "overseas Chinese" style dwellings' (1978a:228). Pavilions from Bang Pa In such as the *Aisawan Thi Phaya* reappear in international expositions and world fairs representing Thailand, and on the covers of silk pillows and tourist books.

The park contains an Italian-style pavilion, a Chinese-style palace made from materials imported from China, and bronze statues imported from Europe (Clarac and Smithies 1972:168). These replicas appear strangely out of context, addressing an unseen (primarily European) audience that could appreciate their cosmopolitan significance.

In 1918, King Vajiravudh (Rama VI) established and administered a miniature city called Dusit Thani, built behind the Dusit palace in Bangkok. It consisted of houses, temples, offices, roads, and canals built to one-twentieth scale, a 'toy' city that only his entourage had access to (Wilayasakpan 1992:75). This small utopian model and experiment in democracy was seldom mentioned in the public press (Vella 1978:75), nor did the public participate in this experiment. It may be thought of as yet another kind of performance art, one endowed with political meaning but without political clout, reinforcing Geertz's argument (1980) about the theatricality of Southeast Asian politics.

Replicas played a part in the initiation rituals of the Village Scouts, a right-wing movement that harkened back to the Wild Tiger Corps of Rama VI whose memory was also invoked in the initiation ritual. During a five-day ritual, styrofoam replicas of Ayutthaya palaces and temples were built and burned to commemorate the wars between Burmese and Thai (Bowie 1997:201). In 1976, theatricality was replaced by brutality, as Village Scouts took a leading role in the massacre of Thai students at Thammasat University in the name of preserving the integrity of the nation.

The complex around Wat Phairongwua in Suphanburi Province was built under the direction of a monk named Luang Phau Khom. It is best known for its graphic depictions of the sufferings of the inhabitants of the numerous hells of Buddhist cosmological fame. The grizzly consequences of adultery are depicted, no doubt without a significant impact on the Thai families visiting the site. Reconstructions of famous Thai Buddhist temples dominate the park, but other buildings including a Christian church, a mosque, a Hindu temple and a Chinese Buddhist temple are located on the periphery of the Buddhist space. The founding monk claims to have attained a spiritual level which qualifies him as a man who is 'truly Thai', 'truly Chinese' and 'truly European' at the same time (Reynolds 1978:198). The park is a most popular pilgrimage site for Thai tourists, who can literally experience Buddhist cosmological space encompassing and engulfing models of other religious buildings.

Concern for authenticity is a particular challenge in a country where instant antiquities representing pieces of the national heritage are faked as soon as they are enshrined as legitimate markers of Thai identity, where leading art historians tolerate the forgeries as one means of preserving 'real' Thai antiquities, and where even the root metaphor for the nation – the thirteenth century Sukhothai inscription – was thought by some to be a fake made in the mid-1800s.

One of Thailand's most elaborate modelling exercises, Ancient City (*Muang Boran*), was not constructed by the state, but by 'Sia Lek' Viryabhum, a wealthy Sino-Thai businessman who made his fortune in Mercedes Benz sales. This 'authentic' model of Thailand's history is located in a 200-acre park on the outskirts of Bangkok. Historical theme parks recreate the experience or look of another place or time by managing buildings, objects, food costumes, and performances that materialize and miniaturize the nation's past and present. Its creator expects that a nostalgic look at Ancient City will have 'a profound effect' on visitors, and that it will secure a permanent niche in their memories (Muang Boran, 1988:6). Ancient City in the late 1980s did not depend on elaborate costuming to set the historical theme, perhaps because of the dizzying speed at which visitors moved through a thousand years of Thai history. Merchandizing was geared not to tourists but to the needs of the thousands of Thai school children passing through the site.

Ancient City was not developed by the Tourist Association of Thailand (TAT) to add another way for foreign tourists to experience Thailand. Rather, the model was intended to educate the Thai public about their history and possibly underscore the fact that the state did not have a monopoly on the construction of heritage. About 10,000 Thai students a month visit the site. In the guidebook on Muang Boran, Sia Lek reveals his Buddhist reasoning for building the site: 'the effect today follows the cause of yesterday . . . the change of tomorrow is what happens to-day . . . therefore man must know the events of the past' or be 'like a vessel without a compass'. He recognizes that 'harm comes from pretending to know but really being ignorant', and looks to Muang Boran '. . . to remedy the existing moral deterioration of human society' (Muang Boran 1980:13–14).

The park is a product of one man's image and imagination about Thai history and its importance for contemporary Thailand. Sia Lek Viryabhum spent around twenty-five million *baht* and several decades reproducing his well-informed vision of what is significant about Thailand's past. An avid student of Thai art and history, he relied heavily on a few professional art historians and archaeologists who supported his view of Thai history.

The park roughly reproduces the shape of Thailand with the entrance gate located at the southern tip of the 'country'. Sites are arranged by a mixture of chronology and geography, with southern monuments ranged along the long stretch of peninsula that serves as a passage into the rest of the site. The chronological framework is laid out in the guidebook and referred to throughout the park. 'Prehistory', acknowledged to be 'fuzzy', includes palaeolithic, mesolithic, and neolithic stages, and ends in the first century AD when the country became Indianized. From this point the country progressed through the eight successive (but overlapping) stages as taught in Thai schools (Mulder 1999):

Dvaravati	fifth – twelfth centuries AD
Srivijaya	seventh – twelfth centuries AD
Lopburi	tenth – twelfth centuries AD
Chiengsaen	eleventh – fifteenth centuries AD
Uthong	eleventh – fourteenth centuries AD
Sukhothai	twelfth – fourteenth centuries AD
Ayutthaya	fourteenth – eighteenth centuries AD
Ratanakosin	eighteenth to present

Muang Boran combines *prawatsat* or modern history of the nation state, with *tamnan*, history as it relates to Buddhism, and *phongsawdan*, history of dynasties (cf. Kasetsiri 1976:1) all overlaid with a significant dose of Thai poetry, fantasy and myth.

Muang Boran establishes authenticity by:

1. Dismantling and removing old buildings from one part of the country and reconstructing them in Ancient City (e.g. authentic but in new locations).
2. Restoring old buildings that were falling apart and reconstructing them in Muang Boran.
3. Reproducing replicas of real buildings in full size or on a smaller scale.
4. Creating imaginative sculptures and tableaus representing Thai myths.
5. Establishing a Lao Song village. The authentic Lao Song houses are occupied by 'real' Thai minorities – but not the Lao Song. The family living its customs in the public eye are Akha, a totally unrelated group of Tibeto-Burman speakers from northern Thailand.
6. Reconstructing the royal palace of the early Ayutthaya period (1448) from Thai and European descriptions plus floor plans of the ruins.

The plans for the reconstruction were reviewed by 'a distinguished panel of Thai historians who testified to the authenticity of the reconstruction' (Muang Boran 1980:70). This reconstruction is particularly important for understanding the relation between successor kingdoms in Thailand. The Sanphet Prasat Palace became the model for the Inthara Phisek Palace in Bangkok (destroyed by fire). Many of the key features of the former capital, Ayutthaya, were recreated at the new capital, Bangkok.

7. Restoring replicas of 'original' palaces and temples before faulty reconstructions could be made by the Fine Arts Department. Research was undertaken to determine their original appearances. Photographs, documents and chronicles were consulted to achieve a copy of the authentic original building (Muang Boran 1980:193).

Sia Lek writes of having panels of Thai experts 'authenticate' his reproductions; that is, to invest them with authority or render them authoritative. In this sense, all the art and architecture reproduced at Muang Boran is authentic. The leading Thai authority on Thai culture history, a member of the royal family, said that he was asked by Sia Lek if there were inaccuracies in any reconstructions. If he found errors, Sia Lek said he would pull the buildings down. While the Prince said he found small errors, he said that he did not have the heart to tell him.

Aesthetic pleasure is the elegant working out of pattern. Muang Boran's builders discover old buildings that were falling (or had fallen) down, buy them, and reassemble the pieces in new contexts, thus saving them. The builders of Sukhothai Historical Park reconstruct Sukhothai buildings in ways that will appeal to park visitors, both Thai and foreign. When the originals collapsed, models had already been reconstructed, saving the exemplars for posterity. Art historians have long deplored Thai lack of motivation for preserving old things or art objects for their own sake, but great concern with perfecting copies and shifting these copies into new contexts. This fits well with Buddhists' preference for constructing a new temple rather than repairing or restoring an old temple. Only the former is considered an important means of acquiring merit because the merit for the repair will accrue to the original builder not to the repairer.

Ancient City is not popular with foreign tourists. The 'authentic' Thai past is so accessible, so well packaged, and so pleasant to explore that there would be no reason for most tourists to brave suburban Bangkok traffic to visit a less accessible theme park. While the Tourist

Authority of Thailand (TAT) did at one time develop a theme park near the airport called TIMland (Thailand in Miniature), and a small display of miniature replicas of famous buildings known as Mini Siam was built near Pattaya, the 'Disneyworld' approach was not successful in Thailand.

In contrast, Mini Indonesia was created by the wife of Prime Minister Soeharto after visits to Muang Boran (Peleggi 1994:68) and Disneyland. Opening near Jakarta in 1975, the park was built to appeal to both foreign tourists and nostalgic Indonesians who longed for home. Admittedly, Ancient City does not have to deal with the ethnic diversity represented in Mini Indonesia, and can merely present a single upland group to stand for all marginalized peoples. Like Ancient City, miniature replicas of national monuments were selected for Mini Indonesia as signs of continuity with Java's past. Pemberton also recognizes this effort as a 'special historicism and concomitant passion for form' (1994:247). Both theme parks miniaturize items of national heritage. But they illustrate differing approaches to and uses of the past. Indonesia must construct a past without colonialism – creating in effect, a contemporary past through the recovery of tradition. Thailand claims to construct an unbroken line from past to present and can risk representing an official past from the dawn of time, as a historical continuity. With no direct colonial rule, Thailand can afford to preserve a few sites of colonial architecture such as the Oriental Hotel and a few nineteenth-century commercial buildings in Bangkok for nostalgia-oriented tourism (Peleggi 1996:444).

The reconstructions at Muang Boran, in addition to the various replicas and models of historical moments described above reveal how old configurations legitimize present and future action. Knowledge of the past is codified in exemplars demonstrating moral knowledge of cause and effect not chronological knowledge of when and where. The correct use of the products of the past is to anchor them into paradigms of Thai history as exemplars of correct moral behaviour or successful political exploits. These exemplars can be reproduced and shifted into new moral and political contexts to legitimize new times, new people, and link them to past moments. These moments cannot and need not be ordered chronologically. Rather, they condense what is important about conditions and quality of life at a particular point in time – much like the Buddhist notion of truth by experience rather than by past examples. Thus the Thai art system, until recently offered few inducements to evolve new art forms, since emphasis was on exact reproduction of received form, rather than creativity, originally, or

individual expression (Mabry and Mabry 1980:350). These values legitimize and encourage the creation and recreation of correct design. Once
a form has been replicated, the original can rot away, crumble off a
cliff, be sold to a tourist, or be stored away on an inaccessible museum
shelf. Prototypes, regardless of when they were made, continually
validate the past by replicating it in a pulsating cycle, rather than a
linear progression.

Replication also brings less than perfect exemplars into line with
existing prototypes to make the fit between object and cultural model
a little closer to perfection, just as the builders of King Mongkut's replica
of Angkor Wat altered the Cambodian temple to meet Thai aesthetic
standards. Muang Boran constantly reconstructs paintings and palaces
'as they should have been'.

These models of and from the past exemplify the state's efforts to
strengthen their rule and claim legitimacy by reproducing in miniature
the buildings of other eras and locations. Miniatures create order, and
are a visible reminder of the present as a conditioned outgrowth from
the past – the operation of *kalatesa* in the realm of material culture. As
expressed by Ancient City's creator:

> Everything has to depend on the suitable position, right nucleus and
> right time. The suitable position means the position that is rightly
> appropriate. The nucleus means growth under limitation. The right time
> means the needed environment at the time . . . This is the state of balance
> according to the law of nature . . . Suitability and beauty have no bound-
> ary in age. (Muang Boran 1988:12–13)

Exhibiting Thailand

At the turn of the century, members of royalty and the Thai elite
travelled to Europe as students of civilization, and took from the
experience not a critique of how they were represented by the Europeans, but a blueprint for how to represent themselves to others. Their
experiences are reflected in various world exhibitions.[7] The Siam
exhibition at the Centennial Exposition in Philadelphia, 1876, was
considered one of the most spectacular at the exposition. King Chulalongkorn sponsored the assembling and inventory of 728 Thai artifacts
and manufactured goods including everyday items (silk and cotton
clothing, basketry, tools, mats, ceramics, samples of wood, minerals,
and rice); royal regalia (symbols of royal rank such as tiered umbrellas,
the royal seal, scale models of the royal funerary chariot and barges);

monk's robes and insignia; and items from Thailand's artistic heritage (puppets, musical instruments, and theatrical masks) (Taylor 1991:13). The Minister of Foreign Affairs, in donating the collection to the Smithsonian Museum after the Exhibition, refers to the objects as '. . . not a collection of Articles of Peculiar excellence, but of articles generally used in this country and of samples of articles of trade of Siamese origin . . .' (Taylor 1991:20).

Another European model borrowed to demonstrate Thai superiority was the evolutionary chart, depicting not their subordinate position among the nations of the world, but the evolution of Thai society from uncivilized to civilized. Evolution is represented in charts and school texts '. . . not only as a change through time but as a willed moral project in which the nation and its citizens advance from the ignorance and disorder associated with animals and slavery toward the knowledge and order associated with civilized human behavior' (Vandergeest 1993:146). Knowledge of *kalatesa* is a critical part of this civilizing knowledge. An evolutionary chart I purchased in the 1980s at a large open market features a skeletal figure beckoning towards an open grave warning the living forms ranged above that 'no one escapes death'. From a rabbit at the lower left side of the chart to a king-like figure at the upper right, each life form denigrates the form beneath: says the king, 'you are a common man'; says the male urbanite in Western dress, 'farmers are low beings'; says the peasant farmer (male) to a wild man with grass skirt and spear, 'you are a forest dweller' who responds to the animals ranged below, 'I am human'. The monkey tells the bear who tells the deer who tells the rabbit, 'you are lower than me'. But the rabbit counters, 'I am master of the small animals'. This is but one variant of the many evolutionary charts available in poster form from market stalls and school supply stores in the country. This adoption of a teleological model common in colonial discourse demonstrated the progressive assent of humans (read males) toward the goal of Western civilization. The Thai elite appropriated this meta-narrative, putting themselves at the pinnacle.

With no direct colonial master, Thailand was not close enough to Europe or important enough for Europeans to attempt to control the way Thailand represented itself. No colonial office dictated or crafted Thailand's public face. Thailand learned from European texts and expositions how to represent her own past and present in a way that demonstrated her exoticism and civilized status simultaneously. Thais had little reason to judge themselves to be uncivilized according to Elias' Eurocentric standards for measuring civilized status (1978), which included control of emotions, disgust of bodily betrayal by sweating and smelling, and sensitivity to one's own bodily space, all hallmarks of Thai construction of self and national identity. Using Elias' standards of civilization, the Europeans were less civilized than the Thais. The Thai state presented itself at World Expositions as civilized but exotic for the European gaze, and continues to do so for tourists.

Tourism and Selling the Land of Smiles

'If we are confident in our own culture, there is no need to be afraid of tourism' (Sujit Wongtet, *Bangkok Post*, 5 Sept. 1990). These words written by one of the foremost promoters of Thai culture suggest an appreciation of the degree to which tourism and public culture are compatible in Thailand. Thai identity is constructed in such a way that it is easily and eagerly consumed by tourists. Thailand is an appealing tourist destination, with over 7.7 million visitors in 1998 embracing luxury tourism, hippy tourism, mass tourism, eco-tourism, and sex tourism in varying proportions (Parnwell 1993; Hall 1994; Cohen 1993). While NGOs expose environmental problems exacerbated by tourism, they also recognize that the industry has provided income for thousands of men and women. Even the tourism industry acknowledges that tourism will destroy tourism if resources such as heritage sites, ethnic diversity, artists and artisans, and women are not managed well. Individual tourist destinations may be damaged by insufficient concern for the environment or certain locations such as hill villages overrun; but the tourist industry's agenda is extraordinarily compatible with the government agenda with regard to national identity and public culture.

There is no enclave tourism in Thailand, with the possible exception of tours to upland minority peoples' villages. Instead, tourists are given the opportunity to participate directly in aspects of Thai life rather than visiting model tourist villages. This is partly related to the tolerance of the Thai for respectful foreigners and their willingness to allow others to pay to 'do their own thing'. Nevertheless, TAT (Tourist Authority of Thailand) advertises 'Lisu Lodge' where visitors can stay in a hilltribe structure (modified with Western toilets and hot water) and observe the daily life of the villagers, 'perhaps even witness a village ceremony presided over by one of the four local witch doctors' (*Thailand Traveller* 1996:15).

The Tourist Authority of Thailand promotes fairs at historical sites with ruins or historical reconstructions as background, as if food and shopping are the only reason for visiting historical sites, the only source of *sanuk* or pleasure (Peleggi 1994:50). Peleggi cites a TAT brochure linking *sanuk* and festivals to the infamous Ram khamhaeng inscription:

> All Thai festivals are characterized by a strong sense of *sanuk*. This has been true since the very earliest days of the nation. A famous stone inscription from 1292, describes how the people of Sukhothai, the first Thai capital, went on merit-making . . . There, seven centuries ago, can be seen the same elements present in nearly all contemporary festivals and public events. (1994:62)

Foreign tourists who seek authentic exotica prefer the ruins themselves to the fairs which offer products packaged for domestic tourists such as pickled *durian* fruit, locally made *phaasin*, or local *nam prik* (regionally distinct chilli paste).

Thai cultural festivals held in both provincial centres and in Bangkok promote traditional culture under state supervision. The fairs feature local foods, herbal or traditional medicines, textiles, music, dances, crafts and often beauty contests. One Thai cultural festival held in April 1992 to celebrate Queen Sirikit's birthday was held in *Sanam Luang*, a large public square that also serves as the royal cremation grounds in front of the Grand Palace in Bangkok. Sponsored by the Thai National Culture Commission, the fair constructed traditional Thai houses from the four regions of Thailand – northern, northeastern, southern and central at a cost of one million *baht* each, while Bangkok migrants from these same regions were losing their homes to modern skyscrapers. 'Traditional Thai' was conceptualized as something that existed in the past but that could still be evoked to 'revitalize the Thai spirit in a modern society'. Visitors to the houses could obtain the 'almost forgotten feeling of what it was like to be Thai' (*Bangkok Post*, 25 April 1992).[8]

The destruction of the regional traditions as part of the pan-Thai movement in the 1940s under Prime Minister Phibun is paralleled today by the reinvention and repackaging of these same regional traditions for tourist consumption. Recognizable regional traits – or traits catalogued as such – are emphasized at these cultural fairs in safe contexts that do not threaten state power or national identity. These safe contexts are largely women's domains – food, textiles, dances – since the skills of food preparation, weaving and dancing are transmitted primarily through women. Yet these acceptable markers of ethnic difference have the potential to threaten the simplicity of Bangkok's dominant hegemonic discourse and male versions of history. Consider, for example, betel chewing which was discouraged by Rama VI and outlawed (ineffectually) by Prime Minister Phibun in the 1940s. While the practice was reviled as dirty and lacking culture, betel boxes are prized craft items, sold at provincial fairs and displayed at international expositions to represent exotic Thailand.

Heritage preservation included the National Culture Commission's declaring certain artists and performers to be 'national living treasures'. Some of these artists performed at the headquarters of the Siam Society and were videotaped so that the public could view them later (Raikes 1990). Thus, commodified by both government and Orientalists, the Thai artistic heritage was made accessible to the public. One wonders about support for current artists and artisans, as royal patronage of the arts gave way to government patronage after the Second World War. Now the tourist is the patron of the arts, according to art historian, Piriya Krairiksh (Alexander 1984:108).

The pastiche of heritage that is incorporated into craft items helps account for the $1,000 million (US) spent on handicraft souvenirs by tourists shopping in Thailand (Parnwell 1993:234). The wide range of tourist items made from pieces of tribal cloth or old silk demonstrate extraordinary creativity; no two pillow covers, shirts or bags are exactly the same. At least some of the money from handicrafts goes directly to artisans outside of Bangkok, and not all products have degenerated into 'airport art'. Jewellery, leather, wood carvings, silk and cotton textiles, and wooden and rattan furniture are among the most popular export goods and tourist purchases.

Products such as handmade textiles, coconut graters, baskets, and ceramics are also in great demand in urban centres to decorate homes in Thai Style (cf. Tettoni and Warren 1989). Rural necessities become urban decor, evidence that the expansion of modern goods into Bangkok and beyond has not resulted in the rejection of Thai goods and aesthetic style. Instead, plastic and bamboo, polyester and silk sit side by side in wealthy urban homes. Ironically, it is the house of Jim Thompson, an American entrepreneur who popularized Thai silk, that exemplifies traditional Thai style for visiting tourists (Peleggi 1996:443).

Buy Thai: Don't! Buy! Thai!

When Prime Minister Phibun called on the public in the 1940s to 'buy Thai' and develop a more 'materialistic culture' as a deterrent to communism, he could scarcely have imagined how well his mandate would be followed. He would certainly rejoice in that aspect of Bangkok culture today, where consumerism flourishes in the new temples of prosperity, shopping malls. No localities where Thai experiences are framed and condensed for locals and visitors alike are more profitable for their owners than shopping malls. And there is no more dramatic change in Bangkok daily life than that centered around shopping malls. The contrast between engaging in unpredictable and undignified bargaining in hot, dark, noisy, disorderly markets for locally made goods, and shopping in bright, light, orderly, air-conditioned department stores soothed by foreign music for the same local goods in addition to foreign-made luxury goods at fixed prices has transformed Bangkok life. The sensory overload in the huge, glamorous malls of Bangkok is matched by their aesthetic potential. Like the department stores that developed in Europe in the mid-nineteenth century, malls are 'dream worlds' where goods on display summon up dream images, filled with objects divorced from their contexts (Featherstone 1991:23). This new site for displaying consumer goods requires no new discipline or skills to penetrate its mysteries, not even money, as much of the pleasure of shopping malls is in the air-conditioned localities themselves, not in the purchase of goods. The high cost of many items puts them out of reach of low-income urban families and rural visitors. But there are always special bins of low-cost goods to appeal to low-income shoppers in even the most expensive Bangkok malls – plastic cups, soap dishes, sunglasses, T-shirts, cosmetics. Shopping malls as sites of signification have replaced cremations and waterfalls as places where Thai from different classes and backgrounds meet. They are also the sites of new leisure-time activities such as video games, which, along with golf, have transformed the Thai landscape. But the old market systems of colourful disorder coexist with the new, allowing people with the skills to meet the challenge of competitive bargaining to move back and forth between the two shopping experiences. Malls have also brought with them the possibility or rather the necessity of choosing ready-made goods over made-to-order goods. In clothing as in food, the home-made is no longer privileged, as mass-produced clothing and fast food is considered more modern and ultimately cheaper.

Malls and markets are filled with objects which cannot be authent-icated. Eight local and international organizations named Thailand as the world's biggest producer of counterfeit goods, with Italy coming in second. French luggage and fashion accessories are the main target of counterfeiters who copy the kind of luxury products that the Thai elite have been bringing back from Europe since the turn of the century.

The Siamese royal family was the only non-European royal house to have religious and household items commissioned from the jeweller, Fabergé (1846–1920) (Support Foundation 1985:Vol. 6, 81). European items were easily adopted as markers of status by royalty, elite and increasingly by middle-class urban and rural households. But luxury objects from exclusive stores are imitated almost as soon as they become symbolic markers of elite status.[9] Instant antiques and fake Rolex watches are prized by tourists who willingly buy into this recycling of status symbols.

Ironically, a campaign to publicize and protest child prostitution in the country urged Americans to boycott products made in Thailand. The Don't! Buy! Thai! campaign of the mid-nineties exposes the excesses of child labour and links it to the global capitalist economy, further evidence of the success of the campaign to Buy Thai.

Conclusions

The marketing of Thai culture domestically and to foreign visitors subsidizes or underwrites the cost of efforts to preserve Thai culture seen to be under threat by Western ways. Like many developing countries with rich heritages, Thailand sells itself abroad by commodifying its culture and tradition (Reynolds 1991:15). Heritage and tradition, materialized as Thai culture are simultaneously trivialized, celebrated and exploited. Similarly, Thai women in their essentialized Bangkok guise have been used both to represent tradition, at times an invented tradition, and as signs of civilization with their high heels and hats. This basic paradox permeates Thai gender representations.

Women's involvement in the tourist service industry and the structure and extent of sex tourism in Thailand has been well-documented (Truong 1990; Cohen 1993; Hall 1994). Chapter 6 examines tourism in relation to prostitution in general and links it more directly with gender relations. Here the connection I want to make is between women tourists and the feminization of royal style for tourist consumption. Thailand is not just a Shangri-La for men. The year 1992 was proposed as 'Women Visit Thailand Year' to allow women to see exactly how their men have exploited 'bad Thai women'. They were encouraged to come and see 'good Thai women' and encourage them to stand up to the brutality they have suffered (Hall 1994:157), in a strange but patronizing attempt to profit from the bad publicity on sex tourism in Thailand.

In 1994, the TAT publication *Thailand Traveller* featured an article

on women travelling alone to Bangkok, identifying hotels that catered
to women's needs by supplying hair grips, pink bathrobes, candy,
fashion magazines, scales, and flowers, among other amenities (Sharples
1994:44–9). Women tourists are encouraged to attend the Oriental
Hotel's Thai cooking school, shop for silk, gems, jewellery, antiques,
and luxurious clothes, enjoy sumptuous afternoon teas or a day at a
beauty spa, and for more local experiences, visit a fortune teller or an
orphanage. International tourism has given women (and other 'quality
tourists') direct access to the life-style and royal perquisites of elite *phuu
dii* (people of quality). The elements of royal, court culture are there
for the pleasure of international tourists, including luxury consumption, the pleasure of the present moment, satisfaction with, even
preference for appearances when relating to those you don't know or
trust, appreciation of nature, and aesthetically elaborated baroque
surroundings decorated with objets d'art – real or fake – from around
the world. The seductive appeal of 'Old Siam' is captured on the cover
of tourist brochures, greeting cards and postcards.

Tourists can also participate in the rituals of 'Old Siam'. For example,
the royal ritual of the first ploughing was revived in the mid-1960s
after many years absence. Changes in the Thai political landscape made
this an appropriate moment to reassert Brahmanic ritual in support of
the monarchy. In the 1980s, the tourist potential of these royal rituals
were developed under conditions that would preserve the Thai significance of the ritual. Tourists were permitted in the inner spaces if they
paid for the privilege and behaved appropriately, but the spaces and
ritual sequences were not significantly altered for their benefit. Royal
rituals served several simultaneous functions, and their meaning differed
for each audience.

The late Chakri dynasty high culture of 'Old Siam' celebrated in state
rituals is replicated in the hotel lobbies of Bangkok, where tourists are
invited to experience '. . . colourful ceremonies, picturesque sights and
sounds, piquant cooking, cheap antiques, plentiful servants and a
"relaxed" attitude on sexual matters' (Anderson 1978a:227). The error,
as Anderson points out, would be to mistake this elite royal complex
of 'Old Siam' dating back no further than 1900, with Thai national
culture.

This chapter has explored some examples of how the Thai state has
invented, modelled, and displayed its history and heritage. Said wrote
of the Orient as an invented, exotic place of haunting memories and
remarkable experiences (1978:1). This also describes the 'Old Siam' that
tourists encounter. These representations of Thailand were not created

for the tourist market, but rather for the European gaze of the nine-teenth century. The discourses of national public culture have simply created an ideal space for tourism.

The materialization of Thai identity does not merely confirm state hegemony. In fact, the constant rewriting and remodelling of history, in addition to Thai skills in manipulating the surface appearance of people and objects, means that no group has exclusive control over the commodification of cultural texts, objects and images. Through the practices of forgery, cultural resources for contesting meaning are freely accessible to a wide range of people. With the exception of a few representations whose meaning is more or less fixed by the state – particularly Buddha images, the government Garuda symbol, and portraits of the King and Queen – representations of Thai culture are not the property of the elite. Or rather, not for long, as objects, images, texts and symbols are effortlessly copied, poached, parodied, displayed, redefined, and sold to tourists. For all the efforts of the elite to fix the signifier, the efforts of entrepreneurs to challenge the ability of elite to fix signifiers are usually more successful. At least there are constant challenges to elite efforts (cf. Coombe 1992). Reproductions for tourist or local consumption present constant challenges to elite Thai efforts to define and circumscribe what they consider to be true Thai, authentic Thai. Authentic Thai is, however, gendered and beautiful, as the next chapter demonstrates.

Notes

1. Orientalism refers to the European discourses on the countries and peoples of the 'orient', constituted as the intellectual authority over the 'exotic other'. The term was further explored by Said (1978), and has been applied to Thai studies by Thongchai Winichakul (1994:7).

2. *Sakdina* refers to a system of feudal ranking based on the amount of rice land and manpower under one's control. *Sakdina* measured the power and dignity of officials from princes with 100,000 *sakdina* to destitute beggar's with 5 *sakdina* (Akin Rabibhadana 1975: 114).

3. His emphasis on race also reflects anti-Chinese bias, as seen in his racist publication, *The Jews of the East* (cf. Anderson 1978a:220).

4. In the late 1960s, I visited a back room in the National Museum where a number of jars containing pieces of the preserved skin of the former kings'

white elephants, part of the royal regalia of each reign, were displayed. King Mongkut supposedly showed Anna Leonowens a piece of the preserved skin of a white elephant that died in 1862 (Quaritch Wales 1931:283). This exhibit was not for Westerners' consumption; several elderly Thai women sat chatting on mats in front of the jars.

5. This may reflect new sensibilities about the country's national image, or the fact that filming would take place on the site of the palace. Among the scenes the Thai officials took offense to is one showing King Mongkut eating with chopsticks instead of a fork. The Minister of Tourism supports having the film made in Thailand in order to have the film-makers co-operate with the Thai in changing unsuitable parts. However, in December, 1998, Fox made the decision to move the filming to Malaysia. In November, 1999, Thai officials raised new concerns about the advertizing for the movie, saying it was still disrespectful to the king.

6. For additional comparisons of the political meanings of miniaturization in Indonesia and Cambodia, see Anderson 1978b, Errington 1997 and Pemberton 1994.

7. World Fairs are an opportunity to condense and display the most publicly appealing representation of a nation state to other nations as public spectacle. They have occurred sporadically since the Great Exhibition in London, 1851.

8. Houses in Thailand and elsewhere in Southeast Asia condense key symbolic meanings and reproduce cultural forms that signify cosmologies and social relations. Errington refers to the nostalgized and idealized displays of the past in the form of typical houses, dances and costumes from regions where diversity cannot be totally suppressed as the Stalinist model of the 'folk' (1997:27).

9. I remember admiring expensive black spandex stirrup pants from Paris in Bangkok boutiques in 1969. On my return to Thailand in 1971, the pants were available in a much cheaper Thai version. By 1974, they were available in the villages in Uthong district, and worn by the wives of the village elite – school teachers, civil servants and nurses, in spite of the great discomfort of wearing black spandex pants in the heat and humidity of Thailand.

f i v e

Deconstructing Display:
Gender and Beauty

Ranking Gendered Surfaces

Appearance matters. Beautiful appearances matter even more. In Thailand, beauty can override family connections, money or class, as well as other ascribed and achieved attributes of women, and to a lesser degree, men. In practice, it is Thai women who are more likely to be affected by judgements about their appearance. As one Thai graduate student explained to me, 'I went into graduate school because I was not pretty enough to be a secretary.'[1] The potential for ranking individuals on the basis of their physical appearance is very strong in Thai society. But the connections between beauty, race, power and rank have not been made in the analysis of gender relations. The moral power of beauty, and the extreme objectification of women intersect in contemporary Thailand, building on the palimpsest of the elite court culture of 'Old Siam' (captured in the postcards described in Chapter 2) where the attributes of gentleness, subservience, silence and virtue are intertwined with the attributes of grace, composure and beauty. It is this *phuu dii* construction of beauty that strengthens the hold of cultural models of the feminine on elite Thai women. Mass media brings these models to rural and minority women throughout the country.

Beauty keeps open the possibility of connections between classes and regions today, as in the past. Movies celebrate the beautiful women of 'Old Siam' who could 'jump the queue' and be associated with elite men, in spite of sumptuary rules which regulated behavior and the consumption of objects such as textiles which were meant to preserve and display hierarchy. Sumptuary rules[2] which displayed hierarchy continue to influence rural and urban ritual since weddings, ordinations and topknot-cutting ceremonies permit breaking sumptuary rules of the past, and dressing in 'royal style' (P. Van Esterik 1980). Even Village

129

Scout initiations use symbols of royalty to evoke royal style (cf. Bowie 1997). Lavish household and public ceremonies are opportunities to assess the appearance of others, particularly women, and are linked to beauty contests and tourism in ways that further the interests of the state.

Beauty contests are not an object of discourse in Western feminist writings. When they are mentioned, it is mostly in response to and protest over a particular contest. Protests against the contests are read, particularly by men, as jealous responses of less than beautiful women. I contributed a chapter on 'The Politics of Beauty in Thailand' (1995), an earlier version of this chapter[3] in a book examining local, national and international beauty contests.

Wolf argues that images of female beauty are used as political weapons against women's advancement. The 'beauty myth' carries on the work of the social control of women, prescribing behavior and not appearance (Wolf 1991:14). Thailand's beauty myths prescribe both. Thus, beauty in Euro-American culture is most directly about men's institutional power in the workplace, and elsewhere. Wolf links the perversions of the beauty myth to religion, sex, violence, and eating disorders, and concludes that only by getting beyond the beauty myth can women enjoy a noncompetitive beauty that cannot be used against them. This Western polemic against the tyranny of beauty argues that women are tired of trying to look beautiful for men. But it leaves aside consideration of women's agency and the aesthetic pleasures of beauty. The caricature of the ugly feminist as 'a big masculine woman, wearing boots, smoking a cigar, swearing like a trouper' (Wolf 1991:18) may well have discouraged young women from identifying with the feminist cause; it certainly discouraged the development of a cross-culturally insightful feminist analysis of beauty.

In 1992, while in Thailand researching this book, two events occurred which altered my thinking about Thai gender ideology. Within the first three weeks of May, Bangkok hosted the Miss Universe Contest, and pro-democracy protests were violently suppressed by the Thai military, culminating in the massacre of May 17–20. During those weeks, I was attending meetings and rallies at Thammasat University in the mornings, and working my way through the protesters to the other end of Bangkok to research the beauty contest in the afternoons. Moving between the two events, cutting articles from Thai newspapers on both the protests and the beauty contest, put me on the receiving end of criticism from Thai colleagues for either dealing with something as trivial as beauty contests when important political work was being done, or by being so foolish as to put myself in danger by attending rallies, from those who were helping me understand the beauty industry in Thailand. But the stories must be read together.

The juxtaposition of the Miss Universe contest and the pro-democracy rallies and reprisals brings into sharp relief dimensions of Thai society that I might otherwise have overlooked as they flowed into the experiences and interpretation of everyday life. Those two weeks in May provide a true moment of polarization, a moment when the super-masculine and superfeminine were opposed and reduced to opposite, essential, narrowly constructed representations' – Miss Universe and Prime Minister Suchinda: Beauty and the Beast. In the streets, the standoff between the male government spokesmen, the male military establishment and the male dominated protest groups, albeit with substantial support from leading women academics and NGO leaders; in the Convention Centre, the display of beautiful women and girls controlled by the few men who run Miss Universe Inc. At stake at one end of the city, the democratic future of a country and the lives of its citizens. At stake in the other domain, the name of the woman to occupy the Miss Universe slot and undertake her endorsement and public relation duties to increase the profits of Miss Universe Inc. Yet neither gender construction exists without the other. They are contexts for each other, no matter how tempting it is to keep them apart for ease of analysis.

This chapter uses beauty and appearance as a bridge linking national identity and public culture to prostitution and sex tourism, and explores how and why these events – the Miss Universe Contest and the pro-democracy protests – separated by a few days in time and a few kilometres in space, were kept apart (at one level), but intimately connected (at another level). Tracing the chronology, representation and interpretation of the two events reveals some of the forces and practices shaping the contemporary Thai gender system. We begin with the political protests.

Deflowering Democracy

The elections of 22 March 1992 brought Suchinda Krapayoon to power as a non-elected Prime Minister on 7 April. Suchinda, part of the Class 5 clique of officers graduating together from Chulachomklao Royal Military College, was the power behind the coup of February 1991, which overthrew the freely elected coalition government of Prime Minister Chatichai Choonhavan and continued the military control of the National Peace Keeping Council (NPKC). Immediately, protests began at this flagrant insult to the electoral process, particularly since Suchinda had repeatedly claimed that he was not interested in becoming Prime Minister. Protests against this continuing military interference took the form of letters, speeches, hunger strikes and rallies. A pro-democracy rally on 19 April brought out 50,000 demonstrators, but the rallies remained peaceful. On 25 April the Student Federation of Thailand organized a protest against Suchinda. Former Member of Parliament, Chalard Vorachat's hunger strike in front of the parliament buildings gained more prominence in the newspapers.

On 4 May Major General Chamlong Srimuang, leader of the *Palang Dharma* party joined the hunger strike, vowing to fast to the death unless Suchinda resigned. Pro-democracy rallies drew 70,000 demonstrators in front of the Parliament buildings, and by 7 May 150,000, to the larger grounds at *Sanam Luang* in front of the Grand Palace. During the week of 4–11 May whole families came after work to pay quiet respects to the fasters, often donating funds to maintain the rally,

Figure 4 Peaceful rallies for democracy in front of Thammasat University, May 1992

offering a quiet prayer, and staying to listen to speeches and entertainment. These speeches turned increasingly anti-government, as people in offices, coffee shops, and markets watched the opposition debate live from parliament on 6 and 7 May.

The first day of parliamentary debates heaped criticism on the National Peace Keeping Council (NPKC) and Suchinda. The NPKC responded to the criticism by attacking the rallies as being organized by the opposition parties and not by ordinary citizens. A leading woman anti-poverty activist brought a coalition of slum groups to protest at the parliament building on 6 May.

In spite of the intense heat of the dry season, the crowds attending the rallies were well behaved and orderly. Volunteers supplied food, water and amenities to the protesters, and kept the crowds in some semblance of order. Women were active in the political protests, and made up 44 percent of the Bangkok based protesters and 34 percent of the protesters from other provinces according to a survey conducted shortly after the event (CUSRI 1992).

Meanwhile, the military, characterized as *Choochok*, the greedy and ungrateful beggar from the Prince Vessantara *Jataka* tale, began preparations for more violent reprisals. Police General Sawat feared that a 'third party' would attempt to instigate unrest at the rally, and if a bad situation developed, then police would cooperate with authorities 'in line with the set plan'. The set plan, called 'operation crush enemies', was launched 6 May by the Capital Peacekeeping Force. A directive by the Internal Peacekeeping Command signed by General Kaset Rojanil empowered the Capital Security Command to order public agencies in Bangkok and upcountry to undertake any activity which would lead to peace and order in Bangkok. The army's 1st Division and the 11th Infantry Regiment were placed on alert in their barracks.

As the rallies intensified through 8 May government agencies dropped propaganda leaflets encouraging the protesters to go home, and attacking the opposition. My diary that day began: 'When fish can read, and bears can fathom the complexities of Thai politics, then the government propaganda leaflets dropped yesterday (May 8) into the Chao Phraya River and the Dusit Zoo will be effective. Meanwhile, hundreds of students, civil servants, factory workers and Thais from all walks of life prefer to judge for themselves the morality of the Thai government, and especially its unelected Prime Minister, Suchinda Kraprayoon.' At the same time, members of the press were called to meet the Interior Minister and asked to be more factual in their coverage of the political crisis. Just in case their warnings were not heeded, British, Japanese and American news services were refused the right to use their regular satellite transmission services from Thailand to their respective countries.

On the night of 8 May demonstrators moved to Democracy Monument on Rajadamnern Avenue, the site of many past protests, and pro-democracy speeches continued all night. Early in the morning of 9 May Chamlong ended his hunger strike, and appeared to call off the rally since parliament had resolved to amend the constitution in four areas, including specifying that the Prime Minister be elected.

Many factors came together to defuse the protests on 8 and 9 May not the least of which was the Miss Universe contest across town gearing up for broadcast to 600 million viewers on 9 May. The Miss Universe contest was initially set for 16 May, the date of *Vesak*, the celebration of the birth, enlightenment and death of the Buddha. This conflict of dates was not discovered until late April when Thai organizers insisted the broadcast date of the Miss Universe contest be changed. Other factors behind the decision to end the protests included the fact that Chamlong ended his hunger strike, and that *Sanam Luang* was needed for a royal ritual and a fair celebrating Buddhist Promotion Week, ending with *Vesak* on 16 May. The will to believe that the constitutional amendments would be effective and the belief that Thailand was indeed a parliamentary democracy and that it was therefore appropriate to give parliament another chance were also factors influencing the decision to call off the protests on 9 May.

By Sunday 10 May *Sanam Luang* and the streets around Democracy Monument were cleaned up in anticipation of the royal motorcade passing by to open Buddhist Promotion Week. Because protesters did not disrupt *Vesak* or Buddhist Promotion week, it was hard for the army to portray them as anti-Buddhist. Meanwhile, each side worked quietly to prepare for the next steps, the pro-democracy movement running seminars on non-violence at Thammasat University, the government coalition inviting radio announcers to dinner to pressure them to support Suchinda, and ordering vocational students, teachers and other government workers not to protest. During that week, the *Bangkok Post* and the *Nation* newspapers provided coverage of the background to the protest and the government's dirty tricks.

The army organized the Promotion of Buddhism week that filled *Sanam Luang* the week leading up to *Vesak* on 16 May. According to the *Nation* (15 May 1992), the monks and lay groups brought in by the army had worked previously with the army's anti-communist programme. Booths displaying bloody photographs of mutilated bodies and open surgical sites were popular attractions, displayed to develop

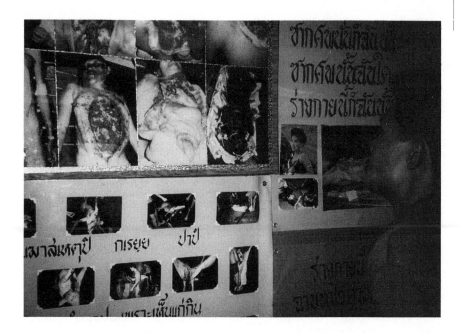

Figure 5 Poster displays of grotesque, damaged bodies, teaching the concept of impermanence at Buddhist Promotion Week, May 1992, Bangkok

understanding of the concept of impermanence (*anicca*). Next to the photographs of the open surgical sites were posters of beauty queens transformed into skeletons and rotting corpses, reminding viewers of the transience of appearances.

On Thursday, 14 May the pro-democracy coalition announced its intention to hold a rally on Sunday to secure a guarantee that the government would not backslide or delay implementing constitutional reforms, but by 16 May it was clear that Suchinda intended to continue as Prime Minister. The government attempted to block the rally planned for Sunday, 17 May by offering free rock concerts at a site distant from the rally, and removing the mobile toilets from the rally site. Suchinda announced that he would dismiss the Bangkok Metropolitan Authority if they allowed demonstrators to use any vehicles, equipment or facilities owned by the city administration. The free rock concert and missing toilets were unable to diminish protesters' desire for democracy.

As people gathered for rallies Sunday evening, 17 May, the English news supplied by the Public Relations department of the Royal Thai Government continued broadcasting old rock music, advertisements about the wonders of Thai golf, and public relations pieces on Thai classical dancing. The announced state of emergency was dismissed very briefly without any explanation about the growing tensions on the streets of Bangkok – simply an announcement that schools and businesses would be closed for three days, gatherings of more than ten people were not permitted, vehicles were ordered off the streets and publications were banned – and then on to discuss the activities of the royal family. Have a nice day and a nice week said the broadcaster, while the army opened fire on unarmed protesters.

On the night of 17 May conflict escalated into the scenes of unprovoked violence shown on CNN, BBC and other international news services. In compliance with the ban on publication, the *Bangkok Post* published their 18 May edition with blank pages where reports of the massacre would have been. The *Nation* reports were quite complete, if one could find a newspaper. In Bangkok, it was possible to obtain CNN coverage, but most early reports consisted of a map of Thailand with telephone contact only. The Thai TV stations repeatedly broadcast a film clip of young men facing the camera while destroying a police truck, but even to the untrained eye, it looked staged. There were no protesters or police in sight – just young men facing the cameras vandalizing a truck in a clearing.

By noon of 18 May the streets away from the protest areas were nearly empty, with a few mostly empty buses and taxis plying the streets. Businesses were grilled shut, with a few disgruntled security guards sitting in front of them. The normally bustling restaurants were quiet. Young men sat dejectedly under trees and on curbs, while a few people bought food from vendors to take home. The spirit of defeat was in the air – dejection, depression, wariness, weariness. Uncertainty was reflected on the faces of those on the street. The pace slows, progress halts, while another military action robs the country of the opportunities to learn the lessons of democracy.

Chamlong, along with over 3,000 protesters, was arrested, but released a few days later to attend a meeting of reconciliation with Suchinda in the presence of the King. Following the end of fighting, as support for Suchinda collapsed, the cabinet quietly rushed through amnesty legislation signed by royal decree on 23 May, before Suchinda resigned on Sunday 24 May. Yet Sunday was not a day of celebration but a day of mourning as the death toll mounted and the numbers of reported missing rose to more than 1,000. (The number killed is still unknown but is probably less than one hundred.)[4] Speculations continued that the army had blocked the streets and moved in trucks to remove the bodies which were reported to have been dumped in Burma or Cambodia where the debris of war would be less visible.

On 25 May, parliament passed the first two readings of the constitutional amendments, including the requirement that the Prime Minister be an elected member of Parliament, and the country recoiled in horror at the cost of life and the length to which the military had gone to maintain political power. On 9 June, a cursing ritual took place in front of Thammasat University, Bangkok, to exact revenge on Suchinda, officials and soldiers who could not be reached by other

Figure 6 Cursing ceremony following the May massacre, June 1992, Bangkok

means. Several women from an NGO arranged the few flowers, inverted ritual objects including monks bowls, and ritual foods in an elegant display, pleasing to those who understood the meaning of the displayed items as well as to those who did not. Tourists being herded into a bus after a tour of the Grand Palace stood transfixed at the sight of this innovative approach to a tragic political event, choking on the fumes of burning chilli peppers and salt (cf. Morris 1998). The following day, Anand Panyarachun was appointed interim Prime Minister, and he set the date for new elections in September 1992.

During the worst of the fighting, banks were closed. As soon as they opened, there was a rush to pull money out of banks owned by the military (referred to as 'the piggy bank of mass murderers'; *Nation*, 23 June 1992). Press coverage stressed the drop in stock market prices, the loss of investment opportunities and decrease in tourist revenue – as if the major casualty of the protests were the national GNP. Violence, it seems, is bad for business.

Within a week of the end of the fighting, the military was back threatening to act against those who were promoting hatred against them. As evidence mounted that many protesters were shot at point blank range or in the back, military spokesmen accused the opposition of paying motorcyclists 300 *baht* (then around $15 (US)) to participate in the protests; others claimed that those missing were paid to stay missing for at least one year. According to the military, soldiers fired in the air but ducked to avoid things thrown at them. This accidently caused rifle barrels to lower and 'apparently harmed a few people'. The videos produced by the protesters provided ample evidence to the contrary.

Figure 7 Replaying the video of the May massacre on Rajdamnern Avenue, June 1992, Bangkok

Right-wing paramilitary groups such as *Krathing Daeng* (Red Gaur) resurfaced after the fighting wearing jackets (embroidered with English words: 'I am righteous – Terminate the Wrong Doers') to map their strategy against the pro-democracy protesters. These gangs are reported to receive high pay, free liquor and brothel privileges, including access to beauty queens.

The Development of Thai Beauty Contests

Beauty contests epitomize a set of performative practices including gestures, body movement, facial expressions, clothing and make-up which exist in popular culture and everyday practice, but are exaggerated, inscribed and more completely embodied during beauty contests. Considering the timing of the pro-democracy protests, it is ironic that the first state involvement in national beauty contests was for the purpose of celebrating democracy and the constitution.

The development of national Thai beauty contests has been analyzed using three periods, the first from 1934 to 1954, the second from 1964 to 1972, and the third, from 1984 to the present (Kobkitsuksakul 1987).[5] As we examine these periods, we should be equally interested in the spaces between the contests and how they were featured in the construction of Thai identity.

Flowers of the Nation, 1934–1954: National beauty contests have been an important part of Thailand's nation building strategy since the 1930s. The first government sponsored contest to choose Miss Siam was held in 1934, two years after the 1932 coup that ended the absolute monarchy. The winner has been named Miss Thailand since 1939. The contest's purpose was political, and it was held as part of the Constitution Day celebrations. A public announcement directed to Thai women read:

> You have shown the country how much you respect the constitution of the Kingdom of Thailand. Therefore you sacrifice your personal happiness to come on stage for public viewing, bringing delight to the atmosphere of the Constitution Celebration. (*Bangkok Post*, 2 March 1990)

The objective of the contest was to support the new concept of democracy, to build the nation, and to increase the status of women. How the contest would accomplish the latter was never made clear. At the same time the contest would provide entertainment at the fair. It seems that democracy and the constitution needed a woman's radiant beauty to increase the power (*serm barami*) and legitimacy of democracy. Seven hundred years of Thai myth and history support this link between legitimate political power and women's radiant beauty, an unusually strongly inscribed palimpsest.

The contest was held at the Rajdamnern Fair in two parks close to the Grand Palace in Bangkok, and was expected to bring a joyful atmosphere to the occasion. The contestants were chosen for their natural beauty. Judges would dip cotton in water to rub off any powder to make sure contestants had good skin. The prizes were insignificant compared with later contests – a crown made from black velvet, a silver bowl, a locket – the honour was enough. The winners were primarily from the families of government officials, and tended to marry government officers.

During the years when Phibun Songkhram was Prime Minister for the first time (1938–1944), the contest served to further his nation-building and political strategy and to provide a setting to display the new Western fashions he wanted Thai women to adopt. Contest photographs showed women in military uniforms and Western-style hats, a fashion accessory that Phibun was promoting. Strategically, the 1939 winner received a kimono from the Japanese Embassy in Bangkok. But in spite of the rhetoric about up-lifting the status of Thai women, the government-sponsored beauty contest displayed women in shorts at least by 1940. No contest was held during the war years, the years of Japanese occupation, and the immediate post-war years (1941–1947).

When Phibun became Prime Minister for the second time in 1948, the contest for Miss Thailand resumed with larger prizes and shorter clothing. The commercial opportunities were beginning to be appreciated, as the 1948 winner received a sewing machine, and the 1950 winner was photographed with her radio, which in addition to 15,000 *baht* in prize money and two tickets around the world, made this a prize worth posing for. As the prizes became heftier, the genteel image of the contest faded. Contestants became mistresses of important, powerful men, particularly military men, including Prime Minister Sarit who used to take his many mistresses – including beauty queens – to *sawan sii chompoo*, his pink heaven, his bedroom (Wyatt 1982:285) .

Beauty contestants in the 1950s began to take on agents, and undergo expensive beauty treatments. By coincidence, the winner of the 1953 contest used the Chantana beauty shop, where Aunt Chulee, who was to become Thailand's most famous beauty pageant agent, worked as a hairdresser. Amara Asavanand, runner-up of the 1953 contest, entered

the Miss Universe contest herself, beginning the association between
the national and international contests.

Getting down to Business, 1964–1972: Just because the national Miss
Thailand contest was not held between 1954 and 1964 did not mean
that there were no beauty contests in the country, only that none were
sponsored by the national government. Many Bangkok communities
held local beauty contests around New Year's celebrations in April
(*Songkran*). These urban contests may have inspired changes in village
beauty contests associated with merit-making rituals following the end
of Buddhist lent and at *Songkran*. These temple beauty contests to
choose the *thepi ngan wat* (temple fair angel), may well have changed
in form during the 1950s to emulate the more Western-oriented urban
contests. A Thai colleague familiar with the literature of this period
noted that these rural contests were ridiculed by urban people in short
stories and novels. New Year's (*Songkran*) beauty contests continued to
be held in cities, towns and villages during the period. *Songkran Wisutkasat* was a particularly well-known Bangkok community celebration
where *Thepi Wisutkasat* was chosen during a beauty contest from at
least 1940. Through the 1950s and 1960s, the contests were held on a
smaller scale than the national contests, but similar in format including
having the contestants wear Western dress. *Wisutkasat* is an area near
Bunglumpoo in Bangkok that used to be a Thai 'red light' district in
the 1950s with cheap brothels and opium dens frequented by senior
military and civil servants. It is interesting that beauty contests should
be popular in this area.

The objectives of the newly re-established (1964) Miss Thailand
contest were frankly commercial with some public relations intentions
to make Thailand better known abroad. Kobkitsuksakul argues that the
beauty contests held during Sarit's (1959–1963) and Thanom's (1963–
1973) terms as Prime Ministers served to entertain the people and close
their eyes to dictatorship. Fashion shows were staged to accomplish
the same purpose (Kobkitsuksakul 1987:135–6). Thailand's close military and commercial relations with the United States during the 1960s
resulted in attracting American development money for investment
and capitalist expansion. And even beauty queens could do their part.

The *Wachirawut* College Alumni Association sponsored a Miss *Wachirawut* contest as part of their charity fundraising strategy, but did not
send the winner abroad to compete in international contests until
1964. With the support of the government, Miss *Wachirawut* became
Miss Thailand, the national candidate for the Miss Universe contest.

Encouraged no doubt by Miss Universe Inc. and TV Channel 7, the association sent Apasara Hongsakul, to the Miss Universe contest, where she won the crown and became a public celebrity. Winning the Miss Universe contest no doubt raised the status of the Miss Thailand contest. It certainly raised the stakes.

With the stakes raised, contestants were prepared to pay the beauty industry for programs that would increase their chances of winning, programs of massage, sauna, exercise, diet and special cosmetics to make contestants (and no doubt any paying customer) beautiful. But these training programs were expensive. 'Beauty is hard work, few women are born with it, and it is not free' (Wolf 1991:151). Enter the professional beauty agent, who would search out suitable candidates, train them in how to walk, talk, sit and smile to international standards, and split their prize money with them, sometimes 50-50, other times 70-30 in favor of the agent. The contestant kept the prizes.

By 1964, the Miss Universe standard of beauty for face, figure and posture was adopted in Thailand. Miss Thailand, like Miss Universe should have shoulders broader than hips, a long neck, straight rounded arms, legs in proportion to hips, straight feet, hair suited to face, long fingers, clean nails, straight back, and breasts not too large or too small. The ideal beauty should be twenty years old, at least 160 cm. tall, and near the golden proportions 33-22-35 inches (Kobkitsuksakul 1987:186).

Miss Universe Inc., 1984-present: The revolutionary democratic ideals of the student uprising of 1973 and the growing women's movement in Thailand discouraged the national beauty contests which were abandoned from 1974 until 1984. Thai feminists were successful in arguing that the contests overstressed the appearance of women and lowered their status. But the growth of tourism in the 1980s encouraged the re-establishment of the national and international contests in 1984, and they continue to be held annually.

The Miss Universe contest of 1992 was held in the Queen Sirikit Convention Centre built for the World Bank meetings in 1991. The construction of the Convention Centre necessitated cleaning out the homes of 'slum dwellers' who lived on the site. The building itself is magnificent – multi-tiered gold and glass shapes reminiscent of traditional Thai architecture with high-tech glass and steel shapes. Inside, the spaces are open, beautifully lit and carpeted luxuriously throughout, with teak carvings and Thai art decorating the walls, and magnificent textile hangings suspended from high ceilings. Spaces are multipurpose and magnificently Thai. Security was omnipresent and thorough for the beauty pageant, as, no doubt for other important occasions. The slum inhabitants are carefully walled out and entrances are well-guarded.

The week before the contest, Thai and foreign Bangkok newspapers kept the public informed about the activities leading up to the Miss Universe contest. Most articles in English newspapers downplayed the display of the women themselves, and emphasized the hard work of the contestants – rehearsals ten hours a day, their careful chaperoning (to keep contestants from alcohol, cigarettes and men) and the emphasis on personality as revealed by the extra interview added to the judging three years ago (to appease the feminists) (*Bangkok Post*, 21 April 1992; *Nation*, 29 April 1992). Public relations personnel worked hard to keep the Miss Universe image clean because there is a thin line between an exploitative sex show and a beauty competition.[6]

For all the rhetoric about the 'balance between inner and outer beauty' (*Nation*, 29 April 1992) and the facade of the contests serving a higher purpose such as the provision of scholarships, attention is clearly meant to be focused on women's bodies and body parts, as women are dismembered into parts perfected for advertising: '. . . there are pointed noses, small noses, full lips . . . perfect figures held up high on long legs, high hips and full bosoms and buttocks . . . and those tiny waists' (*Bangkok Post* 29 April 1992). A pageant press release says that although contestants are 'encouraged not to alter their own natural beauty, no restrictions are placed on cosmetic surgery'. The average size of Miss Universe is decreasing over time, in spite of the fact that women are getting larger. Catalina swimsuits, worn by Miss Universe for the past twenty-nine years, are now provided in one size smaller, with 'fullness at the bust needed by Asian women' (*Bangkok Post*, 29 April 1992). Asian women are now permitted the use of bra padding to provide the necessary bust fullness, and to avoid permanent cosmetic surgery 'which would provoke bad press' (*Bangkok Post*, 21 April 1992). No mention, of course, of the dangers to the women's bodies of such unnecessary intrusive surgery. Wolf cites a clinic's brochure that offers:

'a Western appearance to the eyes' to 'the Oriental Eyelid,' which 'lacks a well-defined supratarsal fold.' It admires 'the Caucasian or "Western" nose,' ridicules 'Asian Noses,' 'Afro-Caribbean Noses ("a fat and rounded tip which needs correction"),' and 'Oriental Noses ("the tip . . . too close to the face").' And 'the Western nose that requires alternation invariably exhibits some of the characteristics of (nonwhite) noses . . . although the improvement needed is more subtle. (1991:264)

Beauty pageants are lucrative industries, linked to the entertainment, advertising and tourism industries at various levels. Miss USA, and Miss Teen USA are produced by Madison Square Garden Event Productions, a Paramount Communication Company. Since 1960, Procter and Gamble company has been the principle sponsor of the pageant, and CBS, the network that has broadcast the pageants live worldwide since 1972. The Miss Universe press kit contained information on TV ratings for the broadcast, estimating a worldwide viewing audience of 600 million in sixty countries, making the Miss Universe telecast one of the most watched event programming in the world. This is prime-time politics, and it is about much more than beauty. The Miss USA contest (1991) achieved a 46.4 rating. The audience composition surveys show that most viewers were young women. Live broadcasts result in some incongruent scheduling, as contestants and audience in Bangkok donned evening clothes by 6 a.m. in preparation for an 8 a.m. telecast. This temporal imperialism allowed North American viewers to have a convenient prime-time viewing slot – 9 p.m. on Friday evening.

When Thailand accepted the contract to host the 1992 Miss Universe pageant, Thai Sky Television of the Siam Broadcasting and Communication Company paid twenty-five million *baht* (then, one million American dollars) copyright fees to Miss Universe Inc. to host the event, and began the task of assembling local sponsors. These included the Bangkok Bank, Kodak, Nestle, Covermark, Nissan, Coca Cola and the Dusit Thani hotels. Sponsors paid between two to five million *baht* cash in addition to the costs of providing their products. Most sponsors said that they did it for goodwill and to promote a positive image of the country, although they expected to lose money.

The commercial side of the Miss Universe contest, run by Miss Universe Inc., is clearly about using women to promote products and places.[7] A three-minute travelogue produced by the Tourist Association of Thailand (TAT) for one million *baht* showed the reigning Miss Universe as she moved through the Thai tourist landscape, stopping long enough to be photographed in all the distinctive places – the beach resorts, northern Thai hill tribe villages, the ruins of Sukhothai, Ayutthaya and Pimai, the Grand Palace in Bangkok, local temples, the floating market, Thai boxing matches, Bangkok 'night life' spots, classical dancing venues, and of course, shopping malls. Culture, in the video, is easily shared, easily transmittable, as Miss Thailand teaches Thai dance to other contestants who wore the long curved nails used in northern Thai dances, and they all splash each other in a parody of the water blessing ritual of *Songkran*.

The final television broadcast shows Miss Universe contestants riding elephants in the Queen Sirikit Convention Centre, and posing on the beaches of Pattaya and Cha'am. As the Miss Universe contestants avoided the steaming piles of elephant dung in the Rose Garden, a popular tourist site, eight middle-aged women dressed in traditional costume rowed decoratively around the pond, work they were ordered to begin an hour before the arrival of the contestants. Here we have both contrived settings for displaying contrived Thai culture, and people performing contrived tasks.

Television viewers and beauty queens were shielded from the struggles for democracy that were occurring as the show was being broadcast. They were shown the other Thailand, the Thailand for sale, 'the enchantment of Thailand, the Orient's most fabled country', and offered 'the magic of eastern fairy tales' (press release, Miss Universe Inc.), images also available on the postcards referred to in the opening of Chapter 2. Contestants reinforced this national representation by praising Thai food, products, and tourist attractions, all scripted for them by the conference organizers. During the broadcast of the final judging, the commentators stressed what made Thailand 'the most fascinating country in the world': shopping, beaches, palaces, food, historical sites, temples, shopping, shopping, shopping.

The stage settings, designed by an American and a Thai firm, also contributed towards the creation of this exotic Thai locality. They constructed a Thai house, a giant ceremonial swing, a rather Japanese-looking bridge, and a Thai pavilion (*sala Thai*) out of which the contestants emerged at different stages in the programme. Participants were protected by figures of giant temple guardians. Other identifying symbols included a pair of royal elephants, Thai orchids, and golden wishing trees (*rajapruk*).

The Miss Universe contest continued to attract newspaper coverage, in spite of the pro-democracy protests in Bangkok. Thai papers featured photographs which go for the jugular, along with a few other favorite body parts. Photographers were particularly active in chasing Miss Belgium who 'showed the most cleavage'. The press can hardly be blamed for focusing on body parts when they were provided with rating sheets to compare their scoring with that of the judges in the Miss Thailand World contest. Scores were assigned as follows: face (30 percent), figure (20 percent), legs (10 percent), walking (10 percent), wit (10 percent), personality (10 percent), and character (10 percent). This may help explain why photographers delighted in taking their photos from unflattering angles and supplying them with rude captions.

These photos – close-ups of thighs and crotches and breasts without heads – are assembled into Beauty Books following the contests, and sold at book stores and newsstands. The photos and captions confirm the fascination with yet contempt for the women who participate in beauty contests.

The Little Sisters of the Miss Universe Pageant who accompanied the contestants during the television program exemplify the growing popularity of children's beauty contests in Thailand. Children were trained and selected for the contest based on their appearance, singing, and dancing skills. They become 'goodwill ambassadors' for companies that sponsor them. Critics of the children's involvement felt that children should not be made up like little adults for other's amusement, particularly considering that the threat of HIV/AIDS has resulted in a demand for ever younger prostitutes.[8]

Throughout the Miss Universe rehearsal, aging ex-beauty queens shouted at the women to pay attention, move along, stop talking or reading. 'All eyes on stage, right Miss Belgium?' The only attention paid to the fact that the contestants probably spoke over thirty different languages was in the few moments when an official translator was called upon to practice translating the judge's question to a contestant who was not fluent in English in order to get the camera angle right. Otherwise, instructions were barked in rapid fire American TV production language. Observing the rehearsal made it abundantly clear that the pageant was merely the occasion for staging 'the most-watched special event programming in the world'. The women might well have been stand-ins, for all the importance accorded to them in rehearsal. They were put through their paces, physically handled and redirected when they made errors on stage. The purpose of the rehearsal was to test the camera angles and other technical aspects of the television production.

On the day when protesters faced off against the military supporters of an undemocratic regime, across the city a six-foot white masseuse and model representing a predominantly black country, Namibia, was chosen as Miss Universe. The contest confirmed the use of Western (white) criteria defining beauty – tall, slim, curvaceous – and the advantage to English speakers. The lone ironic moment came when the only woman of colour to reach the semi-finals lost the crown by lapsing into a moment of honesty. Miss India said that her mind went blank when asked what she would do for children as leader of her country. She answered that she would build sports stadiums for children's use. For a moment, her mind reflected not her condition as an object of beauty for display, but her professional identity as athlete and fitness instructor. As a woman of action, she might indeed build sports stadiums for children. The other two candidates provided vague sentimental rhetoric about children and peace, neither having anything to do with action or practice – so totally committed were they to their display professions.

The headlines on the day after the contest, 10 May (*Nation*, 1992) asked, 'Are the eyes of the beholder truly colour-blind?' The fact that only Miss India was dark complexioned among the ten semifinalists was overshadowed by the election of blond Miss Namibia as the new Miss Universe. 'There are white girls too,' she said in answer to hostile questioning by reporters about the racial composition of Namibia (*Nation*, 10 May 1992). According to one reporter, only the bags of the black delegates were inspected at the airport as the contestants returned home the day following the contest. Thus ended the 'clean peep show that was dedicated to making money, endorsing white supremacy, and denigrating women all in one fell cultural swoop' (Early 1990:296).

National Beauty Contests: From Social Cosmetic to Avon Calling

International beauty contests demonstrate the high value placed on women's beauty. Universal standards of beauty are applied, and cultural identity is reduced to national dress. Naturally, the rewards are much richer in the international contests, and hence the competition is fiercer. Perhaps this is why the role of Miss Congeniality emerges at this level, to mask the very uncongenial conditions prevailing in the international circuit.

National beauty contests are literally a training ground for international contests where women may try out their look, their walk, their runway persona. In many cases women practice for the first time their sexual presentations. Like the international contests, national contests are big businesses with competing organizations developing the Miss Thailand and the Miss Thailand World contests. Famous Thai dress designers compete for the right to design the costumes for the Miss Thailand and Miss Thailand World Pageants.

Avon cosmetics and TV Channel 3 sponsored the Miss Thailand World contest to choose the Thai delegate to the Miss World contest, 1992. Although the contest was covered in local Thai and English newspapers, it did not generate the excitement of the Miss Thailand contest that chose the representative for the Miss Universe contest.

The Miss World contest began in 1951 in England, and prides itself on being more than a beauty contest. The 1992 Miss World contest took place in Sun City, Southern Africa, at the newly opened Lost City, 'an awe-inspiring sort of African Disney World but with a creative cultural background' (according to the organizers, Erik and Julia Morley). 'Beauty with a purpose', the contest slogan, suggests that contestants should be beautiful but should also help society in some way. There is little evidence of this intention in the Thai contest, except that the profits from the dinner and entertainment (which includes the judging of the Miss Thailand World final) are donated to the Narcotics Control Foundation, perhaps the favorite charity of the police general heading the organizing committee. Certainly the gala event (tickets $150 US) attracted many military and police officers in addition to their glamorous wives or escorts.

This is the eighth year of the Miss Thailand World contest. Avon is very involved in the selection process. Avon salespersons sell cosmetics all over Thailand, and are on the lookout for good beauty contest prospects. The forty finalists have found sponsors themselves or have had the sponsoring television channel match them with sponsors. Sponsors like to wait as long as possible to see how the applicants present themselves before signing on. It is to the sponsors' great advantage to sponsor a winner, and thus keep the advertising potential alive as long as possible.

Among the twenty Miss Thailand World finalists who provided the entertainment for the televized extravaganza were two Thai women from the United States, one of whom became Miss Thailand World, and the other, the third runner-up. In the darkened hall, the TV lights shone on an awkward chorus line of young women in black satin leggings, gold sequined vests, and top hats, singing, dancing and parading in front of the gala guests in front, and the press, herded to the corner below the stage. The photographers, mostly male, had no choice but to snap their photographs from below. It is thus not surprising that many shots are of disembodied thighs and rumps. Nevertheless, they clearly enjoyed their vantage point, and loudly evaluated and criticized the contestants from their unlofty vantage point.

The 1992 Miss Thailand contest brought the question of representativeness, authenticity, and Thai *tae (real Thai)* to the fore once again. As a Japanese judge struggled to question the five finalists in Thai, it was revealed that three of the five Thai-Americans could not understand or speak the Thai language. The three from the United States were the

Figure 8 Photographing Miss Thailand World Competition, Bangkok

runners up to the Miss Thailand contest. Two of the three were born to Thai fathers and American mothers. They all felt they were Thai because 'they were raised in a Thai atmosphere, in a house with Thai furniture', says Gina – 'and we eat Thai food'. Gina won a beauty contest in Los Angeles sponsored by Thammasat University Alumni. Reporters complained that they were deprived of the crown because of their mixed looks and their failure to express themselves in Thai. Yet these 'mixed looks' and facility in English are precisely the characteristics that are sought out for success in the international level contests. Their advice for the next lot of Thai-American candidates? 'Take Thai speech classes and study about Thai history and culture' (*Nation Junior*, 19 April 1992). In 1996, a young woman with even less 'Thai blood' but fluent in Thai won the Miss Thailand World contest, raising even more questions about hybridity and embodiment in beauty contests (cf. Weisman 1997, Callahan 1998a:60).

In 1988 when Porntip ('Pui') graduated from Miss Thailand to Miss Universe, her status as a Thai-born, California-raised 'cultural hybrid' was challenged. As in the 1992 concern whether *luk krung* (children of mixed Thai and non-Thai parentage) could be Thai *tae* and represent Thailand, Pui was caught between celebrating her national or her international title. Her cultural hybridity won her the title, but her representation of Thai femininity was problematic. Conflicting notions of beauty also fuelled the controversy over the choice of Miss Orn-anong Panyawong, as the 1992 Miss Thailand. Critics called her 'a national disgrace', 'an insult', and objected to the crown going to a 'local born, dark horse contestant', 'because she looked more Thai' (*Bangkok Post*, 31 March 1992). Miss Orn-anong exemplified the typical Thai beauty according to traditional Thai standards. She is one of the 'rags to riches' success stories that spurs the desires of poor Thai women to enter beauty contests. She comes from a poor family in Chiang Mai, and was the sole income earner for her family of six siblings. In the months after the Miss Thailand contest, she transformed herself from a hesitant, soft woman who could not look people directly in the eye, to a self-assured, confident, professional beauty contestant. She was also a dutiful daughter who sacrificed to help her poverty stricken family, and she excelled at classical Thai dancing, the epitome of feminine grace and skill. In effect, critics were saying that they did not want a typical Thai beauty who met the traditional standards for the ideal Thai woman, but an Americanized hybrid who would strengthen Thailand's chances in the international competition. It is hard to imagine a national beauty queen who could hardly speak the language of the country she represented. In contrast, California-Tongan contestants in the Miss Tonga contest were taunted by the audience for their non-Tongan appearance and behaviour; locals do not want an expatriate Tongan representing Tongan national identity (Teilbet-Fisk 1996:190–1).

Local Beauty Contests

Local contests offer an opportunity to see how indigenous approaches to beauty, appearance, and competition are played out in the absence of international structures, although their standards are increasingly influential. *Songkran* (traditional Thai New Years, 13, 14, 15 April) is associated with beauty contests. The importance of the display of feminine beauty was prominent throughout the celebration of *Songkran* in Chiang Mai (1992), along with a more muted sense of choosing the winner. The parade on the first day set the stage for several contests to be held over the *Songkran* period. The first contest in the morning featured little girls of five or six years dressed in northern Thai *phaasin* and blouses, decked with jewellery, with elaborate hairdos and make-up. They held umbrellas, and looked solemn or terrified, as they rode to the judging platform in bicycle carts. They were spared the worst of the drenchings meted out to their older sisters. They moved very carefully, kept their eyes downcast for the most part, and looked in every way to be in training for adult beauty contests. They all received prizes. The enthusiastic audience at the judging was composed of both men and women.

The next contest featured old ladies in their seventies and eighties, who also rode through the parade and up to the stage in bicycle carts. They, too, were spared drenchings, although many adults poured small amounts of water gently over their shoulders, gave them water to drink, and handed them cool cloths as they passed along the parade route. They were dressed more conservatively in dark *phaasin*, usually white blouses, and shoulder scarves. Again, many looked uncomfortable at being put on display, perhaps at the insistence of relatives. They seldom smiled and showed the same solemnity as the children, with a few exceptions. As the contestants came forward to sit at the front of the stage to be identified, one old lady kept taking the microphone, saying she wanted to win. She chatted to the audience, waved, and generally 'hammed' it up. The male Master of Ceremonies knelt in front of each woman and presented her with a gift. The talkative granny then took centre stage and gave a blessing to the crowd. A second woman made a *sukhwan* blessing, binding the wrists of the Master of Ceremonies with white string, and the event ended. Later, we saw the talkative granny being led away by a relative. 'Did I win' she asked. We *waied* her, asked for her blessing, and poured water gently over her shoulders, much to her delight.

The real competition was for the title of Miss *Songkran*, and the young women candidates representing neighbouring districts and villages were really put through their paces. They all wore beautiful northern Thai dress with the appropriate accessories, and rode in the parade on bicycles, holding umbrellas. This feat of balance was made more difficult, as parade watchers poured water over their shoulders, or threw water on them. With their face and hair elaborately made up, some tried to avoid the water, others stoically accepted the barrages without wavering. These contestants seemed the target of the audience's ire, and the contestants were certainly subjected to substantial abuse. There was no attempt to protect them in any way. Since they had both hands full with their bicycles and umbrellas, they could not protect themselves from water thrown at them. They did not appear to be enjoying the experience, although they showed no emotion except occasionally fear, and more often a hastily repressed disgust at being the target of so much violent attention. Later in the day, they paraded on a large stage in the style of national and international beauty contests, and then sat in numbered rows near the stage, so that spectators could walk up and have a closer look at them at their leisure. The blank stares and slumped shoulders suggested the toll that the day's festivities had taken on them.

While evaluation of the appearance of young women may be 'traditional' in rural Thai communities, it was probably expressed in the past by specifying who lead the communal dancing or performed the first formal *wai khru* (respect to teachers) at temple events. In this context, the audience and contestants would probably reach an unstated consensus as to the most appropriate candidate. No doubt, this had a political element to it, but the idea of measurement and comparison of beauty was probably not central in local competitions.

Thai grandmothers could perhaps think back on the temple beauty contests when they wore their finest family clothing and jewellery, and walked modestly around a temple compound to the rhythm of Thai music, smelling of jasmine and lotus blossoms, knowing that the man they hoped to marry would be watching, admiring from a distance. Perhaps they permitted themselves to be entered in the contest by their children out of nostalgia for those remembered occasions. But their memories must be confused by the parading of women in bathing suits in these modern beauty pageants, parading both their sexuality and their commercial endorsements.

Local contests could be thought of as avenues of social mobility for poor but beautiful rural women. Contestants view beauty contests as a route to economic prosperity; an advertising or entertainment executive might sign them up, or provide product endorsements for them. Local contests are also stepping stones to larger regional and national contests. Young women may well have taken part in over ten contests before entering their present contest. Women who go all over the country seeking new contests are referred to as *nang ngam dern sai* (travelling beauty queens). Each contest provides an opportunity for women to gain experience and grow in self-confidence and assertiveness (to survive walking in high heels and bathing suits in front of men). One feminist alumni spoke of having to avert her eyes when the Thammasat Alumni Association of Chiang Mai held a beauty contest with the contestants wearing bathing suits. While some women alumni objected, the contest was carried out as planned 'because Chiang Mai is famous for beautiful women', as she was told by male alumni.

Provincial governors are encouraged by the Tourist Association of

Thailand (TAT) to hold beauty contests to promote tourism and sales of local products. Provincial beauty contests were used to promote everything from bananas to gem stones. The contests are featured along with local food, local dress, and local historical or pilgrimage sites. For example, a tourist brochure advertised a festival in Siracha, Chonburi Province, featuring local food, local dress, games and a local beauty posing with the mayor and Member of Parliament. (see figure 9)

Figure 9 Provincial beauty queens promote provincial products

In the transformation from local to transnational beauty contests, 'natural' beauty was no longer sufficient, as hair and skin colour could be altered, eye shape changed, eyebrows shaved, and breast size augmented to meet national and international beauty standards. The efforts of contestants to perfect their appearance simultaneously supported the growing beauty industry as beauty shops even spread into remote Thai villages.

Interest in beauty and beauty contests has not diminished in Thailand over the last few decades, however the knowledge and practices that enhance beauty has. Complexion is the beauty asset most elaborated, and light, bright skin was coveted by both rural and urban women, partly as proof that they were exempted from work in the sun. Western cosmetics first began to be imported to Thailand during the reign of Rama V (1868–1910). 'Scientific' perfume, hair removers, creams, blemish removers, lipsticks, rouge, eyebrow pencils replaced local and more natural powders, waxes, herbal mixtures (*samun prei*, which are now being marketed as organic, indigenous, pure Thai products) and flower-based perfumes for those who could afford the high prices. During the reign of Rama VII (1910–1925), white teeth rather than black teeth (from betel chewing) became part of the new criteria of beauty. Beauty shops opened in Bangkok during the reign of Rama 7 (1925–1935) featuring hair styling and perfumes (Kobkitsuksakul 1987:27–31).[9] Nose jobs and eye lifts also became popular among wealthy urban Thai women who wanted to work on their appearance (Kobkitsuksakul 1987:244). Throughout Thailand, there are now 'self-development and personality' courses where young girls can study how to enhance their appearance through make-up, clothing, speech, poise and manners. The courses still build on Thai manners and etiquette of politeness, softness and grace.

As beauty is interpreted less as a natural attribute existing within the body and radiating outward, and more as something that can be purchased, placed on the surface, and enhanced, it becomes the responsibility of women to develop their own beauty potential rather than assume responsibility for meritorious acts that will result in inner beauty.

Incomplete Erasure: The Ideology of Beauty and Buddhism

The international beauty contests, with their huge budgets and media exposure bear little relation to local Thai community contests operating on a much more modest scale. The international and national contests operate in the same conceptual space as the local contests, but when the media covers the international contests, the value of indigenous Thai interpretations of beauty is diminished.

The appreciation of grace and elegance, and the evaluation of beauty is deeply entrenched in Thai culture. 'Thais appreciate grace and elegance; things should be beautiful to be in order, yet this order also requires hard work and dependability. Which is why it is women who are at the heart of Thai life' (Mulder 1992:77). This may help to explain why it is feminine beauty that is extolled in court literature and poetry. Standards of feminine beauty are defined, and these include beauty of manner and behavior as well as form. Voice is also mentioned as a key attribute of women's beauty, as it is in Indonesia.

Beauty is described in the Buddhist canon as one of the five powers of women. But it is also included as one of the powers of men. The Buddhist concept of beauty might be considered sexist if only women's appearance showed the effects of merit collected from past lives and of keeping the precepts. But men's faces show the effects also, in the opinion of several (good-looking) Thai men. It is ethnocentric and Eurocentric to assume that beauty of form is relevant only to women. The court of King Rama VI is a good example of the cultivation of male beauty.

Male beauty is somehow implicated in the power to rule. This is brought out most clearly in the oldest extant Thai poetic work, *Lilit Phra Law*, The Story of King Law. In the story, the handsome king 'lustrous as the moon' prepares to travel to the city of Song to see the two princesses who, driven to distraction by the king's beauty and perfection, cast a spell to attract the king to them:

> The king went to his bath and quickly cleansed himself. He put on fragrances, mixed with gold. He put on his undergarments, finely made, and his outer garments, beautifully decorated. He fastened his shimmering belt, observing the delicate grace of its decoration. His scarf hung, a cascading vine, over garments of diverse colors. He fastened his breast cloth, glowing intensely, and strands of chains over his golden collar. His breast plate shimmered with the light of the dawn, encrusted with magnificent diamonds and jewels. He put on shining bracelets, arm bands in the shaped of the *mangkoon*, dazzling finger rings and a jewelled diadem, shining with pure light. Having put on the royal victory weapons he went forth with the grace of the lion king from the pinnacle of his gem dwelling, and soon arrived at the royal elephant platform . . .. Having

mounted the neck of the great beast, he caused the multitude of his troops to embark. (Bickner 1991:20)

Possession of radiant beauty is evidence of legitimate power – both beauty of self and of mate. This idea, of great antiquity, has great cognitive salience in recent Thai history and even in contemporary Thai politics. Thai women recall that Prime Minister Prem was beautiful and elegant, and ousted Prime Minister Suchinda was supported by some women because he was handsome. In May of 1992, Thammasat University students displayed a poster of Suchinda as a beauty queen, a put-down of Suchinda and of beauty contests that plays with the connections between the beauty of form and political power. Discourses on beauty permeates political rhetoric. The cartoon of Suchinda as a beauty queen is a visual metaphor reflecting the language used to compare politicians to beauty contestants. Thaksin Shinawatra, chief of the Palang Dharma Party (PDP) referred to the leaders of the other political parties as

'ugly' but that their flaws . . . would not prevent them from winning a local beauty contest . . . But if they are to contest the Miss Universe title, they would not be able to win because they would face tough opponents . . . This 'beauty contest' will be decided by the contestants' accessories. If you want your government to look better, you must bring in the PDP. (*The Nation*, 20 Oct 1996: 1)

Wolf refers to beauty as amoral (1991:59). This is not the case in Thailand where beauty is linked to morality through canonical and popular Buddhism and court literature. The naturalness of beauty was further emphasized by astrological predictions. The position of the stars makes women (and men) beautiful. In the past, according to a famous Thai astrologer, beauty contestants would check their horoscopes to discover their beauty quotient before entering contests. With all the various training courses and cosmetic operations available now, the stars can be thwarted. Similarly Suchinda's wife regularly consulted astrologers to alter the course of her handsome husband's political fortune (Callahan 1994:110).

Thai ideas about beauty are also reflected in the *Trai Phum Phra Ruang*. The text describes a *Cakkavatti* or universal monarch who must possess a number of items as signs of his right to rule. One of these possessions is a beautiful gem woman whose beauty is carefully detailed:

Because of the power of the merit of the one who is qualified to be a great *Cakkavatti* king there is a gem woman . . . She comes bringing various kinds of things for ornaments that are replete with the seven gems and are glorious and very beautiful. She comes by air, just like a female *devata*, and comes down to pay her respects and bow down to the great *Cakkavatti* king. This gem woman is neither too short nor too tall, but is beautifully and suitably proportioned. She pleases and gladdens the hearts of the people. Her complexion appears polished and smooth; it is clean, clear, and very beautiful, and even the specks of dust do not settle on it or make marks on it – it is like a lotus being touched by the water. The features of this gem woman's entire body from head to toe are perfect, are beautiful, and please everyone in the human world . . .. The face of the gem woman appears polished and smooth, and is clean, clear, and very beautiful. Her body and skin are soft like cotton that has been fluffed a hundred times and been dipped in clear, very beautiful oil taken from the joint of a special kind of yak oxen called *camara*. Whenever the body of the great *Cakkavatti king* is cool or cold, the body of the gem woman is warm; whenever the body of the great *Cakkavatti king* is hot, the body of the woman is cool. The body of the gem woman has a fragrance like a core of sandalwood and *aloes* wood that has been ground up and mixed with all of the four sweet-smelling essences; this very pleasing smell wafts about in the air at all times. When the gem woman talks or laughs her breath wafts about like the odor of the lotus called blue water lilies and the trees called *chongkolni* when they are in bloom; the breath of the gem woman has that kind of sweet smell at all times. (Reynolds and Reynolds 1982:166)

In the palace tradition, the power to rule was formed and shaped in courts where the beauty of males and females were cultivated. Sunthorn Phu's famous words of wisdom for young women (*Suphasit son ying*) emphasizes the constructedness of women's appearance:

Ensure your attire befits your person
That it may compliment your looks.
When powdering your face and your body,
Consider complexion and be not extreme.
Whoever sees you must surely approve –
Say you are clever and arrayed like a swan.
For though you be young and beautiful,
Ignorance of grooming is beauty wasted.

(Lynch 1978:11)

For all the poem's emphasis on appearance, women who become too absorbed and preoccupied with their looks are ridiculed:

> They are at their mirrors as soon as day breaks
> Combing their hair a thousand times a day.
>
> And though a woman's beauty might decline,
> The goodness of her heart will raise her up.
>
> (Lynch 1978:23)

This linkage between beauty, deportment, morality and status is further complicated by the theme of disguise and masking that is prominent in popular Buddhist tales such as the Jataka stories of the former lives of the Buddha, classical Thai literature, and the poetry of Sunthorn Phu. Appearance must match status. Yet *phuu dii* are encouraged to keep their faults well concealed (lines 92–3), so that the appearance of beauty and refinement is retained. Poor women in stunning finery may be tempted to behave as the wealthy: 'The thought of imitation makes them drool' (Lynch 1978:26). Beneath the concern with surface appearances lies the fear of deception - of beauty that deceives:

> They masquerade among the well-to-do,
> But the nobility does not acknowledge
> Any relationship under the sun.
>
> For those who are really of the nobility,
> Need not declare it to make it true. (Lynch 1978:25)

Conclusions

Beauty contests are both universal and intensely local, showcasing '. . . values, concepts, and behavior that exist at the center of a group's sense of self and exhibit values of morality, gender and place' (Cohen et al. 1996:2). In Thailand, they evoke a trope of royalty in a country where monarchy is both respected and parodied through rituals emulating royal style in both rural and urban communities.[10] The beauty queen has both symbolic and political capital. Village scout initiations elect mock kings, queens and royal attendants (Bowie 1997), at the same time as evoking royalty as sacred symbol. While beauty queens were idealized, at the same time, there is something unsettling about beauty contests, an unsavory atmosphere of excess. Young beautiful women are on public display, their names and measurements made available.

Tourist brochures treat Thai women as part of the aesthetic resources of the country. TAT publications such as *Thailand Traveller* are increasingly conscious of avoiding representations that could encourage sex tourism, instead stressing the ecological and historical resources of the country. Yet publications and posters feature beautiful young women making crafts, dancing, displaying silk and gems, participating in traditional celebrations, and welcoming visitors to hotels ('we recognize the needs of our guests', says a miniskirted beauty advertising Thavorn Hotels in Phuket).

Airlines as well have been quick to capitalize on Asian women's beauty and femininity. 'Singapore girl, you look so good I want to stay up here with you forever . . .', the advertisements croon, and the chairman of Singapore airlines responds to questions about such dialogue: 'We're fortunate in having young people who get a western education, speak English and still take an Asian attitude toward service' (Hochschild 1983:95). Air Chief Marshal Kaset, who ordered the Capital Security Command to put 'operation crush enemies' into effect against the pro-democracy protesters, has announced that Thai Airways, the state enterprise that he controlled, wants more 'bimbo beauties' as flight attendants. He asked the international airline to hire more attractive women 'even if they're not as bright as the mostly college-educated cabin crews,' claiming he has received complaints that the women are not pretty enough, too old, and unsmiling. 'Intelligent women tend not to be good looking.' He ordered recruiters to screen applicants 'in the way beauty pageant judging panels select contestants' (*Daily News* 1991). A Thai cartoon showing a beauty queen racing a turtle in academic robes confirmed the message that beauty contests were a more significant and much faster boost to a woman's status than an education (Kobkitsuksakul 1987:264).[11]

Local beauty contests facilitate recruiting the most beautiful girls into prostitution (*Voices of Thai Women*, 4 Dec. 1990:15), and prostitutes enter contests to provide 'added value' for upper-class customers (Callahan 1998a:57). Even unsuccessful contestants may end up as prostitutes or escorts of prominent politicians. An old term for prostitute, *ying ngam muang* (the beauty of the city), explicitly links beauty and prostitution. The next chapter suggests how conceptions of beauty and concern with the appearance of women underlie the commodification of women that helps prostitution flourish in Thailand.

Notes

1. Prototypes of unattractive, brilliant women abound in classical and modern Thai literature. Female characters in novels, unable to conform to the beautiful, subservient ideal, go abroad to do graduate work (Kepner 1996:8–9).

2. Sumpuary laws regulate consumption and use of goods such as dishes, textiles, umbrellas, and foods in order to maintain control over the presentation of status differences.

3. An earlier draft including my response to the pre-democracy protests was also circulated as a working paper from the Thai Studies Project, York University.

4. Estimates of the numbers of protestors killed is a hotly debated subject. NGOs were accused of inflating the numbers, and the military of deflating them. Further discussion of the politics of numbers can be found in Callahan (1998b).

5. Research on Thai beauty contests is based on the documents assembled in Supatra Kobkitsuksakul's MA thesis (1987) *Miss Thailand Contest: 1934–87* (Thammasat University), *Flowers of the Nation* (in Thai) by Orasom Suttisakorn (1990), the photograph collection (since 1934) in the National Archives, and observation of a number of local, national and international contests in Thailand. There were certainly local beauty contests before 1934 – the Chiang Mai Winter Fair, Miss Lao Song at Nakorn Prathom, and the many community contests held throughout the country at New Years (*Songkran*). These local beauty contests may have become one means for attracting more applicants for the national contests, but there are inadequate records of these local contests before the 1930s when national contests began.

6. Many international beauty contests have to deal with the sleaze factor. For example, two candidates for a recent Miss Italy contest were withdrawn, one, because Italy's most beautiful woman turned out to be a man, born a hermaphrodite and surgically made a woman, and the first potential black Miss Italy had appeared nude in a magazine (*Toronto Star*, 3 Sept. 1992). To improve the image of the Miss China competition, contestants will be asked to give backrubs to homeless pensioners, play with orphans, and comfort the dying (*Toronto Star*, 8 Aug. 1992).

7. This is not just a feature of international contests, for the primary purpose of provincial Thai beauty contests is to promote tourism and sales of local products. Provincial and local beauty contests were used to promote everything from bananas to gem stones. Contestants saw beauty contests as a route to economic prosperity; an advertising or entertainment executive might see them and sign them up, or provide product endorsements for them. The Miss Universe contest fits well into this Thai pattern of commercial beauty contests.

8. The first teenage beauty contest for fifteen- to seventeen-year-olds was recently held in Thailand (*Bangkok Post*, 2 July 1989).

9. Beauty shops in Thailand are not run by male transvestites (*kathoey*), as in parts of the Philippines (Johnson 1997). However, a northern Thai merchant owed his success in the cosmetic business to using *kathoey* as travelling cosmetic salesmen since they looked 'better than most women' and were able to perform femininity in an entertaining manner (Irvine 1982:476).

10. The beauty of the present Queen Sirikit was an asset that enhanced the status of the royal family at home and abroad.

11. Wolf cites a study showing that 'fashion modelling and prostitution are the only professions in which women consistently earned more than men', and she illustrates her point by reference to the income of Miss America (1991:50).

Prostitution and Foreign Bodies

Divergent Voices

Thai studies continues to be criticized for claiming uniqueness in all things Thai. While I am conscious of the dangers of presenting Thailand as the special case, the location of unique particularities, I argue that the Thai sex-gender system has much to contribute to counter Euro-American biases in theorizing gender, sexuality and prostitution. But analyses of the country's sex-gender system cannot be reduced to studies of prostitution and sex tourism. Such reductionism reinforces the good woman/bad woman dichotomy and underplays the importance of local institutions that support gender inequality. If brothels, massage parlours and go-go bars are sites where Thai gender and sexuality are visibly constructed, they are also sites that most Thai women have never visited. Other localities such as beauty contests, workplaces, temples, homes and shopping malls shape Thai gender categories more significantly than prostitution.

When I tell people that I am writing a book about gender and Thailand, inevitably they ask why there is so much prostitution and sex tourism in the country. When I am in the country, both leave my consciousness, replaced by concerns about propriety, manners and admiration for the competence of Thai women. Yet prostitution must figure prominently in the analysis of Thai gender because it articulates with national representations, sexuality, economics, gender categories and marriage in significant and interesting ways.

My perspective on Thai prostitution is not based on systematic field research, but from my review of the academic and popular literature by both Thai and foreign social scientists on aspects of prostitution, conversations with Thai social scientists and women activists on the subject, and observations over a thirty-year period in Bangkok, Pattaya,

Chiang Mai, Khon Kaen and villages in central Thailand. My conversations with prostitutes have been too casual to allow me to use these
experiences to substitute for the voices of the prostitutes themselves.
However, there are a number of anthropologists whose ethnographic
fieldwork focuses specifically on prostitution (cf. Muecke 1992, Odzer
1994, Jeffries 1999). As an analyst, I try to avoid stigmatizing prostitutes
as victims or judging their morality, while critiquing the conditions in
Thailand today and in the past that perpetuate prostitution and gender
inequity, and locating Thai prostitution within broader systems of
meanings, including the Thai sex-gender system.

Discourses on Thai prostitution emerge at the local, national and
international level, from both Thai and foreign commentators. I identified some of these voices in 1992:

- the voices of middle-class women who assume that Thai men need
  prostitutes because of their greater sexual drive, and that the existence
  of prostitution protects 'good women' from rape
- the voices of wives who view prostitutes as less threatening to their
  marriages than *mia noi* (second wives) because prostitutes drain less
  money from the household and do not arouse jealousy, since men
  are assumed not to have emotional attachments to prostitutes
- the voices of Thai legislators who argue that prostitutes are criminals
  who break Thai laws, and therefore must be jailed and fined for their
  actions
- the voices of other Thai legislators who support the development of
  infrastructure necessary for the expansion of the tourist industry such
  as hotels, airports, and places of entertainment
- the voices of social welfare advocates who argue that following incar-
  ceration, prostitutes must be rehabilitated and retrained for alternative
  occupations
- the voices of the Tourist Authority of Thailand (TAT) and tourist
  interests who downplay the negative side of prostitution, but encourage tourists to enjoy the 'service advantages' of Thailand; these voices
  criticize women's groups for giving Thailand a 'bad image' by drawing
  attention to sex tourism
- the voices of lawyers who argue that prostitutes should not be considered criminals, nor prostitution a crime; only rape and kidnapping
  associated with prostitution are crimes and should be prosecuted to
  the full extent of the law
- the voices of young rural women who are devastated by not being
  able to help their parents and siblings financially or to donate

generously at the temple, but are not embarrassed or devastated by taking up prostitution as a source of income

- the voices of some Thai feminists who view prostitutes as independent businesswomen with impressive entrepreneurial skills
- the voices of other Thai feminists who believe prostitution must be suppressed; the profession is an example of sexual exploitation and the commoditization of women perpetuated by a strongly patriarchal society
- still other feminist voices that laud prostitutes as flouting sexual mores and rejecting the image of passive, subservient Thai women, respectful to male superiority
- the voices of women's groups that say prostitution should be legalized in order to give prostitutes the right to free movement, fair treatment, improved working conditions, and adequate medical care
- and the angry retort by other women's groups arguing that legalizing and registering prostitutes will stigmatize them for life
- the voices of economists who see prostitution as a temporary, natural consequence of uneven economic development; as more profitable employment is available for women, prostitution will cease to exist because it will no longer be profitable
- the voices of other economists who point out that the profit from prostitution goes to pimps, brothel owners, and entertainment establishments, not to prostitutes
- the voices of human rights activists who see the necessity of protecting the human rights of prostitutes and ensuring that they have chosen the profession of their own free wills, without coercion; they therefore view policies that force prostitutes to be 'rehabilitated' as violating their human rights (P. Van Esterik 1992b:133–5)

In the few years since these voices were recontextualized and placed in my work, new voices have been raised, including those shaped by international settings, many of them responding to the reality and representation of HIV/AIDS in Thailand.

- critics of the media who argue that the Thai and foreign media are responsible for publicizing prostitution and sex tourism in Thailand, and if the media were silent, the problem would disappear
- the civil servants who view prostitutes as lazy women who do not want to work, but who only want to have fun (on the assumption that because visiting brothels once a week is entertaining for Thai men, it must also be entertaining for the women who have sexual encounters all day, every day)

- the voice of *Bangkok Post* columnist 'Trink' who cautions everyone to lighten up, let men have some fun, because HIV/AIDS is not transmitted through heterosexual encounters with Thai prostitutes
- health promotion campaigns that target prostitutes as the source of disease – (old voice, but new disease)
- the voices of Thai and foreign academics who blame prostitution on 'traditional' Thai values
- the voices of other Thai and foreign academics who blame prostitution on the loss of 'traditional' Thai values
- declarations about the treatment of victims of forced prostitution in the international sex trade

As in many domains of Thai exegesis, there have been few attempts to reconcile opposing views about prostitution. Instead, the divergent discourses stand side by side, becoming more entrenched through time, available for selection by analysts who search for simplifying, overarching explanations for Thai prostitution that will resolve all contradictions.

Some of the divergent views are accounted for by the argument that there are different levels or classes of prostitutes, from children chained in rundown brothels, to silk-clad women in condominium apartments entertaining foreign diplomats. Other discrepancies relate to regional and rural-urban differences. All voices are not equally loud, nor are they all equally heard, particularly in international settings. In fact, the voices are not so much heard as read – voices captured in text.

And the silences on prostitution? Until recently, these surrounded child prostitutes, male prostitutes, bisexual and transvestite prostitutes, overseas Thai prostitutes, foreign prostitutes working in Thailand and part-time casual or student prostitutes. HIV/AIDS has accentuated but not ended these silences.

When prostitutes speak for themselves, their words are embedded in other people's views of Thai prostitution, and may not fit well with either Thai or foreign views of prostitutes, or with feminist paradigms. For example, prostitutes' requests for English or Japanese language lessons to allow them to negotiate the prices for sex acts more directly and effectively with their clients would meet their expressed needs but not the strategic needs of the advocacy groups that labour on their behalf, a dilemma experienced by many Thai women's groups.

The voices of Thai prostitutes, when they are heard, are framed by Thai and foreign mass media. The Thai media rarely examines or condemns indigenous prostitution, but rather documents juicy crimes where prostitutes are the victims, and draws attention to foreign demand generated by the Vietnam war and sex tourism. They look to rural poverty and women's desire for consumer goods to explain the increasing supply of prostitutes (cf. Muecke 1992). Although there are a number of very sympathetic Thai women reporters (particularly Sanitsuda Ekachai) who publicize the evils of prostitution in English language papers (the *Bangkok Post* and the *Nation*), they usually focus on the plight of individual prostitutes, or expose corruption and coercion in the sex industry, giving voice to the prostitute as victim.

Rutnin complains that prostitution is presented in Thai fiction, on stage, in film and on television in the style of romantic realism, avoiding the ugly truths of prostitution (1984:2). The plight of these women is depicted sentimentally in Thai fiction. Rachel Harrison's work on the representation of female prostitutes in Thai literature explores this sentimental romanticism by viewing the image of the pregnant prostitute, for example,

> . . . as a metaphor for the cultural prescriptions concerning Thai women in general and, more specifically, prostitute women. Consciously or otherwise, Thai writers' portrayals of the pregnant prostitute are representative of traditional cultural beliefs about the nature of female sexuality and the need for its control in Thai society at large. (1996:1)

The Thai mass media perpetuates negative images of Thai women generally by publicizing photographs of rape victims, beauty contestants, nude models and victims of gruesome violence (cf. Mulder 1997: 224). Flashy articles on Patpong sex shows do little to untangle the determinants and consequences of prostitution. But they reinforce the perception that Thai culture constructs two kinds of women, the good woman and the bad; the former allows only one man to have sexual access to her for purposes of procreation within marriage, and the latter, more than one man, outside of long-term commitment. Thus the prostitute is more than a metaphor for the bad woman – she is her embodiment.

The foreign media also prefers to portray the more sensational aspects of sex tourism rather than the sexual double standard underlying local prostitution. This latter story is less exotic but requires more understanding of the Thai context than can be framed in a brief film or article. The BBC production, *Foreign Bodies* (1988) is an excellent title for an attention-grabbing film documenting the provision of young Thai women and men for older European men. The film exoticizes

Western men and their relations with young Thai men and women. The 'otherness' of the 'east' is stressed in these videos, as in tourist brochures, including reference to the easy availability of Asian women. As a bar owner explains in the video, visitors feel good because they can find a stable, caring relationship with a Thai woman who does not mind old, dumpy, Western men. And the prostitute feels better because she has made the man happy and helped her family financially. The racism is equally apparent in the interpretation of these purchased bodies as exotic and Oriental. The film begins its exploration of sex tourism in Thailand by referring to Thailand as the 'Brothel of Asia'. Other British, European and North American television documentaries and news shows aired in the 1990s have focused on child prostitution and pederasty in relation to HIV/AIDS and to sex tourism. The government regularly protests the film-makers' representations of Thailand and their failure to emphasize the steps the government has taken to curb prostitution; but they cannot counter the evidence of the institutionalized support for Thailand's sex industry.[1]

The Good Woman of Bangkok, a work of documentary fiction by Australian film-maker, Dennis O'Rourke, is a powerful film depicting in titillating detail the life experiences of a Patpong prostitute that O'Rourke literally 'shopped' for in the Bangkok bars. The movie lingers on the bodies of these 'exotic others' as they dance in a dreamy daze, waiting to be picked up for the night. O'Rourke makes his own position clear, as he sets out to film the experience of falling in love with a Patpong prostitute after his own marriage failed. After making the film, O'Rourke bought a farm for the prostitute, but claims she later returned to prostitution. The movie feels self-serving and calculating, and it is difficult to know how much of the dialogue is directed to the personal relation between the two, but presented as a commentary on Thai prostitution generally. O'Rourke sees prostitution as a metaphor for male and female relations. But the relations explored are not Thai gender relations, but the relations between Western males of different nationalities falling in love with and/or using Thai prostitutes for their own purposes. Manderson argues that the representations of sexuality in these films facilitate and legitimize sex tourism (1997:143).

Media reports of prostitution are important because even superficial treatments of the subject tarnish Thailand's international image. The negative publicity is a more important concern to both the government and to Thai individuals than the lives of prostitutes and the evils of sex tourism. The sex industry is not blamed for this negative image, but rather the foreign media and women's groups that publicize sexploitation are criticized for giving the country 'bad press'. When a Japanese magazine article on Thai prostitution wrote that university students acted as prostitutes and included a photograph of Thammasat University, 'Thammasat and the Thai nation were insulted.' Including students within the spectrum of Thai prostitution was considered an unbecoming act and in poor taste particularly for a foreign nation to make such an observation (Voices of Thai Women 1990:5). Officials are generally instructed not to discuss prostitution when overseas (Truong 1990:187), as if this could silence critics and preserve intact Thailand's international reputation.

The complexity of issues such as Thai prostitution cannot be fully developed in media presentations. They have powerful 'shock' value, but they also entertain, leaving the viewer with an oversimplified picture of the difficulties caused by Thailand's rapid modernization. Although foreign and Thai journalists regularly present exposés on the most abusive forms of prostitution and sex tourism, these analyses are usually built around single events or case studies. Yet Thai women may feel tainted by the media image of Thai women as sexually available. Under the new prostitution law passed in 1996, women travelling abroad could be detained without a warrant, if officials suspect they may be involved in prostitution. One Thai colleague recounted to me her humiliation at the leers she endured at an American airport when she presented her Thai passport. Representations hurt.

Thai social science exegesis on prostitution is rare both for political and intellectual reasons, and it has therefore had little impact on the way prostitution is presented or analyzed by the government. Most research on prostitution by Thai scholars has been framed by health concerns and is strongly positivistic in research design, with the exception of the ground-breaking work of economist Pasuk Phongpaichit (1982) who examined the income of sex workers. There are few indigenous interpretations of Thai prostitution, although there are intriguing comments on the subject. Anthropologist Yos Santasombat has made such a contribution in a Thai monograph, in addition to his suggestive prologue to *Hello My Big Big Honey*, a book of letters and interviews relating the experiences of Patpong bar girls and their customers (Walker and Ehrlich 1992). He identifies several key cultural differences between Thailand and 'the west' which confuse the Western males visiting Patpong prostitutes. First, he argues that Western men view prostitution as an occupation, while 'the girls' have a more open-ended, 'fuzzy' understanding of attachments that can extend into long-term relationships. Second, Westerners consider love and money as mutually exclusive, whereas 'the girls' find overlap between money and gifts; Thai prostitutes view money in the same way they view a gift, not as something having a derogatory connotation. Even gifts are calculated in precise monetary terms. Because of the emphasis on gifts, and the prostitutes' skills in making their clients feel special and sexually attractive, Yos argues that the visiting males do not apply their previous concepts of prostitution to the Thai scene (Walker and Ehrlich 1992:14–17). Instead, many foreign males try to rescue the girl from her plight, help her recover her dignity. (Perhaps she never lost her dignity. Perhaps her clients lost theirs.) Odzer, in her study of Patpong prostitution (1994) calls this the 'Eliza Doolittle syndrome'. For these foreign men visiting Thai prostitutes, then, the line between emotional commitment and material commitment becomes blurred, particularly when they find themselves in the hands of an experienced prostitute, looking for a way out of the business. After age thirty, with ten or more years of work under their G-strings, Patpong prostitutes are unlikely to find Thai husbands who would support them, only men who would use their earnings. But they can hope to catch a foreign male who accepts that their immoral practices are for moral reasons – to support their poverty-stricken families (Walker and Ehrlich 1992:19). In any case, Yos argues, Thai men are less likely to find these women attractive, since many have darker skin, come from northeastern Thailand and act aggressively. The 'ugly women of Patpong' would not fit Thai men's image of beautiful Thai women (Walker and Ehrlich 1992:26). Here, as in the beauty contests, Bangkok sets the standards, and rejects the standards of beauty indigenous to the periphery. Admittedly, Yos' is the voice of a middle-class Thai male academic, perhaps revealing more about the contrast between Thai men and women's interpretation of prostitution, than the contrast between Thai interpretations and Western ones. But he provides important insights into cultural differences in interpreting financial negotiations.

Thai analysts have recognized the importance of Buddhism as part of the ideological context in which Thai prostitution thrives. Yet as documented in Chapter 3, most emphasis has been on blaming Buddhism for tolerating an immoral vocation or even encouraging it because monks accept gifts from prostitutes. Buddhism does not irrevocably damn prostitutes as evil beings.

Chatsumarn Kabilsingh's analysis of Thai prostitution (1991) provides historical and contextual background for understanding contemporary prostitution, but her analysis is based on Buddhist texts and not contemporary social practices. As a Thai woman academic, she has been drawn into discussions outside the domain of textual Buddhism, and here she risks criticism for failing to contextualize Thai prostitution within broader social processes. Her analysis differentiates the Indian courtesans in early Buddhist texts from contemporary prostitutes, stressing the suffering endured by Thai prostitutes today, and warning against equating ancient prostitutes' opportunities to seek enlightenment with Buddhist support for the institution of prostitution. As beings born into the human realm, prostitutes have the same spiritual potential as all of humanity (Kabilsingh 1991:71). Her writing documents the vicious circle by which prostitutes are made aware of their evil life (*chewit baap*), and convinced of the need to make merit to insure a better rebirth. But the only means they have for raising money to make merit is through prostitution. She asks whether it is appropriate for monks to 'turn over their bowls' and refuse to accept gifts from prostitutes. Such an act would deny these women access to the only means at their disposal for merit making, and might well anger other members of the laity who view monks as fields of merit who should not be judging the intentions of givers of *dana*. The effectiveness of gift giving or *dana* depends on the worthiness of the recipient – not the giver (Bowie 1998). Stories of women as generous donors are prominent in early Buddhist texts as well as stories of the early Thai kingdoms.

Prostitution in Thailand could be examined from the standpoint of Buddhist social ethics. Prostitution, along with other immoral vocations *(akusala)* including butchering, fishing and soldiering have inevitable *karmic* consequences. But they may be necessary in order to achieve the four basic supporting conditions of life – food, clothing, lodging and medicine. Under conditions of poverty, these professions are chosen rationally, and are therefore both legal and tolerated in Thai society. In fact, military lifestyles are more than tolerated or socially acceptable; they are admired, sought after, prestigious. According to philosopher Somparn Promta (1993), adult prostitution as a freely chosen vocation is neutral according to Buddhist social ethics: the evil is the poverty which necessitates wrong livelihood. Child prostitution and non-consensual sex is an unacceptable evil from the perspective of Buddhist social ethics. This distinction accounts for the neutrality towards prostitution expressed in the Pali texts, a neutrality that stresses first and foremost the humanity of the prostitute, and the recognition that acting in the real world requires accommodation to gain the necessities of life.

Sukanya Hantrakul's analysis (1988) of prostitution in Thailand begins with an analysis of Buddhism. She stresses that *karma* determines sex, and being born a woman indicates an inadequate store of merit from previous lives. '*Karma* pacifies the despised and leads to prostitute's fatalized acceptance of her profession' (Hantrakul 1988:37). She argues that the most efficient way to attain *nirvana* is by becoming a monk (*bhikkhu*). In the past, Buddhist schools and colleges taught males almost exclusively, thus depriving women of educational opportunities. But prostitution is not directly linked to the availability of spiritual roles for Thai women. Prostitution has been increasing in the country at the same time as women's access to spiritually fulfilling roles is increasing. It is the Thai state and not the Buddhist *Sangha* that has created conditions driving rural and urban women into prostitution.

Historical and Cultural Specificity of Thai Prostitution

What caused prostitution to expand in Thai society in different historical periods?[2] Is it the unequal distribution of wealth? Or the socialization of women? Does it expand in relation to rural poverty or urban affluence or both? Or is it accounted for only by reference to transnational forces? To date, both local and foreign analysts seek answers in the supply of prostitutes rather the demand for them.

Although social historians of Southeast Asia have generally ignored lower-class working women (Warren 1987:150), a number of authors have reviewed the history and cultural context of Thai prostitution. I draw here on the work of Sukanya Hantrakul (1988), Siriporn Skrobenek (1983) and Wathinee Boonchalaksi and Philip Guest (1994) to demonstrate that prostitution in Thailand cannot be accounted for solely on the basis of the Vietnam war rest and recreation businesses nor international sex tourism, although both transformed Thai prostitution.

Siriporn Skrobenek's (1983) history of prostitution in Thailand documents the brothels of Ayutthaya (fourteenth century to eighteenth century), noting that prostitution in Thailand neither developed from temple prostitution as in India, nor from the Japanese 'geisha' system. Reid concludes that in the cities of Southeast Asia prostitution was much rarer than temporary marriage or concubinage until the late sixteenth century: 'In the 1680s a particular Thai official was licensed by the king to run a monopoly of prostitution in the capital, Ayutthaya, using six hundred women bought or enslaved for various offences. This may have been the origin of a Thai tradition of drawing significant state revenue from prostitution' (1988:156). Thus, in the Ayutthaya period, prostitution was legal and taxed by the government. Located in the Chinese community, it was available to both foreign and local men, with both Chinese and Thai houses appealing to both ethnic groups. This form of prostitution serviced Chinese men imported to Thailand without their wives in the nineteenth and early twentieth century for tin mining, building the railroad, and other labour. Traffickers kidnapped or purchased young girls from southern Chinese villages and shipped them to Bangkok and other Southeast Asian ports where they were delivered to brothels or to individual Chinese men (Lai 1986).

Under Rama IV and V (1851–1910), well-run houses of prostitution flourished in Bangkok, operated by managers who supervised the female slaves who serviced their clients well (Boonchalaksi and Guest 1994:3). Mrs Feung, a prostitute working during the reigns of Rama IV and V, built the Bangkok temple, Wat Kanikapol which means the temple built from the profits of prostitution (Boonchalaksi and Guest 1993:4).

Prostitutes served commoners, including Europeans and Chinese in the port cities, not high-ranking men who had concubines and harems. Harems existed in many different contexts, in addition to those associated with Thai royalty during the Bangkok era. In 1890, an agent of the Borneo Company, Dr Cheek had a harem in Chiang Mai licensed by his wife. The girls were housed in a stockade compound and provided with pocket money, nice clothes and jewellery. Farmers received buffaloes in exchange for their daughters. The owner of a harem was admired for the wealth and virility implied by a harem, and their feelings were reflected in rhymes still recited in Chiang Mai:

> Dr Chitt and Missa Louis
> Sleeping with two girls,
> Two nights for fifteen rupees
> Miss Kum asked for silver,
> Miss Huan asked for cloth,
> Miss Noja asked for an elephant.
> Hurry up and finish, Doctor.
>
> (Bristowe 1976: 83)

Ironically, Missa Louis was the son of Anna Leonowens, and when she was governess to King Mongkut's children and harem, he spent several years at school with Prince Chulalongkorn. Perhaps Louis learned the ways of the Siamese court better than the royal children learned the ways of the British.

In 1930, there were 151 licensed brothels in Bangkok – 126 Chinese,

22 Siamese and 3 Vietnamese (Skrobenek 1983: 29–31). Yaowarat in Bangkok's Chinatown is still an important centre for 'teahouses' where child prostitutes are available, and where Chinese own many lucrative brothels. Until the 1950s, 80 percent of the prostitutes in Thailand were Chinese, or if they were Thai, would take Chinese names (Boonchalaksi and Guest 1994:3). The historical links between the overseas Chinese system of prostitution based on subordination and exploitation of Chinese women, and the development of Thai prostitution (particularly in Sino-Thai urban centers) remain to be explored. Jackson writes that 'Higher class night entertainment establishments, tea houses, and hotels at which prostitutes work in Bangkok frequently are owned by Chinese men, whereas brothels are generally owned by Thai women' (1980:46).[3]

Hantrakul (1988) links the growth of Thai prostitution to the large numbers of newly freed slave women who became prostitutes following the abolition of slavery in the late nineteenth century and the end of all forms of debt bondage and corvée labour in 1905. But slaves could 'voluntarily' remain prostitutes after they were freed by registering as prostitutes for a fee and working in a brothel that paid taxes.

In 1908, the Contagious Disease Prevention Act registered brothels in Bangkok to keep them in good order, to control sexually transmitted diseases, and to collect taxes (Boonchalaksi and Guest 1994:4). The Trafficking of Women and Children Act of 1928 outlawed procuring women and children for purposes of prostitution, and the Prostitution Suppression Act of 1960 made brothels illegal. The Entertainment Places Act of 1966 indirectly encouraged prostitution in entertainment places such as massage parlours, nightclubs, bars, coffee shops, tea houses and barber shops (Hantrakul 1988:119). When prostitutes are charged, it is usually under the 1960 Prostitution Suppression Act rather than the Entertainment Act because of the lighter penalties under the former (Boonchalaksi and Guest 1994:21). But under these laws, it is the prostitutes who are punished and sent to rehabilitation centers, not their customers.

Because of the high capital costs in running expensive entertainment businesses, prostitution must be supported by legitimate businesses such as bars, restaurants or massage parlours, so that money can be borrowed from banks. Small entertainment businesses must have legitimate businesses act as middlemen for bank loans (Thai Development Newsletter 1989:26). Nevertheless, banks prefer to lend money for investments in the service and entertainment area rather than in the manufacturing and productive sector, because profits in the former were easier and larger (Hewison and Thongyou 1993:15).

The American military presence in Thailand changed the public display of prostitution. Unlike the more discreet Thai and Chinese customers, American soldiers stationed in Thailand in the northeast and the 70,000 combat troops who visited Thailand for R&R (rest and recreation) between 1962 and 1976 (Phongpaichit 1982:24) treated Thai prostitutes like 'girlfriends', and walked openly with them arm-in-arm down main streets.

During the Vietnam war, American GIs obtained *mia chao* or rented wives to entertain them during their rest and recreation periods in Bangkok, Pattaya, and other Thai cities.[4] Phongpaichit estimates that 70,000 soldiers were entertained on seven-day leaves in Bangkok in 1968–69 (1982: 6). Soldiers were accommodated in new hotels with swimming pools, air-conditioning, 24-hour coffee shops, massage parlours, and bars, all at very cheap prices (Dawson 1988:40). Between 1967 and 1971, the taxes paid to the Thai government by massage parlours, nightclubs, hotels and restaurants amounted to 360 million baht (Meyer 1988:71).

The 'rented wives' of the Vietnam war era appear at first glance to be a modern, Western innovation. But descriptions of arrangements made for foreign traders in Pattani, southern Thailand in 1604, sound strikingly familiar. Local women present themselves to the traders on their arrival, and come to an agreement on payment for the length of time the trader is in port.

> She comes to his house, and serves him by day as his maidservant and by night as his wedded wife. He is then not able to consort with other women or he will be in grave trouble with his wife, while she is similarly wholly forbidden to converse with other men, but the marriage lasts as long as he keeps his residence there, in good peace and unity. When he wants to depart he gives her what is promised, and so they leave each other in friendship, and she may then look for another man as she wishes, in all propriety, without scandal. (van Neck in Reid 1988:155)[5]

The palimpsest is incompletely erased.

The Thai variant on the global practice of prostitution flourishes partly because of the incredible Thai capacity for tolerance and the high value placed on non-involvement in the business of others. It flourishes because of its importance in the definition of Thai masculinity, and its place in Thai males' nonexclusive options of sexual relations – taking a wife and being a husband-father, taking a minor wife or concubine and being a lover-father, and being the client of a prostitute (Jackson 1989:37). Thai prostitution differs from other variants partly because of the place of sex-work in the economic miracle of Thailand: 'The bodies of Thai women have become one of the bases of growth in the Thai economy' (Boonchalaksi and Guest 1994:1).

Boonchalaksi and Guest estimate that between 200,000 and 300,000 women work in the Thai sex industry (1994:32). However, this figure probably underestimates the amount of informal and indirect prostitution occurring outside of sex establishments. Many people who are not commercial sex workers derive income directly or indirectly from the sex industry, including the hotel and restaurant industries (Boonchalaksi and Guest 1994:37). New localities such as luxurious members clubs and karaoke bars have joined tea houses, short-term hotels, and brothels to provide special services for locals and tourists – services requiring different kinds of sex workers. Opportunistic sex workers whose primary occupation is unconnected with the entertainment industry including factory workers and male and female university students, take on sex work when they need extra money (Kanato 1990). Similarly, Cohen argues that a fuzzy 'grey area' exists between prostitution and more emotional relationships between the sexes, including tourist-oriented open-ended prostitution (1987:224).

Who becomes a prostitute? Not all Thai women who are economically marginalized become prostitutes. Most commercial sex workers in massage parlours in Bangkok come from the north of Thailand and are recruited through networks of relatives and neighbours. Their salaries are used to support their parents and siblings. The northeast provides fewest commercial sex workers to the industry, but it is women from the northeast who are most likely to be found in disco bars in Bangkok. They report that they use their earnings to support children (Boonchalaksi and Guest 1994:59,68).

Boonchalaksi and Guest describe the nature of the work in rural and urban brothels and massage parlours (1994:81–7). Brothel workers average four customers a day, massage workers average two. Women have three to five days off when menstruating. Monthly income averages 35,000 baht for commercial sex workers in massage parlours in Bangkok and 6,000 baht for workers in provincial brothels. Brothel workers can go home for visits and seasonal agricultural work more easily than commercial sex workers in other sectors, and presumably more easily than factory workers. Brothel owners are often identified by their sex workers as generous, charitable and ready to intervene to protect their workers (cf. Boonchalaksi and Guest 1994:4).

It is unclear whether the increasing attention on the problem of child prostitution in Thailand reflects an increase in numbers of child prostitutes as a response to the decreasing supply of teenage girls available for recruitment, or increasing media focus on child exploitation. What is clear is that the trade in children is a lucrative and expanding business, and a source of quick cash for agents and parents. While agents or procurers may deceive both parents and children as to the nature of their future occupation, a report from the Centre for the Protection of Children's Rights reported that 63 percent of girls under sixteen were brought to the brothel by their parents (Skrobanek 1990:13). Poverty is not the sole cause of this evil because many families surveyed had adequate income and used the money to purchase luxury consumer goods such as color TVs and VCRs.

Estimates of the number of child prostitutes, both boys and girls, whose virginity can be sold (and resold) for less than three hundred dollars, range from 30,000 (Foundation for Women) to 200,000 (Friends of Women), and the numbers change constantly. To what extent was child prostitution part of the palimpsest of the traditional Thai prostitution system? 'Southeast Asian men preferred their women experienced,' writes historian, Reid (1988:154). Child prostitutes have no special appeal to young Thai men who want more experienced women as partners. Elderly Chinese men in particular believe that intercourse with a young girl will restore or increase their sexual potency (Thitsa 1983: 37). However, there is a tradition of older Thai men 'fostering' a male 'love child' and this has not been condemned in Thai society (cf. Jackson 1989).

The demand for child prostitutes is increasing, particularly from Asian and Middle Eastern tourists who will pay high prices for virgins. Fear of contracting HIV/AIDS is also increasing the demand for younger and younger children, farther removed from the presumed immorality and disease of the urban centers. While successive Thai administrations have not been willing or able to curtail the sex industry, Prime Minister Chuan Leekpai spearheaded attacks on child prostitution in 1992. As campaigns to discourage rural Thai families from selling their daughters into prostitution succeeded, daughters of minorities were increasingly sought out. The photographs and cover of *Time* magazine (July 1993) showing young prostitutes rescued from Bangkok brothels included Burmese and girls from northern minority groups such as Akha. Putting aside the ethics of revealing the girls' identities and intruding into their lives, the Thai government responded not to the report, but to the perceived blow to national pride by banning the magazine.

Minority women entering into Thai prostitution are further disadvantaged by the complex of patrilineal descent, patrilocal residence and bridewealth that makes them particularly vulnerable after divorce.[6] Women divorced because they carried HIV/AIDS infections might not be taken back by their families, leaving suicide as an option to escape disease or a bad marriage. Hmong women, for example, could be discouraged from divorcing because their families would have to repay the brideprice. Relative wealth, the importance of social standing, and patriarchal control protects Hmong women from being sold into prostitution in the first place, although the weakening of the brideprice system might well end this protection (Kammerer et al 1995, Symonds 1999). Akha, Shan and other minority women are being sold into prostitution in local towns and more distant cities. Here they join other women, often from their ethnic groups from neighbouring countries whose economies did not grow as rapidly as Thailand's. The sex industry in Thailand is well-organized to transport these young girls without Thai identity cards into border brothels, karaoke bars, and massage parlours where they have little hope of buying their way out of service. Even paying bribes to officials and police cannot guarantee protection during raids. Poverty has forced men and women into lowland cities to search for work, putting them at risk for acquiring HIV/AIDS. The problem of families selling their daughters into prostitution is spiralling into Laos, Cambodia and Vietnam where families are even poorer and governments cannot spare funds to mount campaigns to counter child prostitution. As these countries open up to tourism, the demand for 'clean' child prostitutes has grown rapidly (*Bangkok Post*, 29 Dec. 1995).

Analysis of prostitution by legislators and service providers has been gender biased, ignoring the fact that boys and men are also prostitutes. Males are seldom included in media discussions of 'the problem of prostitution in Thailand', as if only females meet the criteria for membership in the category, prostitute. For males, prostitution is presented as less a part of their personal or sexual identity, something they do, not something they are. But male prostitution is gaining new visibility in Thailand, encouraged by sex tourism for women and the establishment of special bars, clubs, and massage parlours advertising gay sex. Not all male prostitutes are gay–identified although many are bisexual. They do not necessarily live a gay lifestyle, but rather perform acts with other men for a fee in specially designated localities. What makes the Thai scene characteristically Thai is that men having sex with men is not unmasculine, nor a threat to their masculinity. In the case of bisexual men, it may even enhance their masculinity. Lind van

Wijngaarden (1999) found that Chiang Mai bar boys are in the business for easy work, good money, and a short time commitment.

The interpretation of sexual orientation in Thailand is changing rapid, reinforced through Western media messages about 'coming out of the closet' and the idea that it is healthy to express one's masculine and feminine side. Gay pubs, and a sense of group commonality are recent inventions, as Thailand acquires the institutional structure of the international gay movement. Western imperialism in the form of sex tourism is partly responsible for the incredible proliferation of gay bars, discos, clubs, and massage parlours in Bangkok in the late 1980s. Entertainment places segregating males by sexual orientation has not been part of indigenous Thai sexual practices. Nevertheless, the Thai gender system made the expansion of a category of gay male prostitute possible. But male prostitution would need to be considered within the broader context of Thai male sexuality where a considerable bisexual element was permitted.

Kathoey (male transvestites) have long been features of urban night life in Bangkok. Their drag shows are particularly impressive examples of baroque excess, spectacles of elaborate parodies on Thai gender. The Thai twist on this 'third gender' is the pleasure in disguise, in deceiving the tourist into thinking the *kathoey* is 'really' female, a subject explored further in Chapter 7.

An even more recent feature of Bangkok's night life is the members-only ladies' club. Chippendale's, one of five ladies' clubs in Bangkok in the early 1990s, is in appearance a mirror image of the gay and heterosexual bars around town with dim lighting, loud music, dance floor, and willing partners available. The differences are informative. The male hosts have university degrees or higher vocational certificates in order to interact with the elite business women club members. The drinks are expensive for both patrons and hosts, but staff are prohibited from going off with customers during working hours (*Bangkok Post*, 19 July 1990). Clearly, these clubs are not mirror images of the more numerous night spots catering to Thai and foreign men. Chippendale's has recently closed, one more clear indicator of the differences between establishments catering to male and female fantasies and desires.

Globalization and Sex Tourism

In 1980, the World Bank advised Thailand to develop tourism as a means of accumulating foreign exchange. Building on the supply of both prostitutes and 'entertainment places' in Bangkok, and the demand of male tourists, sex tourism expanded in the 1970s in a form more blatant and diverse than anywhere else in the world. As sex tours advertise, 'Anything goes in this exotic country'. The sexual services provided are geared to the nationality of the visitor: Middle Eastern tourists frequent different brothels than German, American, Australian, Japanese and Malaysian tourists.

Live sex shows are a popular attraction in cities like Bangkok and Pattaya. The degradation of a young heterosexual Thai male performer in a Bangkok sex show who sells himself for the sexual excitement of other Thai males is recounted in the story, 'In the Mirror' by Kon Krailat, exposing the pain underlying the surface detachment visible during the show: 'He feels like a male animal in the rutting season, brutishly copulating with a female animal, right before the eyes of a group of studmasters' (Anderson and Mendiones 1985:213). The sex shows '. . . are no longer only responses to the foreign tourist tide, but have become embedded in metropolitan Thai society' (Anderson and Mendiones 1985:69). There are no links here to any indigenous performance tradition, contrary to Manderson's claims that sex-show dances have their antecedents in ancient northern Thai dances (1992:464). Both rural and urban Thai are exceptionally circumspect and private with regard to sexual activity. In fact, the lack of an explicit indigenous erotic performance tradition makes the adoption of suggestive movements and gestures during the sex shows appear forced, false, and very foreign.

Hong estimated that 60 percent of the two million tourists visiting Thailand in the early 1980s were attracted by the availability of bargain-priced sex (1985:73). By 1989, 89 percent of the visitors to Bangkok were male (Richter 1989:86). Organized tours from European countries and Japan allowed men to choose vacation sex-partners from brochures. Tourists not on organized sex tours could pick up books detailing the location, specialties, and cost of various sexual services in Bangkok or before their arrival in guidebooks such as the *Insight Guide to Thailand* (1991) or on the internet (World Sex Guide). Weekly tourist magazines available in most hotels advertise a wide range of massage parlours and escort services, many with photographs and special discounts for tour groups. These organized sex tours have reportedly decreased in frequency, thanks to the publicity and protest activities organized by local and international women's groups. The policies of the Thai government allow the sex industry to flourish in order to encourage the flow of foreign exchange from tourism. But the government responds quickly to any international reports about the sex industry that threaten Thailand's reputation and thus her tourist and investment possibilities

(Boonchalaksi and Guest 1994:17). When women's groups protest against sex tourism, they face harassment from government officials, tourist authorities, and the police who benefit from prostitution. They are accused of creating a bad image for Thailand abroad, when their real sin is to threaten the profits of officials who benefit from sex tourism.

Since the 1970s, Thai prostitutes have been entering the international sex trade, moving as migrant workers across national borders in Asia and Europe. The internationalization of the Thai economy now includes syndicates with networks of agents who can recruit and place workers overseas. In some cases, the worker is coerced or duped into sex work through debt slavery; in other cases the worker assumes the debt as an investment for future prosperity for herself and her family (Skrobanek et al. 1997). The existence of Thai sex workers in Japan, Germany or the Netherlands reflects back on the construction of the sex-gender system in Thailand. Estimates in the 1990s of the number of Thai sex workers travelling to other countries vary between 100,000 and 200,000 (Boonchalaksi and Guest 1994:39). *Kathoey* in particular number among the most popular window prostitutes of Amsterdam. Renowned for their presentation of female beauty and their ability to arouse heterosexual men, they are in greater demand in northern European cities than female prostitutes.

HIV/AIDS and Prostitution

New locales for sex work proliferate to meet new demands, new expect-ations and new levels of disposable income. And new diseases. HIV/AIDS is having a critical impact on Thailand, one of the hardest hit countries in the world (Gould 1993, Holmes 1993). Koetsawang and Auamkul (1997) estimate that around two percent of sexually active adults in the country were HIV positive in 1995. Thai sexual practices are contributing to the staggering load for families and the state. The HIV/AIDS crisis in Thailand has forced a reconsideration of sexual double standards, prostitution, marriage and gender identity, topics not generally considered in epidemiological models of risk behaviour. Only with the advent of HIV/AIDS have the broader implications of Thai sexual practices been publicly scrutinized.

HIV/AIDS research in Thailand has benefitted from interdisciplinary approaches, including the use of qualitative research methodologies (Morrison and Guruge 1997, Kammerer et al 1995, Kanato 1990). Knowledge of cultural context is particularly important for dealing with questions concerning intimacy and sexuality. However, the biomedical bias inherent in clinical treatments leaves little space for anthropological interpretations in the rhetoric and reality of AIDS policy in Thailand.

According to the official version of Thailand's HIV/AIDS crisis, AIDS was first diagnosed in Thailand in 1984 in a Thai homosexual male returning from the United States. According to Jackson, the early campaign against AIDS was translated into a campaign against homosexual men (1989:274). The disease was later associated with heroin addicts. In March 1989, newspaper reports documented the progress of programs to provide bleach for cleaning needles and equipment to addicts seeking treatment. Although male sex workers and intravenous drug users were considered the first and second wave of groups at risk, it quickly became clear that heterosexual relations accounted for most of the transmission (globally, three quarters of the HIV transmission is through heterosexual contact, Mann 1992). Commercial sex workers (the third wave) were defined as the transmitters of HIV to their male clients, the fourth wave, who then spread it to their partners. Women and their children in the general population are the fifth wave of those at risk of HIV infection (depending whose system of counting used, Weninger and Brown 1996, Ungphakorn 1993 or Beyrer 1998).

Since the mid-1980s, Thailand has moved from denying that AIDS exists in the country in order to protect tourist revenue, to targeting intravenous drug users and homosexual men, to the recognition of the importance of sexual transmission, to concern for people who were living with AIDS, to the development of a broad-based National Health Education Policy on AIDS which emphasizes risk behaviour rather than risk groups. Although early communication strategies used scare tactics to warn against unsafe sex practices, Thailand is now recognized internationally for the success of its prevention programmes, including mass communication about the disease, surveillance strategies, anonymous HIV testing and supplying free condoms to sex workers and clients. By 1994, rates of new infection had fallen nationwide (Beyrer 1998:33). Thailand's 100 percent condom use policy in brothels is cited as a successful policy initiative. Brothel owners are required to enforce the policy, which entitles commercial sex workers to withhold services from clients who will not wear condoms. Reports suggest that condom use has increased markedly in some areas (Rugpao et al 1997); Rojanapithayakorn and Hanenberg (1996), however, argue that condom use is inconsistent at best and reserved almost entirely for prostitutes. Some massage parlours refuse to admit foreigners because they are thought to be the source of HIV/AIDS (Boonchalaksi and Guest 1994:98). In spite of all the AIDS education campaigns, misinformation about HIV/AIDS is still common. Many people still think that mosquitos or monkeys transmit HIV/AIDS, that one can catch the disease by drinking from the same glass, touching, working, eating or studying with an HIV-infected person, and that an effective cure is currently available.

Government motivation for spending money on HIV/AIDS education and prevention includes not only control of the epidemic, but also preserving Thailand's international image as an ideal tourist destination, and combating its equally widespread reputation for the fastest growth of the HIV/AIDS epidemic in Asia (all without dismantling prostitution). The implications of HIV/AIDS for Thai tourism – particularly sex tourism – must have alarmed the government, because in the mid-1980s, it clamped down on publicity about HIV/AIDS, thereby high-lighting the importance of prostitution for tourism (Thai Development Newsletter 1990:63). Critics point out that the media focus on Thai sex tourism was indirectly a means of boosting tourism (Meyer 1988: 73). Popular tourist centres such as Chiang Mai and Haad Yai were identified as areas with particularly serious HIV/AIDS problems. When Ministry of Health officials identified Haad Yai as the worst HIV/AIDS area in the country, the Haad Yai tourist establishment, whose primary income comes from Malaysian sexual forays across the border, was furious. Evidently, the young prostitutes from northern Thailand working in Haad Yai had been convinced that a thorough cleaning after sex was sufficient protection to prevent AIDS, and believed they could easily recognize a client with AIDS simply by observing his skin, hair and facial features. A Bangkok-born prostitute said that she would recognize an AIDS carrier: 'An infected person would have splotches on his body.' Similarly, in Mae Sot, near the Burma border, a reporter quoted a Thai man who frequented the three brothels in the town: 'But we know what precautions to take to stop AIDS. We all take anti-AIDS medicine before we visit the brothels' (*Bangkok Post*, 15 July 1990). Both clients and sex workers remain confident that they can recognize a person with HIV/AIDS by appearance or smell.

Thailand's public health professionals have been marginally concerned with prostitution in the past, with particular interest in hygiene and the sanitary conditions that might endanger clients. They also monitor and treat prostitutes' sexually transmitted diseases; the high rates of sexually transmitted diseases among Thai sex workers may increase their chances of HIV transmission, particularly subtype E HIV, the most common subtype found among people who acquired the disease sexually (Beyrer 1998:182). The rapid spread of HIV/AIDS in Thailand confirmed the fact that frequenting brothels is a part of everyday life in Thailand, particularly northern Thailand (Beyrer 1998:18). For Thai men, prostitution exists as one of a wide range of sexual activities without expectations of commitment. Brown and Sittitrai (1996) estimate three million men visited commercial sex workers as clients in 1990. Particularly in northern Thailand, civil servants, soldiers and police (the most masculine of men, according to Muecke, 1992) visit brothels as group entertainment following a meal and drinking together. Until recently, university student initiations may involve trips to brothels (*khyn khru*, climb on the teacher) accompanied by senior students. Whatever the exact number of Thai men who visit prostitutes, the size of the local sex industry and patterns of seasonal migration contribute to making AIDS in Thailand a pandemic of serious proportions that cannot be 'blamed' on foreign tourists, although their financial contribution to the national economy is greater than that generated by local prostitution.

The HIV/AIDS epidemic in Thailand exposed the illusion of Thai monogamy and the changing structure of Thai families in the 1990s. Thailand is still largely rural, and rural households are often extended, composed of related women whose partners come to live in compounds overseen by matrilineal ancestors who in the past protected the chastity of young women. This traditional picture of matrilocal extended families is changing as land becomes scarcer and policies favour large agribusinesses. AIDS policy assumes Western-style stable nuclear families and underestimates the resulting mobility – rural to urban, rural to rural – resulting from poverty, landlessness, unequal distribution of wealth, and media messages about urban lifestyles and consumer goods. This mobility results in men and women being separated from their regular sexual partners and from the scrutiny of elders and ancestral spirits.

In the past, sexual violations that 'offended the ancestral spirits' (*phit phii*) could be handled through financial compensation. Bridegrooms still pay a substantial bridewealth for obtaining sanctioned sexual access to a young woman. Commoditized sex is not new in Thailand, and its analysis needs to be located in existing complex financial transactions concerning sex and ritual.

AIDS research and policy assumes Western binary categories, male or female, heterosexual or homosexual. But *kathoey*, male transvestites, exist as a third gender, and may be gay or heterosexual – most often bisexual. Current AIDS policy underestimates the importance and extent of bisexuality, ignoring male prostitutes who were most likely gay at work, and heterosexual in their own time. Thai sexual identity is both context sensitive and tolerant of gender ambiguities, as discussed in the next chapter.

Into this context comes Western media displays of overt sexuality in addition to romance. The movie, *Love Story*, reached Bangkok in the early 1970s and was extremely popular, fitting well into the Thai genre of love stories that cut across classes. Subsequently, hand holding among young urban couples became common in Bangkok, with rapid disentangling of hands and graceful reversion to respectful *wai*-ing when meeting an elder acquaintance or relative.

New sexuality and new gender constructions are arising in the context of the decline in the moral authority of monks, elders and ancestral spirits at the time when the need for spiritual resources is greatest. Yet AIDS discourse takes place in a moral void. AIDS, not HIV, is the term used in Thailand – *khon pen ets* – a person is AIDS infected – a death sentence. AIDS research in Thailand acknowledges no moral and ethical complexity in spite of the fact that over 90 percent of the country professes Buddhism, and sickness and death are the basis for under-standing Buddhist concepts of suffering, central to the Four Noble Truths. Ethical questions about who should give birth, how to let people die, who should care for others, is not part of the discourse of AIDS in Thailand. Religious institutions have a minimal hospice role, although individual monks may support community education and care. People living with AIDS are still more likely to be rejected from than cared for by religious institutions on the assumption that AIDS is linked to sexual misconduct. The potential is there and the need is great to develop a Buddhist discourse on AIDS.

Warnings about HIV/AIDS and the 100 percent condom use campaign have reportedly put a damper on Thai and foreign men's enjoyment of the pleasures of Bangkok's lucrative sex-pleasure entertainment industry. In his popular column, Nite Owl, published regularly in the *Bangkok Post* and reprinted in the internationally distributed edition, Trink seeks support for his claim that HIV is not sexually transmitted, and that Thai prostitutes are not infected with AIDS, citing excerpts from any and all experts who argue that it is difficult to transmit HIV through heterosexual relations with a prostitute (*Bangkok Post*, 28 July 1995, 14 November 1997). As recently as 7 February 1998, he provided additional citations to support his position. The responses from readers were interesting. 'How does it feel promoting AIDS in Thailand?' one asks. Trink replies, 'Who, me? I am unalterably against taking drugs and anal sex. Prostitutes may well pass on VD (STD), so I strongly advise using latex condoms when with them' (*Bangkok Post*, 18 Aug 1995). Trink's views support tourism, the sex industry or at least the public, foreign-dominated fun-morality of Patpong and Soi Cowboy entertainment areas. Occasionally, Trink warned his readers that HIV positive prostitutes were continuing to work until just before their three-month HIV examination, when they would quit and begin work at another establishment. He now claims that he has 'never trivialized AIDS', yet ends his column with a sick joke about music, the 'dreaded disease', and band-aids (*Bangkok Post*, 15 Dec. 1995). He has his supporters. One writes that after twelve years of 'dallying', he is 'not withering away yet' (*Bangkok Post*, 17 November 1995).

AIDS has forced the medical gaze onto Thai prostitution, exposing the hypocrisy and sexual discrimination inherent in prostitution suppression laws and policies towards prostitutes. Advocacy groups concerned with prostitution now address the immediate medical needs of prostitutes and their clients. AIDS has also confirmed that current policies are primarily oriented around controlling the bodies of women involved in prostitution, rather than addressing broader questions of equity and Thai gender relations. AIDS policy in Thailand is frankly pragmatic, focusing on protecting male clients of prostitutes, at the expense of women whose infection rates are increasing (Ungphakorn 1993). If women are not protected then children are not protected. Policies assume that women are monogamous, and would not get sexually transmitted diseases that would make them more vulnerable to HIV/AIDS. EMPOWER, the NGO concerned with the welfare of Patpong prostitutes has argued that current AIDS policy is unfairly biased against women prostitutes, and intended only to make the sex trade safer for men. Why not test the men who frequent prostitutes? But when Friends of Women organized a protest against the arrival of another American fleet in need of R&R in Pattaya, accusing them of bringing AIDS, the bargirls organized a counter protest, 'better AIDS than starvation' (Odzer 1994:195).

Currently, the heterosexual monogamous family is being repackaged as a prophylactic social device to protect against HIV/AIDS (Singer 1993:8). In this discourse, Thai wives are to be ready for marital sex twenty-four hours a day in order to keep their husbands from prostitutes, thereby controlling the spread of HIV/AIDS to the general population. Truly monogamous sexual unions are posited as an answer to the epidemic. To insure this monogamy, wives should learn to behave like prostitutes, and be experimental and innovative in their sexual techniques, a challenge to the accumulated wisdom about Thai marriage.

Prostitution and Marriage

Local prostitution in Thailand takes the form it does because of the nature of Thai marriage, and marriage has not been a popular research topic in Thailand. Ironically, it has received less analytical attention than prostitution. When it is considered, it is usually in the context of family planning decision making, the closest most researchers want to get to analysis of marital sex – until the advent of AIDS.

Marriage is the gauge by which the morality of sexual activity is measured. Marriage rules in some sexual practices and identities, and rules out others. Visiting commercial sex workers, having pre-marital or extra-marital affairs and supporting second wives is not ruled out for single or married Thai men. There are few absolutes in sexual morality. All intimate relations are managed with the model of marriage in mind. Same sex couples are advised to marry heterosexually for appearance's sake by advice columnists like Uncle Go (Jackson 1989). The conventional boundaries of Thai marital unions do not preclude other kinds of relationships – same sex or opposite. The institution of marriage matters more than sexual object or orientation, creating a structure which allows other things to transpire, while maintaining acceptable surface appearances intact.

For centuries, Thai/Tai groups made use of strategic political marriages as they strengthened their control in mainland Southeast Asia; women as trophies or as the means to obtain political alliances or key resources remains in the palimpsest of Thai marriage. As does polygamy. While Western visitors read polygamy as a measure of uncivilized behavior, Thai apologists stressed that multiple wives meant that a husband could alternate between wives, never forcing himself on any unwilling wife, and thus accommodating the difference in men and women's natures, a revealing rationale that further reinforces the Thai assumption that women had no interest in or desire for sexual gratification.

De La Loubere, wrote in 1691 that the Thai 'retain wives they love not, and those they love' (Reid 1988:157). Gervaise, sent to Siam as a missionary to Ayutthaya in 1683, noted that polygamy was uncommon among the poor, but the mandarins 'have as many as they wish, and the more they have, the more highly they are considered by the world. All these women are completely virtuous; it is rare to find coquetry or infidelity among them . . .' (1989:55). Another layer of the palimpsest is still visible.

Group courting was practiced in the villages of north and northeast Thailand until recently. A number of young men accompanied the suitor to the home of his intended's parents to carry on a poetic courting duel. And now that group courting has been replaced by groups of young men going together to brothels, the same term is used for both (*aeo saaw*) (Lyttleton 1994a). The palimsest foregrounds men having fun together, a lone woman in the background.

Parents had the right and duty to arrange appropriate marriages for their children, but they usually did so with their children's approval. Marriages arranged without that approval (*klumthungchon*), were permitted until the fifth reign (Chetamee 1995:8). More Thai women are opting to marry late or remain single as a response to the nature of Thai marriage (Thai Development Newsletter 1991:19). Late marriage is also linked to women's increasing opportunities for education and work. The level of celibacy among Thai females is considered among the highest in the world by international standards. However, as more men and women opt for late marriages, the demand for commercial sex workers is increasing. Prostitution allows Thai men to exercize their sexual privilege and power without challenging ideals of female virginity or 'corrupting' good women by pressuring them into sexual relations before marriage.

Many Thai women enter sex work after marriage failure. Boonchalaksi and Guest found that 79 percent of brothel respondents and 48 percent in the massage parlour sector had been or were currently married (1994:62). Urban Thailand is also experiencing an increase in the divorce rate (Mulder 1997:333). In a flyer honoring women for their outstanding contributions to development or commerce, their biographies revealed that the women were often divorced or separated, as if women can succeed best when not weighed down with husbands and families. Neither rural nor urban Thai society stigmatizes single or divorced women to the same extent as in many other Asian societies.

Ethnographies discuss the ideal kinship structure but not the content of Thai marriages. Descent is traced bilaterally, with men marrying in, residing either in or near the compound of the wife's family, with the youngest daughter inheriting the house after caring for her elderly parents. Formal authority rested with male household head, and juniors deferred to seniors in all relations. Couples could get formal approval to marry on payment of bridewealth to the bride's family, or elope without permission and ask for the forgiveness of the bride's family on return. The ceremony itself consists of elders, relatives and friends pouring lustral water over the hands of the couple, followed by a party. The urban version takes place in hotels, often sponsored by a high status patron. The couple may also sponsor a meal for monks. Emotional bonds between husband and wife are generally hidden from outsiders.

With few ethnographic studies available that discuss marital life, insights can be gleaned from letters to advice columnists in Thai newspapers (Owens 1989). The letters relevant to marriage stressed the sanctity of the marriage contract, parental disapproval of matches with a spouse of lower status, decisions whether to remain with an erring husband, and a concern for children, inheritance and material conditions rather than emotional or moral concerns. The letters suggest that men should appear to have the dominant role in the family to save face, even if women control finances or domestic life. Women's collusion in this marital face-saving reinforces the importance of appearance, form, decoration, and display in Thai social relations. Letter-writers express concern with appearance and social conformity rather than with independence or self-sufficiency, and seek an ideal man who is 'handsome, wealthy, knowledgeable and good hearted' (Owens 1989: 64, 65). The weakness of the wife/husband link is also demonstrated in the letters in Hello, My Big, Big, Honey, where Patpong bar girls in letters and interviews make it clear that they prefer to marry foreign men (Odzer 1994, Walker and Ehrlich 1992).

Current research on Thai sexuality confirms that sex with wives, commercial sex workers and *kathoey* are three very separate kinds of experiences, guided by different rules of behavior. Thai men claim they take second wives and visit commercial sex workers because they do not get satisfaction at home and want new experiences, new positions, new flavours. Lyttleton's informant argues that 'sleeping with your wife is like sleeping with a tree' (1994b:269). Yet Kanchana Tangchonlatip argues that Thai men do not expect their wives to be sexually experienced or skilled (1995). Kanchana also found that wives would be ashamed to show sexual desire (1995:4). When Bangkok couples were asked whether they agreed with the statement that in addition to being good at housework, Thai wives should also be 'good in bed', white collar men and women agreed (55 percent, 57 percent) more than blue collar men and women (57 percent, 46 percent) (Tangchonlatip 1995:5). However, it is interesting that wives were more inclined to agree with the statement than their husbands. Both husbands and wives assumed that wives' sexual behavior would be unlike that of prostitutes and would not include oral or anal sex (Tangchonlatip 1995:6). Saengtienchai Champen's informants suggest that normal men need to practice sex so they can do it correctly, although women evidently don't need to and should not practice. One solution proposed to the problem of differing needs and expectations of husband and wives regarding sex was for the husband to let his tired wife sleep while he had sex with her (Tangchonlatip 1995:7).

Marriage and prostitution articulate different but complementary spheres of existence for Thai men. Both are commodified, and reflect the expectation that a man should pay to have access to a woman's body. Daughters repay debts to their parents by marrying wealthy men who can supply bridewealth, or by becoming a prostitute and sending remittances home. In either case, sexual relations are not without cost. Wives, for a variety of reasons, have not ended marriages because of, or even actively discouraged, their husbands' visits to prostitutes as long as the visits did not seriously affect their lives – financially or emotionally. Visiting a commercial sex worker is considered less disruptive than supporting a second wife, particularly if the visits are inexpensive, infrequent and 'protected' by condoms. With the increase in HIV infections among women, it is clear that their partners' use of commercial sex workers can no longer be considered safe (Ungphakorn 1993).

The ordinariness and sociability of visits to prostitutes for both rural and urban married men has already been discussed. Visits initiate men into manhood and sexual activity, and are considered socially acceptable male activities along with drinking and socializing. Since men often socialize in all male groups, the opportunity is there to include a brothel visit if the group so decides. Men who leave their peer group without going on to a brothel are teased that they are gay, or afraid of their wives and made to feel excluded from the group, a serious problem for men. Decisions not to participate are practical (fear of spreading disease or wasting household money) not moral. These male outings are an important part of political networking, patron-client relations, and being part of a group. When Thai men go out for fun (*paj thiaw*) with their friends, a night out might include a meal, card games, drinking and going to a brothel followed by more drinking. Peer pressure is not only critically important in men's decisions to go to brothels, it is intimately connected to men's social and political success, as recent studies have confirmed (cf. Ford and Kaetsawang 1991).

However, a focus group study with slum residents, factory workers and middle-class professionals concluded that many Thai wives do not consider extramarital sex to be normal or acceptable, while men express a greater acceptance (Saengtienchai 1995:5). Frequent use of commercial sex workers is seen as irresponsible to the family. How tolerant are Thai women regarding their husband's use of commercial sex workers? Some claim to be unaware, others unsure, while others realize they do not have the power to influence their husbands. Morrison's research in Chiang Mai (1999) documents the degree to which marital problems are simply ignored to avoid conflict, encouraging more visits to prostitutes to keep peace in the family. But many wives express great anger and pain. Letters to advice columnists express wives' embarrassment, anguish and shame when their husbands are unfaithful (Owens 1989). Thai wives have probably learned to be suspicious and watchful. Some say they can tell from the smell of his clothes if he has slept with someone. They may in fact prefer not to know about the visits, to preserve the illusion that their husbands are faithful exceptions to the Thai rule (Packard-Winkler 1998).

Relations between chief wives (*mia luang*), minor wives (*mia noi*) and mistresses are regularly described and commented upon in Thai newspapers. Wives are blamed for failing to retain their husband's respect when their husbands take second wives, and mistresses are blamed for being immoral temptresses – all presumably caused by arranged loveless marriages. The all-suffering wife who discovers that she is a *mia noi*, but doesn't want to raise a fuss is a common trope: 'We were both government officials with our status to think about' (*Bangkok Post*, 27 Nov. 1989).

The media response to the case of the wives of Supreme Commander General Sunthorn Kongsompong, the leader of the coup that overturned Prime Minister Chatchai in February 1991 is instructive. His first wife (his *mia luang*) Khunying Orachorn chose to sue her husband's *mia noi* to save face rather than divorce her husband, after learning of his second wife. In an interview, his second wife reported that she only wanted to serve and care for him, felt that they must have been husband and wife in another life, and so their union was inevitable. In an unprecedented affront to the first wife, the general's mother allied herself with his second wife and adopted her so that she could use the family name. His name was particularly valuable in her business as a real estate agent.

This was a fight between the women in the absence of the general. If the general is faulted for anything by the press, it is not for his infidelity but for his failure to keep the peace and distance between his *mia noi* and *mia luang*. The affair only became a *cause celebre* when the *mia noi* stepped beyond the boundaries in such a way as to challenge the *mia luang* publicly. 'A wife . . . is like the main Buddha image in the grand hall, deserving respect and deference. They liken the minor wife to an amulet for the owner to take with him wherever he goes' (*Bangkok Post*, 8 July 1991). The logic of mistresses and wives is tied up with face and sexuality in a way that is very difficult to untangle. The novelist, Sidaoru'ang recalls 'understanding the reasoning' of her lover who argued that even when they were living together, he would 'have his eyes on other women' (Harrison 1993:16). However, now that their lovers' or husbands' infidelity may put them at risk of HIV/AIDS, wives' attitudes towards prostitution are changing rapidly.

However, there is also cultural space for celibacy and abstinence for both men and women, legitimized in part by Hindu-Buddhist ideologies. But it is mostly women who are expected to abstain. The cultural ideal of women's virginity before marriage contributes to male demand for prostitution. In their research on the sexual lifestyles of Thai youth, Ford and Sirinan (1993:21) found the young men quite open in their statements that they would not marry a woman who was not a virgin, although they were actively trying to talk their girlfriends into having sex with them.

Conclusions

The greatest contribution that anthropologists could make to understanding HIV/AIDS and prostitution in Thailand is an examination of Thai sexuality – a subject absent from or peripheral to current analyses of marriage, prostitution and HIV/AIDS. Is sexuality dangerous? a renewable or non-renewable resource? a biological given? Before positing a model of Thai gender relations in the next chapter, I will draw fragments of my interpretations about Thai sexuality together into a series of premises to be explored by future research in Thailand.

Thailand provides a sex-positive culture for men not for women – but one without a culturally elaborated erotic tradition. The efforts of Prime Minister Phibun in the 1940s to create a uniform central Thai culture may well have sanitized the more robust sexuality inherent in the Lanna and Isan peripheries. The Thai elite purged this indigenous eroticism of the periphery from the centre, leaving concepts such as *phuu dii* (people of quality), sexual servitude and the dilemma of the opposition between the good and bad woman as analytical tools for interpreting the Thai sex-gender system. Under what social and economic pressures have these upper class, Bangkok-based *phuu dii* values of women pleasing men spread to lower-income and rural women? Sunthorn Phu's mid-nineteenth century discourse on correct behavior for women (*Supasit son ying*) highlights women's need for self-control and restraint with regard to sexual activity. A woman's caring for her body includes preserving her virginity when unmarried and maintaining fidelity when married. Like a precious gem:

Cracked and chipped its value diminishes,
Just as woman's worth may wane.

Choosing a partner decides a woman's worth,
For virginity determines her value.
Once it is lost, it no more appeals,
And cannot conceivably be regained.

(Lynch 1978:10, 15)

This theme of irrevocable loss resulting from improper sexual behaviour reverberates through contemporary discussions of Thai prostitution. For women are required to exercise self-control and good judgement about men:

It is not all wise to be too hasty,
For the fruit always falls when it is ripe.
In the meantime, then, remain with the tree,
And resist being picked too early.

(Lynch 1978:17)

The reason for this self-control is made quite explicit – women owe their parents and must provide for them in their old age, another theme re-emerging in the discourses on Thai prostitution.

When their child is sluttish they are deeply hurt,
The distress and anger breaking their hearts.

(Lynch 1978:16)

Women are also socialized through this *phuu dii* ideology to see and feel sexual desire as 'stains upon the soul', a Christian metaphor that should not resonate so well with Buddhist non-self, no-soul. Women's rights to enjoy sex is not an issue, nor is it part of the discussion on prostitution or marriage.

Thai male sexuality is essentialized as something more driven, more important than female sexuality, conforming to a hydraulic model regulating the exchange of bodily fluids. Both men and women share an assumption about Thai masculinity; that men have insatiable sexual appetites which must be satisfied to protect good women. In the words of a Bangkok police officer: 'the rate of rapes and sex-related crimes might sky-rocket if these men find no place to satisfy their sexual desires' (Boonchalaksi and Guest 1994:8).

This suggests that sexual acts *per se* are not invested with much importance, not elevated to great significance in relationships among men and women. Sex is better thought of as light entertainment than anything too serious. Sexual novelty from new partners can make up for the absence of other sources of intimacy for Thai men in their search for new tastes, new flavours. Expectations of husband and wife regarding eroticism or sexuality are not strongly developed. The non-utilitarian dimensions of sexuality, those concerned with mutual pleasure are particularly underdeveloped. If most Thai men have their first sexual experience with prostitutes, this might explain why erotic traditions are not well established in the Thai cultural repetoir. Recall the words of a rural Thai informant: 'sleeping with your wife is like sleeping with a tree' or those of a young prostitute '. . . when she has sex, she imagines a 500 baht note hung on the ceiling' (Saengtienchai 1995:269, 274).

Emotional support and intimacy comes from same sex peer groups as well as from sexual partners.[7] We have very little understanding of non-sexual same sex intimacy. Yet romance and fantasy is probably more significant than has been appreciated in past research on Thai sexuality. The classical court tradition and regional folk traditions provide ample evidence of an interest in romance and romantic alter-cations. In these romantic traditions, much of the pleasure is in the chase – and that chase is more like a courtship dance than an erotic tryst, with great emphasis on clever speech and turning winning phrases to one's advantage in front of one's peers. Flirtatious banter appeals as well as sexual acts.

In the Thai context, work should be *sanuk* (fun) or new work contexts will be sought. To what extent can sex work be considered *sanuk*? There is no potential for *sanuk* among child prostitutes, or women held against their will. But Odzer (1994) has documented aspects of prostitution that could be considered *sanuk*. These include the public, performative aspects of streetwalking, the opportunities to wear fashionable, Western clothes, jewellery, perfume and make-up, and the lack of monotony – that is, the opportunity to meet new people and have new experiences. The Patpong prostitutes who keep returning to the profession stress the variety of new experiences, how much 'easier' the work is in comp-arison to the boredom of factory or farm labour, even while they are aware of being exploited and victimized (Odzer 1994). Oy, a child prostitute, was described as fond of her job; 'it was hard to make her realize it was not decent' (Thai Development Newsletter 1989:25). One young prostitute in Bangkok told me that she preferred sex work to factory work because on Patpong she could spend her money on food that she enjoyed eating and not eat the food provided by the factory. While it is not politically correct to speak of the appeal of prostitution,[8] this conversation is a reminder of the need to explore the meaning of sex work from a Thai prostitute's perspective.

The moralizing values of Western middle-class oppositional thinking about sexuality and prostitution provide little guidance for interpreting the complexities of the situation in Thailand. While the political economy of sex tourism and Thailand's uneven economic development account for the financial appeal of prostitution, these explanations do not fully address the underlying causes of the subordination and exploitation of women. Marx considers prostitution a specific expression of the universal prostitution of the worker. Utopian socialists build on this logic to argue that work is a source of pleasure. Marx assumes that work without pleasure and satisfaction derived from creativity is prostitution (Truong 1990:31–2). White's study of prostitution in colonial Nairobi analyzes prostitution as domestic labor, illegal marriage. She argues that the definition of prostitution must come from the labour process – prostitution as the occasional work of poor women (1990:11).

Engels (1972) further blurs the distinction between categories of women and work by arguing that a wife differs from the ordinary courtesan only in that she does not hire out her body, like a wage worker, on piece work, but sells it into slavery once and for all. Prostitutes sell reproductive work including conversation, massage, and sexual acts – all transactions available in marriage and paid for out of men's wages. Prostitute groups from industrialized countries argue that prostitution is a freely chosen economic choice like marriage; 'both provide sexual services to men, and the possibility of violence against women is inherent in both' (Sturdevant and Stoltzfus 1992:301). The advantage of Marx and Engel's position is that it breaks down the dualistic opposition so stressed in the middle-class, urban Thai gender system between the good woman and the bad woman, the wife and the prostitute.

Disciplinary power is exercised on the bodies of wives and prostitutes. Body management that render women's bodies more useful to men and the state is obvious in prostitution, as it was in beauty contests and the beauty regimes of women discussed in Chapter 5. But patriarchal oppression – whether western capitalist or indigenous Thai – is insufficient as an explanation for prostitution, as women are so deeply implicated in the expansion of prostitution and the commodification of other women. Prostitution in Thailand is an example of women policing women, judging them, controlling them, exploiting them as commodities. Many of the constraints on women come from other women – more experienced prostitutes, brothel and bar owners, and procurers. This is also true for beauty contestants where women agents mould young women into potentially lucrative winners.

Prostitution cannot be considered in isolation from beauty contests, marriage, tourism and other exchange systems that exploit women. Yet a primary contradiction of gender relations in Thailand is reconciling the competence of individual Thai women with the sexist and oppressive structures which are themselves supported by other women. Singer writes:

> That which is prohibited works to sustain hegemonic social structures: the regulation of prostitution preserves marriage and the sexual and reproductive exploitation of women; pornography preserves advertising; addiction preserves brand loyalty and repeat-purchasing consumer patterns. Regulation inescapably takes place within a system of capital, commodities, and the asymmetrical figuration of differences, including sexual difference, that reproduces hegemonic lines of privilege, dominance and power... Prostitution acts as a regulatory device to discipline wives to satisfy husbands sexually and provide them with other kinds of unpaid labour. They must meet his needs or else... (Singer 1993:42, 49).

The next chapter builds on these initial premises about sexuality, prostitution and marriage and uses them to frame a broader model of Thai gender relations.

Notes

1. A recent Canadian television documentary called *Thai Girls* exposed the complexity of cases of Thai-Lao women working in massage parlours in Toronto, paying off huge debts to members of Asian crime syndicates while trying to send money home to support their families. The women were without options or hope, yet nostalgic about returning to Thailand as wealthy women.

2. Authors differ widely in their definitions of prostitution. Dictionary definitions of prostitution stress payment, promiscuity, and emotional indifference as basic to sex work (Troung 1990:11). These universal features of prostitution are particularly ambiguous in the Thai context where money is also exchanged to compensate for men's sexual transgressions through payment to the spirits (*phit phii*) and through bride wealth; where male promiscuity is part of a double standard that is broader than prostitution; and where emotional indifference is not absent from marriages.

3. The role of Thai women in recruitment and management of prostitutes has not been sufficiently examined. Not all women involved in prostitution lack agency and power.

4. Filipinas were imported to Okinawa to provide sexual services for American troops in order to ensure the safety of the 'respectable' women of Okinawa (Sturdevant and Stoltzfus 1992:308), much as low cost Thai prostitutes protect the reputation of 'good' Thai women. But when American servicemen raped a twelve-year-old Okinawa girl (1995), the island was in an uproar. This raises the question of whether these actions would have been more acceptable if young Filipinas had been attacked. Clearly race, class and ethnicity are all implicated in the servicing of foreign military.

5. Barbara Andaya documents the economic security and social acceptance of temporary wives in early modern Southeast Asia. European traders were dependent on local women to help them with trade before the growth of prostitution. 'But, the stigma attached to common law wives and the condemnation of women who exchanged sex for material gain was not a traditional feature of Southeast Asian societies, but was associated with the spread of world religions (Andaya 1998:12).

6. While lowland rural and urban Thai communities also exchange bride-wealth, some upland minority peoples practice the kind of alliance-exchange that places all authority in the hands of male lineage members, leaving women particularly isolated following divorce.

7. In my experience from living in both rural and urban Thailand, the strongest bonds of trust and affection are between men who go out drinking and visiting brothels together, and women who shop and eat together, rather than between men and women who have sexual intercourse together.

8. Hong Lysa's article on the politics of gender representation in Thailand in academic and popular history misrepresents my position on Thai prostitution. She writes that I contend that prostitution may be a path of liberation for women. In fact I cite and quote Thai sources to argue that Thai prostitutes may not always view themselves as victims. Lysa also says that I have 'given space in Thai studies' to the tendency to see the commodification of women in the sex industry as 'legitimate economic opportunity available to workers who can rationally divorce their work from their personal morality and sense of self worth' (1998:348–9). On the following page, I am then cited to support the idea that prostitutes have agency, can be in control of the situation, and are professionals in their own right. In the midst of her citations of my work as a feminist exploration, is the statement that 'Prostitution thus becomes an acceptable solution to the problems of rural poverty and the subordination of women' (Hong 1998:348). This is not a statement that I would agree with, nor could my work ever support. Prostitution is never an acceptable solution for

those problems. But from the standpoint of feminist anthropology, prostitution could well be an understandable response. Observing that not all prostitutes view themselves as victims, that some exert agency in their lives and operate within a framework of personal morality acknowledges the diversity in contemporary Thai prostitution, and opens 'space' for improving conditions of work that would make that means of livelihood less dangerous.

Part III

Interpretations

Modelling Thai Gender Relations

We have reviewed the material conditions and ideological space for gender in Thailand, and located important sites of gender negotiations, including beauty contests, the sex industry and represent-ations of women in Thai public culture. How do we integrate these disparate pieces into a framework for interpreting the complexity of the Thai gender system? Each provides a part of the story. But how are the parts related to each other and to the past? These examples call for integrated theories compatible with indigenous approaches to gender, rather than piecemeal *ad hoc* interpretations of isolated problems. This chapter develops a model or analytical framework for examining Thai gender.

The model is informed by a wide range of social science theory – some feminist or at least responsive to feminist theory. Theory is a very speculative frame of knowledge that draws us to ask certain questions and not others. We often assume that theory is totalizing, coherent and authoritative. But its power can be judged by its usefulness to guide analyses and critiques of previous theories that have claimed too much, gone too far, accepted without challenge or observation. Models help us 'see the relatively simple in the intricate and the relatively clear in the vague' (Scharfstein 1989:168).

When models simplify, they also erase differences. Returning to the metaphor of palimpsest, regional, religious and ethnic differences in gender models are not discarded and replaced by the dominant dis-courses of gender articulated at the center, but remain accessible in varying degrees to different classes and groups of people. When local models contradict national systems – which may often be the case with regard to gender ideologies – regional variations will probably be suppressed but not erased as has been the case in both the north and northeast of Thailand. They may go underground to emerge as alternate versions at some later point in time (O'Connor 1993).

For example, no contemporary representations of Thai women in the media or elsewhere render earlier readings obsolete. The media dramatically increases access to alternative representations and ideologies of masculinity and femininity, but freely makes use of partial renderings of the past. Like earlier texts on palm leaf manuscripts, representations are written over but still capable of influencing the current text-in-use. This is one important source of contradiction and ambiguity in Thai gender systems. Another is the importance of action and practice, rather than categories in defining gender ideology. These Thai logical tendencies, in contrast with Euro-American expectations of binary, bipolar, clear-cut gender asymmetry makes the analysis of Thai gender a particularly intriguing challenge.

Analyzing Gender

Most examinations of Thai gender, whether written by Thai or foreigners (including my own) have been based on Western approaches to gender, and have ignored the enormous cultural differences in the way body and self are gendered in different societies. Analysts have built on the received categories in Thai gender studies, the clichés that are easy to perpetuate. These assumptions include male promiscuity, the chastity expected of 'good Thai women', and social tolerance for sexual variety (number of partners, sexual orientation, and erotic practices), as long as surface appearances are maintained and rules of appropriate context (*kalatesa*) are observed.

A useful model of the Thai gender system must be grounded in the ideological and material bases of Thai society. Indigenous Thai discourse on the sex-gender system (cf. Rubin 1975) builds on the category of *phet*, a term that conflates sex differences (male and female), gender differences (masculine and feminine), and sexual orientation (homosexual and heterosexual) (cf. Jackson 1999:5). This model of Thai gender identity is body based, starting from the notion of the embodied self and rooted in material conditions and the physiological processes that mark bodies. It does not privilege sexuality above all other criteria in its conceptions of gender; neither end of the sexual spectrum is privileged, according to Jackson (1989). Thai gender can best be represented as a continuum with permeable boundaries, a system that is in essence non-binary but in conventional language provides conceptual space for a third gender. But blurring boundaries neither erases nor emphasizes nor fixes them. The categories are non-exclusive but clearly defined regionally and temporally; what is stressed in the Thai system is the ability of people to move in and out of the categories. It is Thai sensitivity to context – expressed as *kalatesa*, knowing how time, locations and relationships intersect to create appropriate contexts – that allows for the flow of multiple gender identities. Identities slip easily over each other like tectonic plates, alternatively revealing and concealing what lies below.

In brief, surfaces are transformable, temporary and aesthetically pleasing, while the self – who he/she really is – remains hidden and ultimately unknowable, a worldly accommodation to the Buddhist concepts of *anatta* (non-self) and *anicca* (impermanence). The categories and labels for sex roles and acts suggest that a wide range of gender identities and sexual practices are recognized and tolerated, none of which have to be viewed as defining permanent gender categories. Thus, gender is best theorized as a context sensitive process, constructed through interaction with others. Gendered surfaces are carefully and aesthetically presented in public to communicate how one expects to be treated. Yet in this body-based definition of self and identity, what is beneath gendered surfaces is always hidden, inaccessible to observers and intimates alike. The reduction of self to knowable surface is no obstacle to sociability. On the contrary. The sociability and easy access outsiders feel when in contact with Thai men and women is accomplished through the Thai ability to transform the surface, retaining control of both surface appearance and the context in which the appearance is manifested (*kalatesa*). However, the rigidity that appears on the surface of gender interactions is permeated by asexual power differentials that form the basis of gender hierarchies. That is, gender signifies in combination with class and power. And it is power – power to and power over – that must be analyzed more effectively in order to develop an adequate model of gender identities in Thailand. This analysis begins with consideration of bodies and gender.

Inscribing Bodies

Considering the volume of writing on Thai prostitution, consumption and the importance of HIV/AIDS as a policy issue in Thailand, it is difficult to explain the lack of attention to bodies in the analysis of the rapid changes Thailand is experiencing, particularly since Thais are exceptionally aware and articulate about their bodies.

Scheper-Hughes and Lock have proposed that conceptions of the body are basic to substantive and theoretical work in anthropology. They distinguish between three levels of analysis: first, the individual body, the lived experience of the body-self; second, the social body; and third, the body politic, referring to the regulation, surveillance and control of bodies (1987:7). The body politic is clearly a male body in Thailand, and a strongly militarized one.[1] These multiple levels of analysis are necessary for examining institutions as complex as prostitution, sexuality, fashion or marriage. Although the 'social body' and 'body politic' are evoked to explain the tolerance for, or the problem of enforcing laws about prostitution in Thai society, these levels of analysis are inadequate without consideration of the individual body, the embodied self. Errington's model of gender in island Southeast Asia juxtaposes an additional three levels of analysis: local ideas of the body, including both hidden and visible dimensions and discourses on sexuality; categorization, or the combination of signs into identities with identifiable positions in society; and lastly, access of these identities to power (1990:15–18).

While there is a growing literature on the relation between bodies and feminist theory, (cf. Grosz and Probyn 1995, Conboy et al 1997), there are dangers of dehistoricizing and decontextualizing bodies. 'We are invited to overlook the vast differences of culture that separate human beings and find unity in the body: it is portrayed as a ground on which all cultures inscribe significant meaning' (Mascia Lees and Sharpe 1992:2). Butler also warns against the idea that gender is simply written on bodily surfaces, with the body as a 'passive medium' on which cultural meanings are inscribed (1990:8). Her arguments are deeply Western and abstract, strongly psychoanalytic in content, and not easily applicable to Thai logical systems and ideologies. Nevertheless, her work inspires questions key to the analysis of Thai gender systems. She asks if there are ever humans who were not already gendered. 'The mark of gender appears to "qualify" bodies as human bodies; the moment in which an infant becomes humanized is when the question, "is it a boy or a girl?" is answered' (Butler 1990:111). It is interesting in this regard to read Garber's Euro-American evidence that the association of the male infant with blue and the female with pink is a recent convention adopted after World War II. Before that time, the gender and colour associations were reversed (1992:1). This gendering moment is reminiscent of the Buddhist emphasis on human as one level of being among many others, and that the gender of a human 'about to be born' is the last ephemeral 'detail' added, as discussed in the Buddhist textual analysis made in Chapter 3.

Foucault (1980, 1986) has theorized about the docile body from which free will was removed through coercion, a point relevant to the regulation of the male body through military discipline and monastic regimes. Female bodies are more (or less) gently regulated through beauty regimes and manners, and more viciously through the sexual socialization of prostitutes. Some of this discipline is self-imposed; some is imposed and policed by men. But it is convenient to forget that much of the disciplining of women's bodies comes from other women – procurers, brothel owners and the agents for beauty contests. Foucault's work further suggests that it is only through our sexuality that we appear to gain access to our bodies and our identities. I argue that the Thai gain access to their gender identities and their sexuality through their bodies. Bodies as repositories of cultural memories are prior to gender and sexuality. My rural Thai memories include watching mothers and others casually playing with toddlers' uncovered penises while covering girls' genitals with tiny silver mesh 'aprons'; adult males greeting boys by patting their testicles; men patting their patrons on the rump; men walking arm and arm; women walking hand in hand; neighbours asking my husband if he 'slept with his socks on' (meaning wear a condom) to explain why I was not pregnant; considering the 'shaking of the mortar and pestle' on the thin floorboards stretching between the cooking space and sleeping space in our small village house, loudly commented on by neighbours.

These tactile and visual experiential memories suggest the importance of considering the body as the basis for sexual socialization. But these examples also stress the need to distinguish same sex intimacy from homoerotic behaviour. The importance of same sex friendship in Thailand has been insufficiently explored (except as a point belabored in Peace Corps orientations and sensitivity training in cross-cultural communication). Locating the boundaries between same sex intimate friendships and homoeroticism is critical for understanding how bodies structure sexuality, and how sexuality is integrated into the Thai gender system (and also for health or sex education programmes).

Individuals in different societies relate to their bodies in different ways and express different levels of physicality. Both rural and urban Thai exhibit extraordinary bodily awareness, allowing men and women to control the movement of their bodies with consummate grace. Foreigners are painfully obvious on Bangkok streets as they trip off curbs, lurch into other pedestrians and bump into immovable objects. This lack of control of their bodies and lack of awareness of how they move through space illustrates Westerners' different orientation to their bodies. Thai appear to be much more 'in' their bodies than do Westerners, suggesting that the core of Thai self is strongly embodied and effectively socialized. Invading the personal space of others is a violation requiring apology, but is also an indication of lack of control.

This sense of physicality and embodiment, body awareness and body control is built into the socialization of Thai children, and is an import-ant part of gender performativity and the definition of beauty. Teaching children (and foreigners) to *wai* correctly and to reproduce the hand motions of classical Thai dance are lessons in transferring body-based skills. I recall watching children in a central Thai village dressed in their school uniforms *wai* their grandparents, on their knees, heads bowed, and then take off their uniforms and treat their grandparents in much less respectful ways, as if by shedding their school uniforms, they were shedding *kalatesa* and the rules of etiquette associated with their schooling. A Thai television drama (*Ban Taek*) solved the 'problem' of a daughter adopting male dress and courting a female singer by having the girl's family dress in drag; whereupon the daughter decided she would become a girl again (Jackson 1997:177).

Phillips' original work on Thai personality (1965) was sensitive to body issues. He stressed the importance of motoric self-discipline, the inviolability of every person, and the importance of the body in human and social relationships. Thai 'tend to be aware of physical bearing, beauty, and ugliness, as well as the use of the body as a communicative device' (1965:45). The fluid movements of a northern Thai dance were once seen as a form of bodily tribute, a mode of making the self more beautiful, more *suai* (Morris 1994a:134, 309).[2]

The 'sheer factualness of the human body . . . lends an aura of realness and certainty to cultural constructs' (Mascia-Lees and Sharpe 1992:146), and fits well with Thai notions of embodiment. The pragmatic accept-ance of bodily functions requires sensitivity to *kalatesa*. For example, Thai concern with propriety does not preclude talking about body functions with those of equal status – urinating, defecating, farting, spitting. I recall a monk talking about defecating and constipation. It shocked me at the time, but why should it? The Vinaya's monastic rules are very explicit about cleanliness and elimination. A university student who would not talk about her English homework without blushing with embarrassment would talk in English or Thai about the pressure she felt to urinate at inopportune times. Natural body functions are not a source of embarrassment per se, but only if one neglects to consider the time and place where the conversation is taking place, if one forgets *kalatesa*. *Khii* (shit) is elaborated metaphorically in Thai to refer to a number of bodily dregs including *khii muk* (nose mucus), *khii fan* (scum and particles in teeth), *khii hu* (ear wax), *khii lep* (dirt under fingernails), *khii lom* (dandruff), in addition to describing personality traits such as *khii nio* (stingy).

Paradoxically, performativity and embodiment draw attention to Buddhist notions of non-self and impermanence. While bodies are impermanent and trivial forms of identification, they are clues to *karmic* status and are the stage upon which appearance and reality are played out. For example, the terms for man and woman – *phuu ying, phuu chai*, humans possessing either vaginas or maleness (which a Thai colleague once translated to me as penis)[3] – are descriptions of temporary manifestations in the human realm, signifiers of difference that reinforce popular Buddhist speculations about rebirth status, rather than permanent identities for all of eternity.

Awareness of the body's surface appearance is basic to Thai gender identity. Until recently, elaborate tattoos inscribed on its surface a wide variety of cultural messages. Thai bodies are constituted by appearance; *taeng tua* refers to dressing or making or composing the body. 'Everybody regardless of gender, makes their body up on a daily basis and in accordance with culturally defined norms of masculine and feminine appearance' (Morris 1994b:37). It is not only *kathoey* who '*taeng tua*'; '. . . dressing is less a modification of the body than a construction of the embodied self' (Morris 1994b:24). This is why Phibun's cultural dictums on dress discussed in Chapter 4 were so offensive as a means of social control.

The importance of being fashionably attired is not lost on Bangkok shop owners where young Thai women literally reconstruct their identities in Bangkok's shopping malls. Particularly striking are the endless stalls of make-up and jewellery in shopping malls, department stores and vender's booths near factory dormitories. Avon and Amway are exceptionally popular in Thailand as venders of make-up. Fashion standards move rapidly into rural areas where only the most powerful of advocacy from women's organizations and financial constraints can slow the rush to dress and make up one's appearance to match urban and media representations of women (see also Mills 1997).

An insightful story by a Thai feminist writer tells of rural teenagers gradually coming to understand that beauty comes from within, that their rural dress has a natural beauty to it, and that the only people who benefit from cosmetic sales are the urban companies making the products. In an attempt to raise their consciousness, the teenagers are urged not to be slaves to foreign countries and urban Thai, and to throw out fake materials like cosmetics (Pruksathorn 1982).

Buddhism does not demand strict visible compliance to religious rules of dress for women as Islam does.[4] Thai and tourists alike, both men and women, are expected to follow rules of comportment and dress around palaces and temples – closed shoes or no shoes, covered shoulders and modest clothing (honoured more in the breach than in the observance in some locations). Thai women are free to arrange and decorate their bodies according to income, taste, and occupational standards of dress. In the past, these arrangements were also constrained by sumptuary rules restricting the use of some textiles to royalty.

It is restating the obvious, then, to say that Thai Buddhist women are not veiled. Consequently, their clothes and body shape are accessible to public gaze, to male gaze. Thus, Thai women have had to learn how to move and interact in the public sphere, bathing, eating, dressing and courting in sight of others. Both women and men are exceptionally skilled at using clothes or cloths to protect their bodies from exposure.[5] The skills of handling *phaasin* for bathing and changing clothes modestly are learned with some difficulty by *farang* women, many of whom have grown up without the need to adopt bodily habits of modesty because they were socialized in houses with private spaces for urinating and bathing. I was reading out of sight at sunset near a river in central Thailand when my eyes were drawn to the sight of two young women and two young men entering the river to bathe. Leaving would draw attention to myself and cause us all embarrassment, and so I watched a daily ablution dance of about five minutes duration. In those few minutes, they turned away from each other, soaped down their dusty *phaasin* and trousers, washed arms and face, swam to rinse, came ashore to fetch their clean clothes, stepped back in the water to keep feet and legs clean and perhaps modestly out of sight, pulled the clean, dry clothes over the wet dirty clothes, deftly pulling the latter off from underneath and giving them a final soaping and rinsing, and walked back to the village, their bathing and laundry complete and modesty gracefully preserved. When I tried the same dance the next night, it was an immodest disaster with an older village woman telling me I would have to bathe alone if I could not manage the wet cloth with more skill. I am sure I am not the only foreign woman who has had a rural woman place a hanky on her knee when wearing a short skirt instead of a *phaasin* in rural areas on public transportation. This nostalgic memory of the modesty of rural Thailand in the 1970s as opposed to the developed 1990s also contrasts the construction of 'traditional' (*samai gorn*) in oppostition to 'modern' (*samai mai*, cf. P. Van Esterik 1988).

Habits of modesty allow Thai women to bathe and change clothing in public with no exposure. The stripping away of bodily habits of modesty as well as clothing from Patpong nude dancers is thus a double loss. Do strippers return to this skilled use of *phaasin* on return visits to their villages? The book cover of *Patpong Sisters* by Cleo Odzer shows two sides of a prostitute's display, one, strip dancing in a bar, and the other on her return to her village in the northeast, where she bathes in her *phaasin* but is photographed with it pulled up to reveal her underwear pants.

Bodies are made-up and constructed, and many religious, state and familial institutions are concerned with regulating this process. Traditional Thai medicine acknowledged the link between human bodies and astrology. Hindu-Buddhist cosmology expressed through Thai court Brahmanism links bodily protection to deities: early in the morning, the protecting deity is in the forehead and mouth, at noon he is in the breast and heart, and in the evening, in the feet. By washing the appropriate part of the body at the appropriate time, protecting deities remain within the individual, keeping him or her happy and safe from enemies (Quaritch Wales 1983:2).[6]

Colours of clothing can also bring the wearer into harmony with astrological forces. Sunthorn Phu, the Thai court poet writing in the reign of Rama III codified these associations with the days of the week (*swasdi raksa*): Sunday – red, Monday – light yellow, Tuesday – purple, Wednesday – yellow, red or multicolor, Thursday – yellow or green, Friday – blue or grey, Saturday – black.[7] In a world of uncertainty and change, where surface is illusion, *kalatesa* smooths social relations by providing rules for ordering surface appearances of bodies.

Fragrant Bodies

People of different cultures inhabit different sensory worlds, and become accustomed to their own and their group's smell (Classen 1993:80). The senses of taste and smell are deeply integrated in Thai bodily identity. Smell is seldom considered in the analysis of personhood, although scent is inescapable in a way distinct from sight or sound. The least researched of all the senses (Classen et al 1994, Classen 1993), smell communicates the essence of both people and places. It is almost impossible to disguise or mask, and is certainly less superficial than sight which can be deceptive. Incense is one way to transform or mask smells in public places; deodorants and perfumes mask smells and transform people's bodies.

Body odours escape through orifices – the skin is porous rather than a barrier to outside influences. Thus, perspiration causes the skin to smell, and the smell of urine and feces need to be controlled through bathing. Smell of body and breath may be controlled by altering one's diet, as the smell of garlic, durian and butter reveals past repasts. Anyone travelling on Thai buses quickly learns to stand beside a Thai rather than a foreigner.[8]

The smell of bodies is important to self identity, both the absence of offensive smells and the application of soothing and healing perfumes. (*Hom* means a good smell, to sniff or to kiss). Cleanliness is metaphorically and literally an important part of Thai bodily orientation. Washing the body is an intrinsically social act, as anyone who failed to bathe before dinner in a Thai community would be reminded. Bodies should be bathed before eating and before sex: thus, a reference to bathing in classical theatrical performances stands for the intention to consent to sexual relations. Prostitutes complain about the smell and dirt of their clients, particularly foreigners.[9] Being able to bathe a client before sex is one stated reason why prostitutes prefer working in massage parlours compared to bars. Massage parlour prostitutes were less likely to change their place of employment, and those who did would shift to another massage parlour, in spite of the fact that they generally had more expenses than brothel prostitutes. Those working in Bangkok massage parlours devote 8 percent of their expenditures to purchasing cosmetics, including perfumes (Boonchalaksi and Guest 1994:77, 92).

In the BBC television documentary *Foreign Bodies* (1988), a Thai businesswoman described the girls in the massage parlour she operated as very clean since they bathe with their customers every day. This clean image is extended metaphorically to cover much of the sex industry in Thailand. I recall an evening spent in a raunchy, low-life dive near the docks in Bangkok. A blond seaman, encouraged by his friends, chose a bar hostess to accompany him to a curtained off back room, from which he emerged about five minutes later to the cheers of his friends. Following behind him was the hostess who alternatively held her nose, and gracefully flicked imaginary sweat from her armpits, with a look of utter disgust on her face. This disgust with the smell of foreigners is also evident from the stories in Odzer (1994) and Walker and Ehrlich (1992).

Body Fragments

Bodies are bounded, but males and females differ in the firmness and impenetrability of their body boundaries. Women's bodies are penetrable through intercourse, childbirth and even through breastfeeding. Thai masculinity is constructed on the premise that men must constantly resist allowing penetration of their bodies, and must constantly work to strengthen the outer surfaces of their bodies through tattoos, amulets, meditation practices, mantras and avoiding the passive role of the penetrated in anal intercourse. This submissive position likens men to women, and lowers their hierarchical position in the field of sexual identities. But as one can never be sure about one's invulnerability, men must test those boundaries and risk the discovery of vulnerability. Hence the self-testing *nakleng* (thug), and the men who drive too fast, drink to excess, and refuse to wear condoms in spite of the risks of unprotected sex.

In addition, there is a fascination with grotesque bodies at every level of society. Walking through Chulalongkorn University with a very senior social scientist, we diverted from our path so that she could look at a display of colour photographs of car accidents and their victims. Newspapers and posters display images of the open body – the body exposed and cut or damaged in some way. 'In a reversal of western censorship standards, representations of the sexualized body are suppressed throughout Thai society, while representations of the mutilated and decaying body are commonplace, as images of murdered and mutilated bodies appear regularly in magazines that are devoted to their depiction' (Hamilton 1993:524). The exceptions to this are the sexy posters advertising liquor, movies and posters for Patpong sex shows. Yet even these latter appear less than erotic and more like cartoon caricatures.

Bodies figure prominently in the depiction of decay and imperm- anence, reflecting the importance of the concept of *kayagatasati* (Pali), observing the unpleasantness and unsatisfactoriness of the body, seeing the body as a container of filth (Jackson 1993:17). Buddhism teaches detachment from the body through emphasis on the decay and imperm- anence of its physical form. The body is illusion, appearance only. 'Beauty as an abstract quality does not decay, but what perceives it does, as well as the object of beauty' (Khantipalo 1990:20). This approach to physical appearance does not distinguish between the decay of male and female bodies.

Face (*naa*) and heart (*chai*) are the two body parts which condense the greatest amount of information about a person's state. Faces are made, made up, put on, the interface between the public and private self, and the basis of metaphors elaborating on the idea of 'saving face'. '*Naa* is not representation of subjectivity but a presentation of public order' (Morris 1994b:37). Face is the gendered surface displayed to the public; it is face that is protected by rules of *kalatesa*, and face that is reworked as contexts change. Similarly, heart (*chai*) is a key metaphor to express feelings, relations and emotions. Glossed in English as heart, *chai* is never really separated from mind, a succinct summary of the differences between English and Thai approaches to body and mind. Information, both emotional and technical, must 'enter the heart' to be understood (*khaw chai*). Moore (1992) discusses over 330 heart phrases in Thai, revealing how much thinking, feeling and talking takes place through the heart. Unlike the 'soft-hearted woman' and 'hard-hearted man', Thai hearts can be soft or satisfied, hard or heavy, wicked or withered; the states are not gendered.

Gender Categories

How do bodies relate to other aspects of sexuality and gender? Europeans and North Americans privilege sexuality above all other criteria in their conceptions of gender. Ortner and Whitehead acknowledge that 'the degree to which cultures have formal, highly elaborated notions of gender and sexuality is itself variable' (1981:6). My model suggests that in Southeast Asia, and specifically in Thailand, gender is not as dominant an organizing principle as relative age, wealth, or merit store. Further, sexuality per se may be weakly integrated into Thai gender identities.

While sex is a marked category in the West, 'burdened with an excess of significance' (Rubin 1984:279), it is much less so in Thailand, and much less problematic. Thailand offers a taken-for-granted unrepressed social atmosphere towards sex, at least for men (Jackson 1989), rather than a sex denying social atmosphere. Men's sexual activities, regardless of object choice, confirm their power and masculinity. Women's sexual activities, unless within marriage, are stigmatized or trivialized. Talking about sexual matters, particularly in mixed groups is not polite (*phit kalatesa*).[10]

Eurocentric concepts of self, sex and gender identity make it difficult to address questions regarding Thai gender adequately. What are the elements of Eurocentric models of gender identity that bias the task of analyzing gender in Thailand? They include the search for binary, bimodal sex classifications based on genitalia, and classifications based on binary object choice (same sex, opposite sex, or assumptions that naturalize a heterosexual norm). They work on the logic of exclusivity (either/or) rather than the logic of a continuum or non-exclusivity (both/and), and have been broadly critiqued by anthropologists and others (MacCormack and Strathern, eds 1980, Ortner and Whitehead 1981, Rubin 1975, Vance 1991, Moore 1994). This emphasis on bipolar opposition is quite recent in Western gender analysis, as in the past, homologies between men and women were stressed rather than differences, including arguments that male and female bodies were inversions of each other (Laqueur 1990). But in the last few years, assumptions that male and female are the most basic binary oppositions, that each form can be defined by some essential characteristics, and that the forms are non over-lapping have been challenged (cf. Fausto-Sterling 1993). These challenges to the idea of fixed, bounded categories are more compatible with Thai logic. This model proposes that Thai gender identity is a much more ephemeral part of self identity, and much more context sensitive, than Western constructions. Although sexual organs are part of the materiality of bodies and even the naming of gender identities, what you do with those organs is much less relevant to gender identity than it is in the modern West, and until recently, much more your own business. Further, sexual organs are not the only basis for gender identification.[11] *Winyan* (spirit essence), *kam* or *karma* and *chai* (heart) are also important determinants of gender identity, and account for differences between people. These multiple influences on gender can be further modified by habit, teaching by example, and practices such as merit making, mediumship and *sukhwan* rituals designed to keep the life force firmly lodged in the body. Jane Hanks pointed out the importance of these multiple interpretive frameworks for understanding individuality over thirty years ago (1964, 1965). Current gender analysis will benefit from incorporating her insights into individual behaviour into more postmodernist approaches to gender performativity.

Individuals having the appearance of male or female humans move back and forth over multiple lifetimes, in and out of gender and sexual identities as contexts change. People behave in a strikingly different manner when they leave each other's presence. It is the contexts of social life that are strictly rule governed and situationally defined, not the consistency of the individual moving through these social contexts. That is, individuals move in and out of fixed contexts. The fluidness of gender identities in Thailand is also enhanced by the acceptance of alternative ways of expressing masculinity and femininity, the linkages between sexuality and play, and the potential for experiencing former and future lives as man, woman, or *kathoey*.

Thai tolerate an extraordinary fluidity of desire along with a range of personal decisions without exercising jural control. As a Thai student pointed out to his American teacher in a discussion on freedom, Americans are not free because they do not have freedom to spit (Hollinger 1977:62), implying that Thai who spit where they want are free. 'To do as one pleases is to be genuinely Thai' (Podhisita 1985). Embree (1950) glossed this lack of regularity and discipline as individualism and 'loose structure'.

The situatedness of gender identity and sexuality is not unique to Thailand. Southeast Asia has been identified as 'the most tolerant area of the world with respect to variant sexuality' (Whitam and Mathy 1986:144). From colonial times, the Dutch in Indonesia were shocked at the 'natives' incorrigible addiction to pederasty and homosexual sodomy' (Anderson 1990) and commented on their shared passion for these vices. Chou Ta-Kuan, visiting the Khmer empire in 1296–7, recorded: 'In this country, there are many homosexuals, who every day wander by in groups of more than ten in the market place. They constantly try to attract the Chinese for rich presents. It is hideous. It is vile' (Briggs 1951:247). Anderson writes of the ability of Javanese power to concentrate opposites, represented iconographically as the dynamic and simultaneous incorporation of male and female opposed characteristics in a single entity (1992:29) – one that is neither hermaphrodite nor merged. Many representations of gender in Southeast Asia are ambiguous as well as androgynous.[12]

What Western analysts read as tolerance or confusion, may simply be the recognition that throughout Southeast Asia, the diversity of gender traditions presents a sharp contrast to the essentialism of Euro-American binarism. Tsing (1993) addresses important questions about power among the Meratus Dayak from the assumption that males and females share a universal humanity that is essentially feminine. Atkinson (1990:88–93) describes a category of mixed gender status among the Wana of central Sulawesi. This casual but uncommon gender shifting, open to men or women, is based on dress or work preference rather than sexual preference. However, since men and women are considered to be very much the same, a man's extra edge is his penis, a badge that empowers its owner to certain advantages. She speculates that no man would become a woman because he would have to sacrifice his penis (although he might adopt women's appearance). Male to female cross dressing, more prevalent than female to male cross dressing in Southeast Asia and elsewhere, provides men with access to a wider range of gender expressions and still appears to be hegemonic, a further example of male privilege and power according to Garber (1992:51). In Southeast Asia, clothing and cloth marks gender and transgendering, and both are linked to local performance traditions and healing.

Like many features of Southeast Asian life, sexual identities are very much open to negotiation and constructed through interaction with others. Consider the case of *kathoey*, whose identities are highly ambiguous. *Kathoey* had an original biological denotation as a being with indeterminate sex or a hermaphrodite, although the meaning has been expanded to refer to transvestites, transsexuals, and homosexuals. In northern Thai origin myths, *kathoey* seems to be neither male nor female but both (Morris 1994b:19). *Kathoey* is a transgender category, a true third sex rather than a variant of male or female (cf. Herdt 1994).

Kathoey who dress as women and believe they have a woman's heart can become transsexuals through expensive operations to 'correct a mistake'. One 'lady-man' paid 45,000 *baht* for genital surgery and 20,000 baht for breast surgery (Walker and Ehrlich 1992:106). 'Lady-men' are assumed to have superior knowledge of feminine fashion and comportment: *kathoey taeng tua phuuying dii kwaa phuuying* (*kathoey* compose a female body better than do women) as an informant explained to Morris (1994b:24). I have also heard overdressed women accused of looking like *kathoey*, in a parody of reversals.

In the Thai gender system mapped here, *kathoey* may be included as a third gender, but one that cannot easily or usefully be assimilated to either the male or female end of Western gender binarism (cf. Garber 1992:10). Effeminate male transvestites (*kathoey*) are referred to as *phuu ying praphet song* (the second kind of woman) perhaps because they were considered as safe sexual outlets for Thai men (Jackson 1997:173). More significantly, *kathoey* challenge Western notions of binary thinking, and even the term continuum seems distorting and arbitrary.[13] *Kathoey* change surface appearances without breaching gender boundaries. Rather, they underscore the different positioning of boundaries in Thai and Euro-American logic, the different need for boundaries in different societies, and the ability of individuals to move in and out of identities.

There are choices available to Thai men and, to a lesser degree, to women regarding how they exercise their sexuality, provided they are the dominant partners. Thai men have a wide range of sexual options open to them – heterosexual fidelity, polygyny, homosexuality, bisexuality or celibacy, options which Morris (1997:63) reads as compulsive masculinity. Until the recent HIV/AIDS pandemic influenced public opinion, persons preferring homosexual relationships were not considered dangerous or subversive, were not the target of violence for their sexual preferences, and faced no legal or religious interdictions (Jackson 1997:175). Morris (1997) documents the increasing violence and discrimination against the public expression of gayness, including the banning in 1996 of homosexual students from the major teacher training school, the Ratchabat Institute.

Celibacy or sexual detachment is also an option for Thai men. Consider, for example, the sexual restraint of political figures such as Chamlong Srimuang, who are perceived as even more powerful when celibate. Monks who withdraw from society provide a model of young, sexually active men who gain power and prestige by abstaining from sexual activity. This pattern of ascetic restraint coexists with the *sya bi* (bisexual predator) model and the more common 'hydraulic pump' model of Thai male sexuality. Just as non-violence conjures up the image of the opposite, perhaps the controlled celibate reinforces the idea of masculine control over sexual expression.

Until recently, Thai did not have nouns to designate people who preferred same sex relationships who were not also transvestites, but only verbs for homosexual behaviours (cf. Jackson 1997:170). Sexual orientations were best understood as phases people move in and out of, rather than fixed sexual strategies. Homosexual acts do not turn boys into homosexuals (Jackson 1989:18). 'Having homosexual tendencies or desires does not necessarily entail perceiving these tendencies as integral to one's selfhood or personhood, to which they can remain peripheral and isolated' (Jackson 1989:100). Wijeyewardene writes of *kathoey*: 'Men who will be appalled at the suggestion that they are homosexuals will flirt with them in public – at least in a joking way, and in local communities, they fit into a recognizable public role' (1986:158). Anyone, male or female, could have been *kathoey* in a former life. But bisexual males and *kathoey* have the flexibility to return to the advantages conferred by male gender. The key point is that Thai definitions of masculinity do not preclude homoerotic behavior and practice.

Thai terminology with regard to sexual identities is both changing rapidly and regionally specific. Naming and labelling are critically important clues to understanding the organization of sexual knowledge; however, naming categories does not guarantee access to meaning. Recently, a set of terms derived from international gay culture have made their way into the Thai language. These terms privilege sexual acts in defining categories of people and make these categories appear more permanent than Thai logic encourages.

Jackson's extensive research on the historical basis for gender categories and labels includes reference to male authority figures who abuse their position with young boys and *len tua dam* (play with black beans);

a man's love child (luuk sawaat), a less negative term; *gay king*, an active, dominant gay-identified man of masculine appearance; *gay queen*, an effeminate, passive gay-identified man (1989:19–21). Yet this listing appears too static, too rule-governed to reflect currently changing terminology. Jackson has also noted the use of a new term, *quing*, to designate flexible, sexually versatile gay-identified men, further linguistic evidence that Thai are not satisfied with binary categories. Thai use of the term, *Tut*, from the movie Tootsie to refer to both male and female cross dressers is doubly ironic as the movie featured a male to female cross dresser (and tootsie roll is slang for a phallus, Garber 1992:9). Garber (1992) notes that the real message of Tootsie is that feminist ideas are much less threatening when they come from a man. The movie was not intended to be a feminist film but a film about trans-vestism within the Hollywood codes of female impersonation. Toot is a term that is most likely to be applied to a 'gay queen' or a non-crossdressing male. (Jackson also points out that *tut* is phonemically close to slang for 'anus' 1997:175). Same sex gender roles derive their meaning from heterosexual gender roles. Real men dominate women and/or submissive men by controlling active sex acts such as anal penetration or oral sex. Age is a factor in status relations, allowing young men to service older men for money while seeking dominant sexual relations with women on their own time. Men who take submissive roles for money can still be real men. According to Morris, *kathoey* may pass for gay men or women, and move back and forth between these identities (1994b:28).

The term *kathoey* is rarely used to denote female transvestites or lesbians, although the original meaning of the word may have included them. More likely, the phenomenon was simply ignored as it has been in gender studies elsewhere until recently. Morris points out that although lesbianism is more repressed and more reified in Thai discourse, the range of options in gender identity and sexual practice for women has received little attention (1994b:30). This is partly because Thai lesbian-identified women are rarely involved in commercial sex work or public forums about sexuality, but meet discretely for social support and comfortable surroundings. Their interactions are less commercialized than those of gay men. There are few public spaces for gay women who want to express their erotic selves romantically, but many spaces for women to enjoy each other's company. Again, this underscores the need to distinguish between same sex intimacy and homoeroticism. Women's relations with other women are assumed to be a form of friendship (*len phuan*, play with friends), nothing that would inhibit her from fulfilling other social obligations including marriage (Morris 1994b:30).

Anthropologists have recently begun the task of redressing the balance of research on this subject with ethnographic studies of lesbian lifestyles and lesbian activist groups such as *Anjaree*. Thai concepts of the family persist in determining the shape of lesbian relationships. *Tom* (from tomboy) labels masculine identified lesbians who dress and interact like men; *dii* (from lady), feminine identified lesbians who meet Thai expectations for feminine behavior and appearance. *Tom* are not expected to have relations with other *tom* but with *dii*, who may also be in relationships with men.

A study of the sexual values of students and factory workers reveals that there is more acceptance of homosexual relationships between women. These relations are valued because '. . . you will never get pregnant or contract a disease. You are safe and secure . . . it is a good thing so that no one can interfere with you and exploit you . . .' (Soonthornthada 1995:3). Her work suggests that there is a continuity between close, same sex friendships where women share similar interests and seek companionship, and homoerotic sexual relations. Relations between women were viewed as natural, unlike the attraction between men which was considered disgusting. In a national survey which included questions on sexual attitudes, both male and female respondents indicated that it was slightly more acceptable for a married woman to be involved in a sexual scenario with another woman than with a man (Boonchalaksi and Guest 1995:Table 2). While most respondents agreed that both were wrong, it may be that only sexual indiscretions with another man constitute adultery.

Jackson writes that 'the key to understanding the subjugated status of *kathoeys* and women in Thailand lies in their both being denied the active bisexuality which is the ideal and acme of sexual power in the Thai system of sexuality' (1989:216). This argument calls for more ethnographic research but fits well with the model of gendered surfaces developed here. What is clear is that 'the political economy of sex in Thailand is structured for male consumers, whether those consumers are comprised of heterosexual men seeking women's bodies and beauty, or homosexual men seeking male or *kathoey* bodies and beauty' (Morris 1994a:36).

Labels and categories reflecting sexual orientation are changing rapidly, reflecting style and fashion rather than permanence and substance. The influence of international gay culture including new media (magazines and videos) may be increasing the numbers of category labels, but is breaking down the diversity in the Thai gender system to stress identity based on object choice, heterosexual or homosexual. In Thailand, as in other parts of the world, exposing what should be private to the public gaze entails a loss of face. Rules of *kalatesa* help preserve face and keep what is meant to be private, private, as identities play across gendered surfaces; however appearances can be deceiving.

Disguise

Another key to understanding the Thai gender system can be seen in a Pali loan word, *lakka phet*, meaning to disguise one's true identity or position by cross-dressing; for example, a man who lives as a woman, a woman who lives like a man, a monk who pretends to be a layperson, or a layperson who pretends to be a monk (Jackson 1989:21). This potential for disguising the surface is at the heart of the Thai attitude towards gender categories, and being 'taken in' by someone who is not what he/she seems is a constant source of tension and amusement. The *kathoey* as trickster enjoys deceiving unsuspecting tourists who think they have been approached by a beautiful woman. The greatest joke is the king disguised as demon, the sweet young thing as the evil temptress, the ugly body hiding a great mind. These illusions are the basis of ambiguity in theatrical performances. Disguise itself is of interest since the person disguised often intends to be recognized. Similarly, the graceful, powerful and refined appearances of royal heroes and heroines in classical literature and theatre revealed their true identity and gave them away even when characters tried to disguise themselves as common people (Kriengkraipetch 1993:7). The pleasure lies in disguising the surface, but *karmic* status – being born superior in this life – always shows through.[14]

Nagavajara (1994) reminds us of the importance of the performing arts in Southeast Asia in schooling the public in the social poetics (cf. Herzfeld 1997:xx) of gender shifting and the flexibility of gender boundaries. He contrasts the all-women dance-drama troupes of the *lakhon nai* (theatre of the inner circle) with the all-male troups of the *lakhon nok* (theatre of the outer circle). The ability to play male and female roles is considered a demonstration of artistic prowess. *Lakhon nai* was originally performed by a troup of female dancers considered part of the royal regalia (Wilayasakpan 1992:28). Later, *lakhon nok* had to add females to their troups to compete with *lakhon nai* female troups who, in 1855, were permitted outside the palace (Wilayasakpan 1992: 32). Formerly, within each troup, a single gender must play the full range of gender-differentiated parts. In these performances, power is invested in what Westerners might consider effeminate male characters. There is no assumption that supermasculine robustness is the only route to power. On the contrary, intelligence, spiritual strength, and beauty can and do substitute for size and strength. But in the world of performance, gender usurpation operates in one direction only – with feminine attributes being transferred to a man (Nagavajara 1994b:xxi).[15]

Where Thai court performance traditions feature disguise and masking, the stories do not focus on males disguised as females or vice versa. Instead, they shift across class lines, blurring boundaries between nobility and peasant, prince and pauper. Western theatrical performances provide examples of transgender disguise. The Thai production of *As You Like It* provides some insight into contemporary approaches to disguise. Shakespeare's play, featuring Rosalind – a man playing a woman who is disguised as a man and then pretends to be a woman – was translated into Thai by King Rama VI, himself known for gender bending. The play is a perfect vehicle for exploring the situatedness of gender identities. Rosalind passes through the state of being a man in order to become a woman but would originally have been played by a boy, the term used to describe the players who took the parts of women in Shakespeare's day. Boy is also a code word for the third sex (Garber 1992:10). Rosalind is the epitome of a cross-dressed woman, 'an infinite regress of representation, of which the transvestite ... is a powerful and inescapable reminder' (Garber 1992:76).

The Thai director chose to express the system of differences that sexual stereotyping depends on through costumes consisting of breastplates and arm and leg bands that could be easily taken on and off. Female identity was depicted by full breasts on a removeable breastplate, and less 'puffy' muscles; male identity, through more muscular breastplates and heavier 'spiked' muscle bands (Wayne 1994). The Thai production staff used the construction and reconstruction of bodily surfaces as the key to gender identity. Gender identity was represented as a system of differences that could be put on and taken off, and the site of this transformation was the surface of the body.

Performances featuring disguise are easily read by a wide range of individuals and classes because of the effectiveness of sumptuary laws in reducing gender and class ambiguity. While contemporary Western dress codes or sumptuary laws aim to 'class up', requiring a higher class of dress – ties, shirts, jackets, shoes – the sumptuary laws of premodern Thailand, like those of medieval Europe, were meant to 'dress down' social climbers who were trying to dress above their station; the laws thus reinforced the existing social hierarchy (cf Garber 1992:23). Whereas actors were allowed to violate the sumptuary laws on stage, Thai villagers violated them during rituals such as weddings and ordinations where participants carried regalia such as tiered umbrellas and jewelled swords and dressed in royal style, wearing pink and gold silks, and embroidery normally reserved for royalty. By changing clothes, spirit mediums crossed both class and gender boundaries during trance. In Chiang Mai, mediumship is on the rise, with most mediums being female or *kathoey* possessed by male spirits who speak primarily to women clients (Morris 1994a:51). Cross-gendered possession provides another glimpse into how appearance creates gender identity across time and space.

Butler's analysis of 'Subversive Bodily Acts' raises questions about impersonation. If impersonation is a key fabricating mechanism through which the social construction of gender takes place (1990:136), then *kathoey* mock the notion of Thai masculinity and femininity. However, we know little about the eroticism of Thai cross dressing, *kathoey* as agents of destabilization of gender identities, or the relation between transvestism and sexual orientation. Transvestism occupies contradictory social sites in the drag spectacles of Pattaya and Bangkok, the *kathoey* beauty pageants of Lampang, the sex shows on Patpong Road and in the royal courts of the past. Are these gendered performances about males usurping female bodies, about the aesthetics of female appearance or about females having more opportunities than males to express aesthetic taste in appearance? Or, as Morris asks, 'are maleness and femaleness the only aspects of identify at stake in transgendering and cross dressing'? (1995:583)[16]

These gestures and acts, performative of gendered bodies, raise a very Buddhist question about the ontological status of the body apart from the masquerade which constitutes its reality. In fact, the politics of bodily appearances reinforces the Buddhist emphasis on non-self, impermanence, illusion and the deceptive nature of appearances. Bodies, like self and ego, are constituted as 'nothing but' appearance and illusion.

Gender Unfinished

If gender is contingent and fluid, modelling gender relations will be an endless task, always unfinished and tentative. This model still lacks an adequate discussion of sexuality, and how power shapes both gender and sexuality. Morris (1997) warns against nostalgia for an imagined

moment when sexual identities were not binary, and homoerotic acts
not prohibited in Thailand. Current interest in sexuality is framed more
by discussions of the need for sex education to prevent the spread of
HIV/AIDS than by the need to understand the nature of sexuality itself.
Jackson's research on Thai sexuality suggests that sexual desire may be
thought of as a mood, an emotion that comes over one, a temporary
emotional state in need of release, more like an itch than a romance,
and unconnected to love and commitment (1989:38, 74). It is as if
desire is the prerogative of males only who have to respond to their
drives, with women feining or experiencing no desire, expecting no
pleasure. Current understandings of sexuality essentialize male sexuality
as something more driven, more important than female sexuality. How
has this hydraulic model of sexuality come to be shared by Thai men
and women?

I have argued, as have others, that Thai gender, sexual orientation,
sexual practices, and identity should be thought of as context-sensitive
choices shaped by a number of factors, not as inevitable outcomes of
characteristics fixed from birth. What is fixed is the importance of power
in all relationships. Thai masculinity and prestige is partially derived
from the control and objectification of women, whether they be young,
unprotected tenant farmers, employees, beauty queens, prostitutes or
mistresses. The logic of slavery never left some aspects of Thai gender
discourse and practice; the logic of play never left others.

Notes

1. Relating the body-self back to the body politic, provincial governors were
known as royal spittoons; 'each subordinate is the symbolic recipient of his
superior's spittle' (Phillips 1987:280).

2. Standard Thai differentiates *suai* (raising tone) meaning well-dressed, nice-
appearing, beautiful, graceful, from *suai* (low tone) meaning poll-tax or tribute.

3. I regret not checking the etymology more carefully before writing that
phuu chai could be glossed as human with a penis, or male. However, several
authors cited my work because it also made sense to them.

4. I separate these discussions of dress and appearance from the prohibitions
of women entering temples in some parts of the country. These prohibitions
may be more olfactory than visually based. Women's exclusion from sacred

places may be partly based on the bad smells supposedly emanating from women's bodies after childbirth and at menstruation. Women take special herbal medicines to ensure they are sweet smelling to others.

5. Europeans viewed public bathing as an indication of moral laxity and immodesty because they were 'ignorant of the strict codes that governed bathing practices' (Andaya 1998:22).

6. Some Asian systems of medicine combined physiognomy and astrology, resulting in the forehead corresponding to Mars, the right eye to the sun, the left to Venus, the right ear to Jupiter, the left to Saturn, the nose to the moon, the mouth to Mercury' (Magli 1989:111). European systems of physiognomy such as Lavater's (1741–1801) linked moral and intellectual traits to physical appearance. Renaissance artists praised the beauty of the body as a sign of inner goodness – the integration of physical and moral beauty. The equation of God, beauty, and goodness is also reiterated in St Augustine's *Confessions* (Synnott 1993:18, 83).

7. Ploi, the heroine of Kukrit Pramoj's *Four Reigns*, ridiculed this system when her husband dressed for a palace party from head to toe in pink, a colour also associated with Tuesday. There are differences in the assignment of colours and days. These may be regional or temporal differences. The key point is that colours, clothing and astrology were related in the palace, and these associations were well known and used in Central Thai and Lao communities, particularly for costumes for beauty contestants.

8. Research on perfume purchases in Thailand could provide interesting evidence to support or refute the argument that both men and women expend resources and energy to de-odorize and re-odorize themselves for reasons beyond the heat of Thailand.

9. In a television documentary, *Thai Girls*, shown in Toronto in November 1998, a Thai prostitute working in Toronto complained that her Canadian customers were rude and smelly.

10. This is rapidly changing in the context of HIV/AIDS. However, it is not at all uncommon for very intimate questions to be asked of relative strangers, a habit that has both embarrassed and facilitated the work of anthropologists. Women past menopause are also freer to express a frank ribald nature.

11. And even gender organs can be altered. However, in systems where femininity and masculinity are more nuanced, surgery may not be considered necessary except for aesthetic reasons. In 1950s Thailand, Jane Hanks viewed a man's ordination as equivalent to childbirth; (1963:77); in 1990s Indonesia, Anderson sees the sex change operation as the moral equivalent of childbirth (1996:294).

12. A fascinating example of this is the androgynous beauty of the thirteenth-century Buddha images that Nagavajara argues were modelled on women

(1994:xxi). He is surely referring to the Sukhothai walking Buddha figure. In an effort to understand why this image was seldom reproduced in drawings or modern sculptures, I asked a monk who blessed new images and oversaw their casting in Sukhothai. He told me that they were too perfect and could not be reproduced by contemporary artisans; they could only be cast in the time of the Sukhothai kingdom when there was more moral goodness in the community. Further discussions of androgyny are found in Scharer 1963 (for Borneo) and Peacock 1968 (for Java).

13. For example, Jackson (1989) has analyzed lesbian-identified feminine women (*dii*) and gay-identified masculine men (*king*) as wayward heterosexuals, super passive and super dominant, two extremes along a continuum of temporary sexual identities, rather than permanent gender categories. This is a further argument for Thai plasticity surrounding gender identities, and the capacity of individuals to shift in and out of categories. Ong (1989:298), too, sees the gender continuum as offering the possibility for individuals to engage in gender switching. She sees transvestites as dramatizing the fluidity of gender permitted in prestige structures.

14. A popular poster and postcard for sale in Bangkok reproduces a photograph of King Chulalongkorn pretending to be a simple peasant on his trips upcountry, but everyone knew he was the king.

15. Javanese court performances show similar flexibility in gender ascription. Yogyakarta court culture required men to play men and women; Surakarta's dance drama required females to play men and women (Hughes-Freeland 1995:183). As in Thailand, true talent is the ability to display the full range of gendered performances (although physique may make the fit easier at one or another end of the spectrum).

16. Cross gendering may be easier than crossing ethnicity. I was singled out from the Thai members of my Buddhist meditation class and barred from entering the grounds of the Temple of the Emerald Buddha with them for a service (although I was appropriately dressed) because tourists were not permitted in the temple grounds that day. I could pass as a Buddhist but not as a Thai. A comparable conflict developed at a magnificent Bangkok drag show I attended in 1992 with a Thai friend. More significant than the blurring of gender categories inside the show was the attempt to cross the categorial opposition between Thai and non-Thai that took place before the show. My Thai friend tried to get me in to see the show paying the lower Thai admission price rather than the tourist price, claiming that I lived in Bangkok, spoke Thai, and was studying gender. What finally permitted me to pay the Thai admission price was the conversation my Thai friend had with the manager, who, it turned out had some connection with her school and knew someone she was related to. This time, I was permitted to pass as a Thai for the evening.

I felt more uncomfortable in my ethnic/racial drag than the drag queens looked on stage and off, as they posed with male and female Japanese tourists after the show.

Context and Continuity: Grasshoppers, Turtles and Feminists

A s I was revising this conclusion, a number of Thai prostitutes, part of the expansion of the international sex trade into Canada, were arrested in Toronto. Once again, I was called upon as an 'expert' to answer questions about Thailand and Thai women. The questions could be reduced to, 'What is Thailand like that it could produce this industry?' and 'What draws Thai women to prostitution?' They raised a memory of villagers in Supanburi Province, after hearing our explanation of what anthropology is, asking us at every opportunity, 'how about Canada?' They demanded a snapshot of what made our home and native land different from theirs. We were unable to come back with anything better than, 'how about Thailand?' Another villager asked who were the stupidest people in the world. When we were unable to provide a definitive answer to that question, they gave up on trying to figure out what anthropology was about. Both sets of questions raise the problem of cultural context and difference; or as recalled from undergraduate anthropology courses, other fields, other grasshoppers (Geertz 1973:53).

'Other Fields: Other Grasshoppers'

'Other fields: other grasshoppers' is an analogy for different contexts. Cultural context is at the heart of anthropology and yet is more clearly defined and operationalized in archaeology and linguistics than in social anthropology. Context as background renders form interpretable and is key to the work of ethnographic analysis. Its etymology draws attention to things that are woven together, connected, coherently

227

linked. The weaving together of words, ideas and strands into back-grounds and foregrounds provides a very different metaphorical base than the Thai image of the intersection of time and space expressed by *kalatesa.*

Archaeologists use context to refer to the depositional matrix from which an artifact is recovered, and to the information gleaned from the environment about the conditions of deposition. Context can also refer to the events, actions, social organization and cultural practices that resulted in a particular placement of objects. In linguistic usage, context refers to what comes before or after a phoneme, word or passage to 'fix' its meaning. Briggs views context as the 'waste' created from our extraction of texts, and, to focus attention on the strategic process of discourse production, proposes three transformations of the concept: entextualization, shaping texts into bounded units amenable to insertion in other discursive settings; decontextualization, the removal of text from its setting; and recontextualization, the subsequent reinsertion of text into discourse (Briggs 1993:405–6).

Cultural anthropologists use the term more loosely than linguists and archaeologists to refer to that which frames something and renders it interpretable, once again, relying on a textual analogy. But as Appadurai points out, contexts are produced from both discursive and non-discursive practices. Since the establishment of fieldwork as the authoritative basis for ethnography, context has come to mean the 'thick description' of field locations and conditions, including texts, structures and practices. The non-discursive practices of settings have often been overlooked.

Appadurai focuses attention on localities as contexts which them-selves produce other contexts. His refinements in defining context differentiate between neighbourhoods as historically grounded social forms, and localities as properties of social life. The former are contexts that at the same time require and produce contexts:

> . . . as local subjects carry on the continuing task of reproducing their neighbourhood, the contingencies of history, environment and imagination contain the potential for new contexts (material, social, and imaginative) to be produced . . . neighbourhood as context produces the context of neighbourhoods. (Appadurai 1996:185)

Context as frame or setting, and the contingencies of history provide potentials for new contexts. But the danger of context, as every thesis-writing student quickly learns, is that everything is connected to everything else. Contexts are infinite regressions and permutations. Everything is a context for something else depending on the level of abstraction chosen. For example, Buddhism is a context for gender and has the potential to create new contexts such as Buddhist feminism.

Strathern initiated an extensive discussion of context in *Cultural Anthropology* (1988) which was primarily concerned with the writing of British Social Anthropologists, the social context of their writing, and how these social settings have shifted. Writing creates contexts for other writing. 'All contexts are alike insofar as they give rise to the situated statement, are the frames for people's performances . . .' (Strathern 1988:269). Strathern identifies the problem of rendering ideas and concepts from another culture 'within a conceptual universe that has space for them, and thus of creating that universe' (1988:256). Anthropologists imagine themselves moving between two cultures – the culture being studied and the culture being addressed (Strathern 1988:261). This double perspective means that nothing can be taken 'out of context'. There is no local untouched by the global, and no context so fixed that it lacks a history.

Turtles

Geertz inspired a second metaphor, this one drawing attention to explanations of historical change:

> There is an Indian story . . . about an Englishman who, having been told that the world rested on a platform which rested on the back of an elephant which rested in turn on the back of a turtle, asked . . . what did the turtle rest on? Another turtle. And that turtle? 'Ah, Sahib, after that it is turtles all the way down. (Geertz 1973:28–9)

I use this metaphor to draw together some arguments concerning Thai concepts of time and history, the search for the continuities under gender surfaces, and how they are shaped by past structures. If new meanings always emerge as a response to and a commentary on old meanings (McKinley 1979: 316), some things in the past make some things in the present more likely.

If it is 'turtles all the way down', history is the only guide as to when to stop. (This is particularly important for me since I have been accumulating so many turtles.) History provides one dimension of cultural context, although it cannot be reduced to cultural context (cf. Roseberry

1989:9). In the cases developed here, history provides contexts. Indian-ization is, perhaps, the earliest elaboration of the argument that Thai public culture has selected and absorbed models from outside Thailand – Sukhothai from Khmer, Ayutthaya from Khmer and Sukhothai, Bangkok from Ayutthaya and Europe, Bangkok's gays from the inter-national gay movement. What Prime Minister Phibun did in the 1940s to update the appearance of Thai women is part of the same strategy that kept Thailand free of colonial rule and kept competing elites in check while centralizing power. Foreignness validates and is an integral part of the construction of Thai identity. 'Where India abhorred the outside as polluting and China disdained it as barbaric, Southeast Asia appropriated foreign borrowings as the idiom of urban rule . . . foreign fad becomes an indigenous hierarchy' (O'Connor 1995a:35). In addition to adopting what is thought to be civilized from the outside, ruling elites also link what happened in the present to what has happened in the past in an ancient Southeast Asian strategy of legitimation by exemplary pasts. Founder cults become princedoms, become nation states in a sequence of adjustments to founding myths. Even the name of Bangkok appropriates the kingdoms and cities of the past.[1] Past legitimizes present syntagmatically by linking events chronologically, or paradigmatically, as relations are established metaphorically between events as members of classes of actions (cf. Valerio 1990:157). Past merges with present in many different ways. The problem of repres-enting the past has emerged throughout this book.

This approach to the past contrasts with Euro-American approaches, according to Foucault who writes of European history: 'Between each of the epistemes is a gulf so deep as to be beyond meaningful dis-cussion . . . Epistemes are like islands separated by an unbridgeable gulf of water going down to uncharted depths' (Tilley 1990:291). The lack of connection between these periodic epistemes, the 'forgetting' of past epistemes, may make sense in Foucault's analyses of Euro-American institutions, but it does not fit with Thai notions of historical periodicity and paradigm shifts. Pasts may be evoked for communal solidarity, manipulated to reorder events, or rewritten to demonstrate continuity with the present. How the past is used and what it is used for is what matters most to anthropologists. Understanding uses of the past, the nuances of time (the pragmatics of temporality in Fabian's phrase, 1991:228), helps avoid the biases of allochronism (the denial of co-temporaneity). Visualism, the domination of sight to the detriment of sound, taste, smell and touch also contributes to detachment and distancing from the other (Fabian 1991:201–4). When we attempt to enter into other temporal concepts, we orient ourselves to others. Homi Bhabha writes of '. . . the moment of transit where space and time cross to produce complex figures of difference and identity, past and present, inside and outside, inclusion and exclusion' (1994:1). At this point in time, at the edge of the century, we are restless, disoriented, caught in 'a disturbance of direction' characterized by terms such as postmodernism, postcolonialism, postfeminism . . . (1994:1).

Negotiating Temporal Differences

Time passes quickly in Bangkok, in spite of the fact that much of it is spent trying to get somewhere. Fortunately for those caught in time and traffic, social time and interactional time take precedence over organizational and institutional time. Pleasure and skill in synchronizing interaction time is visible in the punning and verbal give and take of courting language and poetry duels. It is still visible in the admiration for those who are smart talkers (*kuey geng*). Westerners may feel profound discomfort when subjecting themselves to the intensity of Thai interaction time. Interaction time which synchronizes people's lives however briefly in time and space – taking turns, as children phrase it – is experienced as discontinuous punctual moments overlaid with synchronicity and embedded time. Outings or day trips provide an example of the intersections of time and space; getting there is literally half the fun. Trips may require hours in a crowded bus to visit a place of pilgrimage for half an hour followed by a shared meal. Cars caught in Bangkok traffic jams for hours are equipped to make getting there as pleasant as possible, with potties, coolers and games to distract occupants from the passage of linear progressive time and the waste of institutional time.

By stressing the Thai sensitivity to the quality of the present moment, the intersection of time and space, rather than institutional and organizational time, I appear to support a stereotypical version of a cultural relativism that calls for a multiplicity of times. I am not arguing that Thai live in different temporal universes, but that they are culturally equipped to attend to more aspects of time, and that these different representations of time add nuances to shared events. Differences among Thais and between individual Thais and individual Canadians are not attributable to different conceptions of time. Thai notions of correct time in qualitative terms co-exist with other measures of time intervals and measure the progress of universal perceptual time in comparable units to other industrialized nations. However, their cultural time-handling system (Gell 1992:85) is enriched by reference to Buddhist cosmological definitions of time and space.

Thai constructions of time and space come together and intersect as points to provide stability in an otherwise uncertain and unknowable world. These points, lines, or grids are guides to locating and recognizing appropriate temporal contexts, transient points dependent on relationships between people. Uses of space and time then are related to social practices. Time-handling systems cannot be shunted off to apply only to the domain of ritual and cosmology, but rather colour the quality of social interaction and the interpretation of gender through the application of concepts such as *kalatesa*.

Other Feminisms

This book ends with no grand narrative, no total scheme that accounts for gender relations or women's status in Thailand or elsewhere in Southeast Asia. Rather it is a reminder that there are many stories to tell. As in the Buddhist texts, they take us in many different directions. The greatest error is in reading part of the story, usually the part shaped by Eurocentric gender concerns as the real story, or the only story. Neither prostitution nor beauty contests reveal the truth about Thai gender. Each piece reveals and fails to reveal part of the shifting gender landscape in Thailand. The relevance of gender remains open and undecided. Nevertheless, Thailand has something important to say about gender in Southeast Asia and gender theory.

Analyses of Thai gender system are situated directly in some of the most important arguments in international feminism and feminist anthropology concerning the sexual division of labour, elite versus peripheral representations of women, embodiment, sexual double standards, gender and sexual categories, colonialism and gendered representations, the commodification of women, and the dangers of politically correct feminism. Further, Thai gender research demonstrates how local and international issues for women (such as consumerism, violence against women, and sex tourism) are linked through processes of globalization. Examination of the Thai gender system, Thai sexuality and the Thai women's movement can redirect and enrich Euro-American dominated models of gender and sexuality.

For example, if colonization has an impact on the way gender is represented, how was the Thai women's movement affected by the fact that Thailand was never directly colonized? First, in Thailand, there was no clearly defined single relation between the colonizer and the colonized, no single colonial agenda against which Thai nationalism struggled, in spite of the fact that Thailand's borders were colonially determined. Thai women were not constructed as objects of colonial benevolence in the same way as Hindu women were under British colonialism (cf. Grewal 1996:180). South Asian feminists remind us that the feminist transformational process did not start in the West, nor did Asian women wait for the development of Western feminism to struggle against their oppression (Bhasir and Khan 1986).

The Thai women's movement did not emerge from nationalist struggles. Women as citizens and icons were appropriated not for the struggle against colonizers but for the struggle to construct Thai national identity, as Prime Minister Phibun's initiatives in the 1940s emphasize. This frees Thai feminist groups to selectively borrow Western feminist discourses to resist male-biased nationalist discourses, or take up nationalist ones to resist Western feminist ones.

Western gender models brought in by royalty or elite women and men were often resisted (recall *mam kapi*, the smelly women who dressed in Western-style clothes, the old women who wore *chongkraben* under their sarongs). In fact, Western women and Western gender relations were not idealized, perhaps because they were not as well known as they were in countries experiencing direct colonial rule.

Euro-American feminism has been accused of being culturally imperialist, internally racist, and representing middle-class white experience only, neglecting considerations of race, class, and other differences (Anzaldua 1987, Moraga and Anzaldua eds., 1981). Feminism, grounded in difference, is now accused of masking difference. Academics working on gender issues in third world countries have also been accused of using the experience of the other to 'fill in the gaps' in the global feminist agenda (Lazreg 1988:82). Critics of Western feminists argue that the struggles of third-world women are appropriated by white women academics in a form of colonization (Mohanty 1991:53). The stinging words of Trinh Minh-ha ask, 'Have you read the grievances some of our sisters express on being among the few women chosen for a 'Special Third World Women's Issue' or on being the only Third World woman at readings, workshops, and meetings? It is as if everywhere we go, we become someone's private zoo' (1989:82).

Amadiume (1987:10) views the collection and publication of third-world women's stories by white women as the usurpation of people's struggle and anger, as the theft of words, as exploitation. But these words and experiences are equally easily appropriated by elite women in their own societies, by funders, by multinational corporations and governments, and they can do much more damage with them than well-intentioned academics in Asian studies or women's studies (cf. Lazreg 1988:81).

Are Western feminist anthropologists still reproducing racist or colonial discourses or appropriating the struggles of Asian women by trying to learn from their experiences in order to 'correct' their own Eurocentric understandings of feminism and broaden their understandings of the position and condition of women? In the past, perhaps. But, as Atkinson, whose work in Sulawesi was relevant for thinking about transgendering in Thailand, reminds us, the use feminists make of ethnography has been changing:

> In the sixties and seventies, ethnography had relevance to feminists as a source of examples to either confirm or disprove universal statements about women or as documentation of evolutionary or historical schemata. Increasingly, the relevance of ethnography has become to document the way certain national, international, multinational and transnational structures and processes impinge on the experience of people in different locations . . . (Atkinson 1996:188).

The attack on Euro-American feminism puts third-world feminists and academics in difficult positions. An African scholar expressed problems with the use of the term, feminist, saying that African women who call themselves feminists are '. . . stigmatized and called parrots of western women. They are considered to be simply regurgitating the ideas of Western feminists . . .'(Ogundipe-Leslie 1991, also Mikell 1997). Sri Lankan scholar, Kumari Jayawardena, counters that 'those who want to continue to keep the women of our countries in a position of subordination find it convenient to dismiss feminism as a foreign ideology' (1986:1). By blaming the West, elite women of the south absolve themselves of their responsibilities for the inequalities in their own societies. The accusation of cultural imperialism can easily be used against any form of women's protest in Asia and elsewhere. But 'the West' is less the source of inspiration for the Thai women's movement and more the source of transnational processes that exploit women and encourage state institutions that damage Thai gender complementarity.

Butler argues that the political assumption that there must be a universal basis for feminism, one which must be found in an identity assumed to exist cross-culturally, often accompanies the notion that the oppression of women has some singular form discernible in the universal or hegemonic structure of patriarchy or masculine domination (1990:3). The Thai case sheds light on questions about patriarchy and male dominance as part of a universal core of global feminism. Thai feminists seldom use patriarchy as a singular, totalizing concept, but rather articulate cultural notions of male prestige using indigenous concepts such as *barami* (perfections, in canonical Buddhism; power, in more colloquial usage), specific instances of male power, authority and control over women, while simultaneously acknowledging the existence of female and feminine power. The practices of Thai women's groups would not provide support for the argument that patriarchy is part of a universal core of feminist values valid in all societies.

In 1987, I struggled with trying to make sense out of concepts like 'the status of Thai women', arguing that the position and condition of women varied depending on what domain one considered – education, politics, religion – and how those domains are differentially valued. Within each domain, we could compare how males and females were ranked – as inferior, superior or equal (P. Van Esterik 1987:599). Looking back, I should have had more to say about regional, ethnic and class differences in ranking domains, and more about comparisons within domains. Ortner's work on *Gender Hegemonies* carries the argument further: 'Every society/culture has some axes of male prestige and some of female, some of gender equality, and some (sometimes many) axes of prestige that have nothing to do with gender at all' (Ortner 1990:45).

Bhasir and Khan suggest that some forms of women's oppression are broadly shared, and others are local (1986:6). Assumptions about universal feminist values are based on the idea of women as an already constituted and coherent group with identical interests, suffering under the same oppression (Mohanty 1991). 'Women elsewhere are, it seems, the image of ourselves undressed' (Rosaldo 1983:79). Travelling theorists – feminists included – may be a legacy of imperialism, but the travel is no longer one way.

The Thai women's movement has avoided both the extremes of universalizing women and of overstressing differences, albeit at the price of privileging central Thai and Bangkok women when representing Thai gender. Women's groups accomplish this balance by positioning feminism as political action requiring strategic alliances among women and men occupying very different positions in society. Thai feminists actively resist narrow self-interest at the expense of others, but stress the forms of relatedness individuals sustain with each other (cf. Ferguson 1984:199). While factionalism in the Thai women's movement is rampant, each faction's unwillingness to commit to a single ideology keeps potential for cooperation open. The movement also provides an interesting example of how groups that insist on avoiding confrontation can collaborate with groups that must confront. Neither feminist nor anti-feminist groups were institutionalized in Thailand, making it easier for groups with vastly different agendas to coexist, thus prefiguring the plural consciousness demonstrated in the Thai women's movement today. Plural consciousness reaffirms the need for a more relaxed feminism to accompany theoretically complex feminist work on gender performativity, representation, and positionality. Similarly, African feminism is concerned with bread, butter and power issues, not essentialism, patriarchy or sexuality (Mikell 1997). Relaxed feminisms would provide space for the clarity necessary to act politically when necessary.

For me, the benefits of trying to communicate across differences outweigh the dangers: 'By presenting informants' stories, we help marginal groups intervene in global narratives by putting into circulation alternative circuits of discursive power' (Ong 1995:354). Ong acknowledges that feminist research on Asian women has distanced 'us' feminists from the Asian other, the oppressed women, an opposition which reinforces the cultural superiority of Western feminists (1988:85). 'We begin a dialogue when we recognize other forms of gender-and culture-based subjectivities, and accept that others often choose to conduct their lives separate from our particular vision of the future' (Ong 1988:90). Her position does not privilege the insider, although others have read her work in that way. Behar, commenting on Ong's work, questions the notion of 'privileged nativism', arguing that 'being positioned as some kind of insider to the culture does not predispose one to producing a politically correct ethnography of the Other' (1995:22).[2]

In 1975, Ardener proposed that women were a muted group, unable to articulate notions of self outside the idiom of the dominant male discourse. Over the last decade, feminists have effectively sought to insure that women's voices could be heard, and have included both their own voices as researchers with biases along with the voices of the subjects of their research. Now, under postmodernist attack, their authority for this 'giving voice' is being questioned, along with the right of anthropologists and researchers to represent the 'other'. Feminists' efforts to present life histories and other local texts have confirmed the multiplicity and multivocality of these voices; the self-reflexivity of the women's movement and postmodernist anthropology have appeared to coincide. But, as Hartsock (1987) has pointed out, just as women have begun to speak, postmodernists have argued that there is no dominant voice, no true text, no authority. 'Postmodern is a man in woman's clothing' (Lutz 1995:257).

Behar and Gordon have noted the inadequacies of endless 'dichotomies between Subject and Object, Self and Other, the West and the Rest' (1995:7), and called for the recognition of sameness in the other, always the self in the other, in a feminist discourse that does not oppose self-other in dyadic confrontation. The key concept in this non-oppositional, non-dualistic imagined reality is the practice of joint action and caretaking – a coherent form of co-operative activity acknowledging our relatedness to others. This the Thai women's movement exemplifies, *par excellance*. The core of Thai feminist practice is the mutual realization of people. This concept emerges from feminist practice because it stresses the creativity and responsibility of nurturing. Nurturing here refers not to a personality trait attributed to women or a romanticized metaphor for mothering. The Thai verb, *liang*, to nurture or support with food is an excellent example of nurturing practice. I acknowledge that this is a conceptual tool I find useful, but one that annoys Thai feminists who read back into my words the tourist discourses that entice men to experience the pleasure awaiting them at the hands of nurturing Thai women. The appropriation and commodification of *liang* – this capacity to relate to others in a supportive way – I find even more reprehensible than my essentializing or romanticizing *liang* (cf P. Van Esterik 1996).

The Thai sex-gender system provides a space for a non-dualistic view of reality, whether or not the male-female binary is disrupted. Opposition of masculine and feminine principles intended to show complementarity, inevitably lead to hierarchical ordering of people as superiors, inferiors, or equals. Third gender, bisexuality and androgynous symbols coexist in Thailand in the midst of hierarchy and exploitative and sexist institutions. Thai palimpsests of feminine power are hard to erase.

The Last Turtle

Would I have been another kind of anthropologist if I had gone to Tunisia instead of Thailand? If people who are the subject of anthropological enquiry end up resembling the anthropologists who study them (Moore 1994:130), perhaps the anthropologists also come to resemble the people they study. Is it locality or luck, theories or talent that shapes the life work of anthropologists? Fabian writes:

Dilemmas appear when we consider the consequences of our work –
before and after. Precisely because critical anthropology demands that
the research process be open, dialectical-interactive, historically-situated
and therefore contingent, there is no way of knowing in advance what
kind of consequences – changes in ourselves and in the people we study
– our projects will bring about. (1991:247)

Looking back over Thai lessons learned amidst Bangkok traffic,
academic and state mismanagement of money, sex tourism, devout
prostitutes, shopping malls, classical poetry, fortune tellers, and historic
sites, I could not have predicted how Thai experiences would shape
my personal[3] and anthropological life. How do my lessons reflect back
on anthropology at the end of the millennium?

First, a strong commitment to ethnographic endeavours as a valid
way of knowing about the human condition. A privileged position,
perhaps, and certainly only one of many ways of knowing about others,
but one that should be valued and transformed, not ridiculed and
abandoned in some postmodernist angst about truth. Life is too short
not to be accepting of partial truths. Atkinson acknowledges that
anthropologists will seek to characterize the experience of 'others', but
concludes, as I do, that the ethnographic enterprise is valuable.

Flawed and politically suspect as ethnography in far-off places may be,
it does provide a needed counterpoint to conversations generated 'at
the center' . . . Much better, I think, to have critiques that are informed
by first-hand knowledge and experience rather than distanced and
jaundiced skepticism by those who regard research beyond their own
social milieu as a wrong-headed enterprise. (1996:195).

In the same breath, ethnography carries the heart of anthropology
in a specifiable relation to the rest of the discipline, and the refiguring
of subfields that will emerge as needed if the discipline is to thrive.
Sanskrit etymologies, ancient pots, AIDS-related syndromes are all part
of the layers of context that enrich ethnographic interpretation in
Thailand and provide the often unacknowledged strength behind what
other disciplines and the general public find powerful and appealing
about anthropology. With the explosive expansion of knowledge in
anthropology's traditional subfields, it becomes more, not less, important
to know what linguists, archaeologists, physical anthropologists and
ethnographers seek to explain, even if it is impossible to know what
they each know. In-house interdisciplinarity, if you will. Trivialize this

diversity, and we become literary critics with passports.

Second, a commitment to the heuristic value of the concept of culture, or better, the cultural, which stresses context sensitive contrasts and situated differences, '. . . difference in relation to something local, embodied, and significant' (Appadurai 1996:12). Culture as a noun, reifies, while cultural as an adjective, differentiates; it was a constant struggle to resist reifying 'Thai culture'. It is easily objectified by outside analysts because it is so completely objectified by insiders and delivered, thinglike, prepackaged with shiny surfaces that attract for both theoretical and aesthetic reasons.

Third, I seek a new perspective on holism, configuration, pattern, style, even while knowing that pattern is beyond view – the underlying assumption that things are interrelated even when the relationships are not fully grasped. Not filling in the missing pieces of some mystical comprehensive ethnography, but allowing for, accounting for their absences; not presenting a coherent pattern of the interconnectedness between Buddhism and feminism, beauty contests and historic theme parks, prostitution and marriage, *The King and I* and military control, but assuming that connections exist, and that the inevitable gaps are signposts towards future research. At some level, monks, marriage and malls are all part of the same system of differences that allow us to recognize the boundaries of what is Thai. Contradictions, loose ends and counterdiscourses are only recognized when set against pattern, and anthropologists will not see pattern as long as they continue to view symbolic analysis as irrelevant to material analysis (cf. Herzfeld 1997:23).

Lastly, the search for pattern reconnects us with history and comparison, the connections that Thai studies has not always made. Anthropology swings back and forth between emphasis on differences (pre-disciplinary travellers' tales), to emphasis on similarities (universals of culture), and back to differences (in the guise of localities, specificities, and subaltern voices). New concerns about human rights and globalization are pulling us back to universal questions about the human condition. The need for frameworks that allow us to explore tensions between particularities and uniqueness, local and global, similarities and differences within and between societies has never been greater. If the global is only experienced in the local, then multi-sited ethnographies need to be combined with new methodologies for linking global and local.

O'Connor calls for regional comparisons between mainland and island Southeast Asia, historical perspective and deductive logic to produce testable models, not in the sense of more fieldwork-driven empiricism but to raise new questions that will organize knowledge about Thailand differently. 'An anthropology that abandons regional questions has nothing better to say or, worse, reifies culture as national purists do' (O'Connor 1995b:987). If presentism is the way Thais draw history into their lives, then it is presentism anthropologists must study. By searching for pattern in time and space – in Bateson's terms, the pattern that connects – anthropologists and other observers of the human condition oversimplify and reify, frustrated by their inability to communicate about the whole, about pattern. But if anthropologists reject the possibility of holism and pattern as a valid framework for interpretation (cf. Harries-Jones 1995:197), they lose the potential for leading the social sciences out of a spiral of nihilistic and reductionary thinking, and relegate the discipline to a reflexivity devoid of praxis, leaving us with one less way to understand the human condition.

Notes

1. I am grateful to Richard O'Connor who provided me with the full name of Bangkok: *Krungthep mahanakorn amorn ratthanakosin mahinthara ayutthaya mahadilok phopphanaphrat ratchathani burirom udomratchaniwet mahasathan amornphiman awattornsatit sakka phathorn wisanu kammarasit.*

2. I recall the confusion and anger colleagues and I felt on hearing a Thai student lecturing Canadians interested in Southeast Asia about being racist for delivering research papers on Southeast Asia when they were not themselves Southeast Asian nationals. White guilt combined with Canadian politeness tolerated this opportunistic confusion of ethnicity, nationality, knowledge, and political correctness. Tongchai Winichakul (1994) has also warned against this danger of assuming you have to be a Thai in order to understand Thailand, an issue that Thai studies is beginning to come to grips with.

3. Personal lessons are harder to identify I measure my differences against a Thai standard that I constructed to make sense out of that locality. Thais taught me that each day, the slate is clean, and that people behave according to how you treat them. Assumptions that others are your enemies or your friends are impediments to enjoying new experiences in new contexts. Finally, I learned to let go. The inability to let go of texts, while acknowledging errors, incomplete arguments, paths not taken, yellow stickers on citations of citations means never publishing a book.

Bibliography

Alexander, D. (1984), 'Immediate Antiques as Good as Gold are a Thai Specialty', *Smithsonian* 15(1):100–8.

Amadiume, I. (1987), *Male Daughters, Female Husbands: Gender and Sex in African Society*, London: Zed.

Andaya, B. (1998), 'From Temporary Wife to Prostitute: Sexuality and Economic Change in Early Modern Southeast Asia', *Journal of Women's History*, 9(4):11–34.

Anderson, B. (1977), 'Withdrawal Symptoms: Social and Cultural Aspects of the Ocotober 6 Coup', *Bulletin of Concerned Asian Scholars*, 9(3): 3–30.

Anderson, B. (1978a), 'Studies of the Thai State: the State of Thai Studies', in E. Ayal (ed.), *The Study of Thailand: Analyses of Knowledge, Approaches, and Prospects in Anthropology, Art History, Economics, History, and Political Science*, Athens: Ohio University Centre for International Studies, Southeast Asia Program.

Anderson, B. (1978b), 'Cartoons and Monuments: The Evolution of Political Communication under the New Order', in K. Jackson and L. Pye (eds), *Political Power and Communication in Indonesia*, Berkeley: University of California Press.

Anderson, B. (1983), *Imagined Communities*, London: Verso.

Anderson, B. (1996), 'Bullshit! S/he Said!: The Happy, Modern, Sexy, Indonesian Married Woman as Transsexual', in L. Sears (ed.), *Fantasizing the Feminine*, Durham: Duke University Press.

Anderson, B. (1990), *Language and Power: Exploring Political Cultures in Indonesia*, Ithaca, N.Y.: Cornell University Press.

Anderson, B. and Mendiones, R. (eds). (1985), *In the Mirror*, Bangkok: Duang Kamol Books.

Anderson, J. (1990), 'AIDS in Thailand', *British Medical Journal*, 300:415–16.

Anzaldua, G. (1987), *Borderlands/La Frontera*, San Francisco: Spinsters/Aunt Lute.

Appadurai, A. (1986), 'Theory in Anthropology: Center and Periphery', *Comparative Studies in Society and History*, Vol. 28:356–61.

Appadurai, A. (1988a), 'Introduction: Place and Voice in Anthropological Theory', *Cultural Anthropology*, 3(1):16–20.

Appadurai, A. (1988b), 'Putting Hierarchy in Its Place', *Cultural Anthropology*, 3(1):36–49.

Appadurai, A. (1996), *Modernity at Large: Cultural Dimensions of Globalization*, Minneapolis: University of Minnesota Press.

Ardener, E. (1977), 'Belief and the Problem of Women', in S. Ardener (ed.), *Perceiving Women*, London: Dent and Sons.

Atkinson, J. (1990), 'How Gender Makes a Difference in Wana Society', in J. Atkinson and S. Errington (eds), *Power and Difference: Gender in Island Southeast Asia*, Stanford: Stanford University Press.

Atkinson, J. (1996), 'Quizzing the Sphinx: Reflections on Mortality in Central Sulawesi', in L. Sears (ed.), *Fantasizing the Feminine in Indonesia*, Durham: Duke University Press.

Barmé, S. (1993), *Luang Wichit Wathakan and the Creation of a Thai Identity*, Singapore: Institute of Southeast Asian Studies.

Barmé, S. (1995), 'Talking Women: Early Twentieth Century Discourses on Women in Siam', Paper presented at the conference on Gender and Sexuality in Modern Thailand, Australian National University.

Barthel, D. (1988), *Putting on Appearances: Gender and Advertising*, Philadelphia, Penn.: Temple University Press.

Bartholomeusz, T. (1992), 'The Female Mendicant in Buddhist Sri Lanka', in J. Cabezon (ed.), *Buddhism, Sexuality, and Gender*, Albany: State University of New York Press.

Basham, R. (1989), 'False Consciousness and the Problem of Merit and Power in Thailand', *Mankind*, 19(2):126–37.

Batson, B. (1980), 'Siam and Japan: the Perils of Independence', in A. McCoy (ed.), *Southeast Asia under Japanese Occupation*, Yale Southeast Asian Studies, Monograph 22.

Behar, R. and Gordon, D. (ed.)(1995), *Women Writing Culture*, Berkeley: University of California Press.

Benedict, R. (1952), 'Thai Culture and Behavior', an unpublished wartime study dated September 1943, Data paper 4, Southeast Asia Program, Cornell University.

Beyrer, C. (1998), *War in the Blood: Sex, Politics and AIDS in Southeast Asia*, Zed Books: London.

Bhabha, H. (1994), *The Location of Culture*, London: Routledge.

Bhasin, K. and Khau, N. (1986), *Some Questions on Feminism and its Relevance in South Asia*, New Delhi: Indraprastha Press.

Bickner, R.J. (1991), *An Introduction to the Thai Poem 'Lilit Phra Law* (The Story of King Law), Special Report No. 25, Northern Illinois University, Center for Southeast Asian Studies.

Bloom, A. (1996), 'A Perspective on Buddhism and Women', in *Yasodhara: Newsletter on International Buddhist Women's Activities*, Vol. 14, 1(53): 5–8.

Boonchalaksi, W. and Guest, P. (1994), *Prostitution in Thailand*, Institute for Population Studies, Mahidol University, Bangkok.

Boone, S. (1986), *Radiance From the Waters: Ideals of Feminine Beauty in Mende Art*, New Haven, Conn.: Yale University Press.

Boonsue, K. (1989), *Buddhism and Gender Bias: An Analysis of a Jataka Tale*, Thai Studies Project, Working Paper Series, No.3, York University, Toronto.

Boonsue, K. (1992), *Women's Development Models and Gender Analysis: A Review*, 'Gender Studies' Occasional Paper No. 2, Bangkok: Asian Institute of Technology.

Boonsue, K. (1998), 'Gender Planning for Thailand's Industrial Labour Force', Unpublished PhD dissertation, Asian Institute of Technology.

Boserup, E. (1970), *Women's Role in Economic Development*, New York: St. Martin's Press.

Bowen, J. (1995), 'The Forms Culture Takes: A State of the Field: Essay on the Anthropology of Southeast Asia', *Journal of Asian Studies*, 54(4):1047–78.

Bowie, K. (1992), 'Unraveling the Myth of the Subsistence Economy: Textile Production in Nineteenth-Century Northern Thailand', *The Journal of Asian Studies*, 51(4):797–823.

Bowie, K. (1993), 'Assessing the Early Observers: Cloth and the Fabric of Society in 19th-century Northern Thai Kingdoms', *American Ethnologist*, 20(1):138–58.

Bowie, K. (1997), *Rituals of National Loyalty: An Anthropology of the State and Village Scout Movement in Thailand*, New York: Columbia University Press.

Bowie, K. (1998), 'The Alchemy of Charity: Of Class and Buddhism in Northern Thailand', *American Anthropologist*, 100:469–81.

Bowring, J. (1857), *The Kingdom and People of Siam*, London: John W. Parker and Son.

Bradley, W. (1981), *Siam Then: The Foreign Colony in Bangkok Before and After Anna*, Pasadena, Ca.: William Carey Library.

Brailey, N. (ed.) (1989), *Two Views of Siam on the Eve of the Chakri Reformation*, Whiting Bay, Arran, Scotland: Kiscadale Publications.

Brenner, S. (1995), 'Why Women Rule the Roost: Rethinking Javanese

Ideologies of Gender and Self-Control', in A. Ong and M. Peletz (eds), *Bewitching Women and Pious Men*, Berkeley: University of California Press.

Briggs, C. (1993), 'Metadiscursive Practices and Scholarly Authority in Folkloristics', *Journal of American Folklore*, 106(422):387–434.

Briggs, L.P. (1951), *The Ancient Khmer Empire*, Philadelphia: The American Philosophical Society, (Volume 41, Part A).

Bristowe, W. (1976), *Louis and the King of Siam*, London: Chatto and Windus.

Brown, T. and W. Sittitrai (1996), 'The Impact of HIV on Children in Thailand', Program on AIDS, Thai Red Cross, Bangkok.

Buehrer, J. (1995), 'Sukhothai: Thailand's Camelot', *Thailand Traveller*, 5(38):32–7.

Butler, J. (1990), *Gender Trouble*, New York: Routledge.

Cabezon, J. (1992), *Buddhism, Sexuality and Gender*, Albany: State University of New York.

Callahan, W. (1994), 'Astrology, Video, and the Democratic Spirit: Reading the Symbolic Politics of Thailand', *Sojourn* 9(1):102–34.

Callahan, W. (1998a), 'The Ideology of Miss Thailand in National Consumerist and Transnational Space', *Alternatives*, 23(1):29–61.

Callahan, W. (1998b), *Imagining Democracy*, Singapore: Institute of Southeast Asian Studies.

Cannell, F. (1991), 'Catholicism, Spirit Mediums, and the Ideal of Beauty in a Bicolano Community', Philippines. PhD dissertation, University of London.

Caplan, P. (1989), 'The Cross-cultural Validity of Feminism: A Case Study from Tanzania' *Garcia de Orta, Sér. Antropobiol*, Lisboa, 6(1–2):49–58.

Caplan, P. (1987), 'Sex, Sexuality, and Gender', *The Cultural Construction of Sexuality*, P. Caplan (ed.), London: Tavistock.

Carrithers M., Collins S. and Lukes S. (1985), *The Category of the Person*, New York: Cambridge University Press.

Chaloemtiarana, T. (1979), *Thailand: The Politics of a Despotic Paternalism*, Bangkok: Social Science Association of Thailand/Thai Khadi Institute, Thammasat University, Bangkok.

Chamberlain, J. (ed.) (1991), *The Ram Khamhaeng Controversy: Collected Papers*, Bangkok: The Siam Society.

Chetamee, M. (1995), 'Concepts of the Family and Lesbian Lifestyles', Paper presented at the Conference on Gender and Sexuality in Modern Thailand, Canberra, Australia.

Clarac, A. and Smithies, M. (1972), *Discovering Thailand*, Bangkok: Siam Communications.

Classen C. (1993), *World of Sense*, London: Routledge.

Classen, C., Howes D. and Synnott A. (1994), *Aroma*, London: Routledge.

Coedès, G. (1964), *The Indianized States of Southeast Asia*, Honolulu: East-West Center Press.

Cohen, E. (1986), 'Lovelorn Farangs: The Correspondence Between Foreign Men and Thai Girls', *Anthropological Quarterly*, 59(3):115–27.

Cohen, E. (1987), 'Sensuality and Venality in Bangkok: The Dynamics of Cross-Cultural Mapping of Prostitution', *Deviant Behavior*, 8:223–34.

Cohen, E. (1993), 'Open-ended Prostitution as a Skilful Game of Luck', in M. Hitchcock, V. King and M. Parnwell (eds), *Tourism in South-East Asia*, London: Routledge.

Cohen, E. (1996), 'From Buddha Images to Mickey Mouse Figurines: The Transformation of Banthawai Carvings', in *Traditions and Changes at Local/Regional Levels, Vol. 1*. Proceedings of the Sixth International Conference on Thai Studies, Chiang Mai, Thailand.

Collins, S. (1982), *Selfless Persons*, Cambridge: Cambridge University Press.

Compton, C. (1992), 'Lao Poetics: Internal Rhyme in the Text of a Lao Sithandone Performance', in C. Compton and J. Hartmann (eds), *Papers on Tai Languages, Linguistics and Literatures*, Northern Illinois University Center for Southeast Asian Studies, Paper No. 16, Dekalb, Illinois.

Conboy, K., Madina N. and Stanbury S. (eds) (1997), *Writing on the Body: Female Embodiment and Feminist Theory*, New York: Columbia University Press.

Cook, N. (1991), 'Thai Identity in the Astrological Tradition', in C. Reynolds (ed.), *National Identity and its Defenders*, Monash Papers on Southeast Asia, No. 25. Monash University, Clayton, Australia.

Coombe, R.J. (1992), 'Author/izing the Celebrity: Publicity Rights, Postmodern Politics, and Unauthorized Genders', *Cardozo Arts and Entertainment Law Journal*, 10(2):365–95.

Copeland, M.P. (1993), 'Contested Nationalism and the 1932 Overthrow of the Absolute Monarchy in Siam', Ph.D. dissertation. Australian National University.

Cortes, R. (1984), 'Thai Society and Culture in the Ayudhaya Period as Seen Through the Eyes of a European', in *Customs and Traditions: The Role of Thai Women*, International Conference on Thai Studies, Bangkok.

Da Grossa, P. (1989), 'Kamphaeng Din: A Study of Prostitution in the All Thai Brothels of Chiang Mai City', *Crossroads* 4(2):1–7.

Dawson, A. (1988), *Patpong: Bangkok's Big Little Street*, Bangkok: Thai Watana Panich Press.

De la Loubere, S. (1969), *The Kingdom of Siam*, New York: Oxford UP (1697).

Donaldson, L. (1992), *Decolonizing Feminisms: Race, Gender, and Empire-Building*, Chapel Hill: The University of North Carolina Press.

DuBois, E. and Gordon L. (1984) 'Seeking Ecstasy on the Battlefield: Danger and Pleasure in Nineteenth-century Feminist Sexual Thought', in C. Vance (ed.), *Pleasure and Danger: Exploring Female Sexuality*, Boston: Routledge and Kegan Paul.

Early, G. (1984) 'Life with Daughters: Watching the Miss Universe Pageant', *The Kenyon Review* 12(4):132–45.

Eberhardt, N. (ed.) (1988), *Gender, Power and the Construction of the Moral Order*, Monograph 4, Madison: University of Wisconsin, Center for Southeast Asian Studies.

Eisen, A. (1984), *Women and Revolution in Vietnam,* London: Zed Books.

Elias, N. (1978), *The History of Manners*, New York: Pantheon Books.

Embree, J. (1950), 'Thailand – A Loosely Structured Social System', *American Anthropologist* 52:181–93.

Engel, F. (1972), *The Origins of the Family, Private Property and the State*, New York: International Publishers (1884).

Errington, S. (1990), 'Recasting Sex, Gender, and Power: A Theoretical and Regional Overview', in J. Atkinson and S. Errington (eds), *Power and Difference: Gender in Island Southeast Asia*, Stanford, CA: Stanford University Press.

Errington, S. (1997), 'The Cosmic Theme Park of the Javanese', *Review of Indonesian and Malaysian Affairs*, 31(1):7–35.

Everingham, J. (1984), 'A Thai Specialty: Making Instant Antiques', *Smithsonian*, 15(1):100–8.

Evers, H.-D. (ed.) (1969), 'Loosely Structured Social Systems: Thailand in Comparative Perspective', *Cultural Report Series No. 17*, New Haven, Conn.: Yale University Southeast Asia Studies.

Fabian, J. (1991), *Time and the Work of Anthropology*, Switzerland: Harwood Academic Publishers.

Fausto-Sterling, A. (1993), 'The Five Sexes: Why Male and Female Are Not Enough', *The Sciences*, March/April 1993:20–5.

Featherstone, M. (1991), *Consumer Culture and Postmodernism*, London: Sage Publications.

Ferguson, K. (1984), *The Feminist Case against Bureaucracy*, Philadelphia:

Temple University Press.

Finklestein, J. (1991), *The Fashioned Self*, Philadelphia: Temple University Press.

Fitzgerald, K. (1992), 'Buddhism needs Feminism', *Sakyadhita*, 3(2): 5–8.

Florida, N. (1996), 'Sex Wars: Writing Gender Relations in Nineteenth Century Java', in L. Sears (ed.), *Fantasizing the Feminine in Indonesia*, Durham: Duke University Press.

Ford, N. and Kaetsawang, S.(1991), 'The Socio-Cultural Context of the Transmission of HIV in Thailand', *Social Science and Medicine*, 33(4): 405–14.

Ford, S. and Saiprasert, S. (1993), 'Destinations Unknown: The Gender Construction and Changing Nature of the Sexual Lifestyle of Thai Youth', Paper presented at the Fifth International Conference on Thai Studies, SOAS, London.

Foucault, M. (1980), *The History of Sexuality*, Volume I: *An Introduction*, New York: Vintage Books.

Foucault, M. (1986), *The History of Sexuality*, Volume 2: *The Use of Pleasure*. New York: Vintage Books.

Futrakul, P. (1989), 'The Environmental History of Pre-Modern Provincial Towns in Siam', Unpublished Ph.D. dissertation, Cornell University, N.Y.

Garber, M. (1992), *Vested Interests*, New York: Routledge.

Gardiner, H. and O. Gardiner (1991), 'Women in Thailand', in L. Alder (ed.), *Women in Cross-Cultural Perspective*, New York: Praeger.

Geertz, C. (1960), *The Religion of Java*, Glencoe, Ill.: Free Press.

Geertz, C. (1966), *Person, Time and Conduct in Bali: An Essay in Cultural Analysis*, New Haven: Southeast Asia Studies, Yale University.

Geertz, C. (1973), *The Interpretation of Cultures*, New York: Basic Books.

Geertz, C. (1995), *After the Fact: Two Countries, Four Decades, one Anthropologist*, Cambridge: Harvard University Press.

Geertz, H. (1961), *The Javanese Family: A Study of Kinship and Socialization*, Glencoe, Ill.: Free Press.

Gell, A. (1992), *The Anthropology of Time*, Oxford: Berg.

Gervaise, N. (1989) (1688), *The Natural and Political History of the Kingdom of Siam*, Bangkok: White Lotus.

Gould, P. (1993), *The Slow Plague*, Cambridge, MA.: Blackwell Publishers.

Grewal, I. (1996), *Home and Harem: Nation, Gender, Empire, and the Cultures of Travel*, Durham: Duke University Press.

Gross, G. (1986), 'Buddhism and Feminism: Toward Their Mutual Transformation', *Eastern Buddhist*, 19(1):44–58.

Gross, R. (1993), *Buddhism after Patriarchy*, Albany: State University of New York Press.

Grossman, R. (1979), 'Women's Place in the Integrated Circuit', *Southeast Asian Chronicle*, No. 66.

Grosz E. (1998), 'The Intervention of Feminist Knowledges', in B. Caine, E. Grosz and N. de Lepervanche (eds), *Crossing Boundaries: Feminisms and the Critique of Knowledges*, Sidney: Allen and Unwin.

Grosz, E. and Probyn, E. (eds) (1995), *Sexy Bodies: The Strange Carnalities of Feminism*, London: Routledge.

Grow, M.L. (1996), 'Tarnishing the Golden Era: Aesthetics, Humor, and Politics in *Lakhon Chatri* Dance-Drama', in P. Durrenberger (ed.), *State Power and Culture in Thailand*, New Haven: Yale University Southeast Asia Studies.

Hall, C. Michael (1994), 'Gender and Economic Interests in Tourism Prostitution: The Nature, Development and Implications of Sex Tourism in South-east Asia', in V. Kinnaird and D. Hall (eds), *Tourism: A Gender Analysis*, 143–63, Chichester: John Wiley & Sons.

Hamilton, A. (1991), 'Rumours, Foul Calummies and the Safety of the State: Mass Media and National Identity in Thailand', in C. Reynolds (ed.), *National Identity and Its Defenders*, Monash Papers on Southeast Asia, No. 25, Monash University.

Hamilton, A. (1993), 'Video Crackdown, or The Sacrificial Pirate: Censorship and Cultural Consequences in Thailand', *Public Culture*, 5(3): 515–31.

Hamilton, A. (1997), 'Primal Dream: Masculinism, Sin and Salvation in Thailand's Sex Trade', in L. Manderson and M. Jolly (eds), *Sites of Desire-Economies of Pleasure: Sexualities in Asia and the Pacific*, Chicago: The University of Chicago Press.

Hanks, J. (1964), 'Reflections on the Ontology of Rice', in S. Diamond (ed.), *Primitive Views of the World*, New York: Columbia University Press.

Hanks, J. (1965), 'A Rural Thai Village's View of Human Character', in *Felicitation Volumes of Southeast Asian Studies*, Volume 1, Bangkok: The Siam Society.

Hanks, L. and Hanks J. (1963), 'Thailand: Equality between the Sexes', in B. Ward (ed.), *Women in the New Asia*, Paris: UNESCO.

Hanks, L. (1972), *Rice and Man*, Chicago: Aldine.

Hantrakul, S. (1988), 'Prostitution in Thailand', in G. Chandler, N. Sullivan and J. Branson (eds), *Development and Displacement: Women in Southeast Asia*, Monash Papers on Southeast Asia No. 18 Clayton, Australia: Centre of Southeast Asian Studies, Monash University.

Haraway, D. (1991), *Simians, Cyborgs and Women: The Reinvention of Nature*, New York: Routledge.

Harries-Jones, P. (1995), *A Recursive Vision: Ecological Understanding and Gregory Bateson*, Toronto: University of Toronto Press.

Harrison, R. (1994), Introduction. in *A Drop of Glass, and Other Stories*, Sidaoru'ang. Tr. R. Harrison. Bangkok: Editions Duang Kamol.

Harrison, R. (1996) 'The 'Good', the 'Bad' and the Pregnant: Why the Thai Prostitute as Literary Heroine Can't be Seen to Give Birth', Proceedings of the Sixth International Conference on Thai Studies, Chiang Mai, Thailand.

Hartsock, N. (1987), 'Rethinking Modernism', *Cultural Critique*, 7:187–206.

Heine-Geldern, R. (1956), Conceptions of State and Kingship in Southeast Asia, Data Paper No. 18, Southeast Asia Program, Cornell University, Ithaca, N.Y.

Hennessy, R. (1993), *Materialist Feminism and the Politics of Discourse*, New York: Routledge.

Herdt, G. (ed.) (1994), *Third Sex: Third Gender: Beyond Sexual Dimorphism in Culture and History*, New York: Zone.

Herzfeld, M. (1997), *Cultural Intimacy and the Nation State*, New York: Routledge.

Hewison, K. (1987), 'National Interests and Economic Downturn: Thailand', in R. Robison, K. Hewison and R. Higgott (eds), *Southeast Asia in the 1980's: The Politics of Economic Crisis*, Sydney: Allen and Unwin.

Hewison, K. (1989), 'Bankers and Bureaucrats: Capital and the Role of the State in Thailand', *Yale University Southeast Asian Studies Monograph Series, No.34*, New Haven, Conneticut: Yale Center for International and Area Studies.

Hewison, K. (1992), 'Thailand: On Becoming a NIC', *The Pacific Review*, 5(4):328–37.

Hewison, K. and Thongyou M. (1993), 'The New Generation of Provincial Business People in Northeastern Thailand', Working Paper No. 16, Asia Research Centre, Murdoch University.

Hochschild, A. (1983), *The Managed Heart: Commercialization of Human Feeling*, Berkeley: University of California Press.

Hollinger, C. (1977), *Mai Pen Rai Means Never Mind*, Tokyo: John Weatherhill, Inc.

Holmes, K. (1993), 'The Changing Epidemiology of HIV Transmission', in L. Corey, (ed.), *AIDS: Problems and Prospects*, New York: WW Norton and Company. (p. 31–49)

Hong, E. (1985), *See the Thirld World While it Lasts*, Penang, Malaysia: Consumers Association of Penang.

Hong L. (1998), 'Of Consorts and Harlots in Thai Popular History', *Journal of Asian Studies*, 57(2):333–53.

hooks, b. (1984), *Feminist Theory from Margin to Center*, Boston: South End Press.

Hughes-Freeland, F. (1995), 'Performance and Gender in Javanese Palace Tradition', in W.J. Karim (ed.), *'Male' and 'Female' in Developing Southeast Asia*, Oxford: Berg.

Hutheesing, O.K. (1990), *Emerging Sexual Inequality Among the Lisu of Northern Thailand: The Waning of Dog and Elephant Repute*, Leiden: E.J. Brill.

Ireson, C. (1996), *Field, Forest and Family: Women's Work in Rural Laos*, Boulder: Westview.

Irvine, W. (1982), 'The Thai-Yuan "Madman" and the Modernizing, Developing Thai Nation as Bounded Entities under Threat: A Study in the Replication of a Single Image', Ph.D. dissertation, University of London.

Jackson, L. (1980), 'Prostitution', in J. Lebra and J. Paulson (eds), *Chinese Women in Southeast Asia*, Singapore: Times Books International.

Jackson, P. (1988), 'The Hupphaasawan Movement: Millenarian Buddhism among the Thai Political Elite', *Sojourn*, 3(2):135–70.

Jackson, P. (1989), *Male Homosexuality in Thailand*, Elmhurst, NY.: Global Academic Publishers.

Jackson, P. (1997), '*Kathoey*><Gay><Man:The Historical Emergence of Gay Male Identity in Thailand', in L. Manderson and M. Jolly (eds), *Sites of Desire-Economies of Pleasure: Sexualities in Asia and the Pacific*, Chicago: The University of Chicago Press.

Jackson, P. (1993), 'From *Kamma* to Unnatural Vice, Thai Buddhist Accounts of Homosexuality and AIDS', Paper presented at fifth International Conference on Thai Studies, SOAS, London.

Jayawardena, K. (1986), *Feminism and Nationalism in the Third World*, London: Zed Press.

Jeffrey, L. (1999), 'Sex and Borders: Gender, National Identity and Prostitution Policy in Thailand', unpublished Ph.D., York University

Johnson, M. (1997), *Beauty and Power*, Oxford: Berg Publishers.

Josselin de Jong, P.E. de. (1965), 'An Interpretation of Agricultural Rites in Southeast Asia with a demonstration of use of data from both continental and insular areas', *Journal of Asian Studies*, 24(2):283–91.

Jumsai, M. (1973), *History of Thai Literature*, Bangkok: Chalermnit Press.

Kabilsingh, C. (1984), *A Comparative Study of Bhikkhuni Patimokkha*,

Varanasi: Chaukhambha.

Kabilsingh, C. (1988), 'Menstruation: Buddhist Perspective', Newsletter on International Buddhist Women's Activities, 15:10–14.

Kabilsingh, C. (1991), *Thai Women in Buddhism*, Berkeley: Parallax.

Kabilsingh, C. (1995), 'Helping the Daughters of the Buddha', Newsletter on International Buddhist Women's Activities, 11(3):3–5.

Kammerer, C., Hutheesing, O., Maneeprasert, P. and Symonds, P. (1995), 'Vulnerability to HIV Infection among Three Hilltribes in Northern Thailand', in Han ten Brummelhuis and G. Herdt (eds), *Culture and Sexual Risk: Anthropological Perspectives on AIDS*, Luxembourg: Gordon and Breach Publishers.

Kamphibol, N. (1987), 'Policies about Thai Women in the Period of National Construction of Marshal P. Phibulsongkram (1938–1944)', M.A. Thesis, Faculty of Liberal Arts, Thammasat University, Bangkok.

Kanato, M. (1990), Becoming Opportunites Commercial Sex Workers: An Anthropological-Epidemiological Study. M.Sc. Thesis, McMaster University, Hamilton.

Kanokpongchai, S. (1988), *Museum of Folk-Culture*, Bangkok: Muang Boran Publishing House.

Karim, W. (ed.) (1995), *'Male' and 'Female' in Developing Southeast Asia*, Oxford: Berg Publishers.

Karim, W. (ed.) (1995), 'Bilateralism and Gender in Southeast Asia', in W. Karim (ed.), *'Male' and 'Female' in Developing Southeast Asia*, Oxford: Berg Publishers.

Kasetsiri, C. (1976), *The Rise of Ayudhya: A History of Siam in the Fourteenth and Fifteenth Centuries*, Kuala Lumpur: Oxford University Press.

Keeler, W. (1987), *Javanese Shadow Plays; Javanese Selves*, Princeton: Princeton University Press.

Kepner, S.F. (ed.) (1996), *The Lioness in Bloom: Modern Thai Fiction About Women*, Berkeley, California: University of California Press.

Keyes, C. (1984), 'Mother or Mistress but Never a Monk: Buddhist Notions of Female Gender in Rural Thailand', *American Ethnologist*, 11(2):233–41.

Keyes, C. (1991a), 'The Proposed World of the School: Thai Villagers' Entry Into a Bureaucratic State System', in *Reshaping Local Worlds: Formal Education and Cultural Change in Rural Southeast Asia*, Monograph 36, Yale Southeast Asian Studies.

Keyes, C. (1991b), 'The Case of the Purloined Lintel: The Politics of a Khmer Shrine as a Thai National Treasure', in C. Reynolds (ed.), *National Identity and its Defenders*, Monash Papers on Southeast Asia, No. 25, Monash University, Clayton, Australia.

Khantipalo B. (1990), *The Garden of Dhamma, Radical Conservatism: Buddhism in the Contemporary World*, Bangkok: Thai Interreligious Commission for Development.

Khiang, M. (1984), *The World of Burmese Women*, London: Zed Books.

Kirsch, A.T. (1969), 'Loose Structure: Theory or Description?' in Hans-Dieter Evers (ed.), *Loosely Structured Social Systems: Thailand in Comparative Perspective*, Yale University: Cultural Report Series No. 17, Southeast Asia Studies.

Kirsch, A.T. (1982), 'Buddhism, Sex-roles and the Thai Economy', in P. Van Esterik (ed.), *Women of Southeast Asia*, Center for Southeast Asian Studies, Northern Illinois University: DeKalb, Illinois.

Kirsch, A.T. (1985), 'Text and Context: Buddhist Sex Roles/Culture of Gender Revisited', *American Ethnologist*, 12(2):302–20.

Kobkitsuksakul, S. (1987), Miss Thailand Contest: 1934–87. MA thesis, Thammasat University, Bangkok. (in Thai)

Koetsawang, S. and Auamkul, N. (1997), 'HIV and Women in Thailand: Severity and Services', *International Journal of Gynecology and Obstetrics*, 58:121–7.

Komin, S. (1989), *Social Dimensions of Industrialization in Thailand*, Bangkok: NIDA (National Institute of Development Administration), Bangkok.

Komin, S. (1990), *Psychology of the Thai People: Values and Behavioral Patterns*, Bangkok: NIDA (National Institute of Development Administration), Bangkok.

Koset, S. (1962), *The Study of Thai Customs,* Pranakhon: Radchaband-ittayasathan. (in Thai).

Kriengkraipetch, S. (1993), 'Characters in Thai literary Works: "Us" and "The Others"', Paper presented at the Fifth International Conference on Thai Studies, SOAS, London.

Lai, A. (1986), *Peasants, Proletarians, and Prostitutes*, Research Notes and Discussion Paper No. 59, Institute of Southeast Asian Studies, Singapore.

Landon, M. (1944), *Anna and the King of Siam*, New York: John Day and Co.

Laquer, T. (1990), *Making Sex: Body and Gender from the Greeks to Freud*, Cambridge: Harvard University Press.

Lazreg, M. (1988), 'Feminism and Difference: The Perils of Writing as a Woman on Women in Algeria', *Feminist Studies*, 14(1):81–107.

Leach, E. (1961), 'The Frontiers of Burma', *Comparative Studies in Society and History*, 3(1):49–68.

Leach, E. (1965), *Political Systems of Highland Burma*, Boston: Beacon Press.

Lefferts, L. (1992), 'Contexts and Meanings in Tai Textiles', in M. Gittenger and L. Lefferts (eds), *Textiles and the Tai Experience in Southeast Asia*, Washington DC: The Textile Museum.

Leonard, T. (1990), 'Male Clients of Female Street Prostitutes: Unseen Partners in Sexual Disease Transmission', *Medical Anthropology Quarterly*, 4(1):41–55.

Leonowens, A. (1870), *The English Governess at the Siamese Court*, Boston: Fields, Osgood & Co.

Leonowens, A. (1873), *Siamese Harem Life*, Boston: J.R. Osgood.

Lepowsky, M. (1993), *Fruit of the Motherland: Gender in an Egalitarian Society*, New York: Colombia University Press.

Lim, L. (1978), 'Women Workers in Multinational Corporations: The Case of the Electronics Industry in Malaysia and Singapore', Michigan Occasional Papers in Women's Studies, No.9.

Lind van Wijngaarden, J. (1999), 'Between Money, Morality and Masculinity: Bar-Based Male Sex Work in Chiang Mai', in *Lady Boys, Tom Boys, Rent Boys: Male and Female Homosexualities in Comtemporary Thailand*, P. Jackson and G. Sullivan (eds), New York: Haworth Press.

Ling, T. (ed.) (1993), *Buddhist Trends in Southeast Asia*, Singapore: Institute of Southeast Asian Studies.

Lutz, C. (1995), 'The Gender of Theory', in R. Behar and D. Gordon (eds), *Women Writing Culture*, Berkeley: University of California Press.

Lynch, J. (1978), 'Sunthon Phu's Advice to Women: an Annotated Translation', Honours Thesis, Faculty of Asian Studies, Australian National University.

Lyttleton, C. (1994a), 'Knowledge and Meaning: The AIDS Education Campaign in Rural Northeast Thailand', *Social Science and Medicine*, 38(1):135–46.

Lyttleton, C. (1994b), 'The Good People of Isan: Commercial Sex in Northeast Thailand', *The Australian Journal of Anthropology* 5(3):257–79.

Mabry, M. and B. Mabry (1986), 'The Role of the Arts in Developing Countries: Thailand, a Case Study', in W. Wendou (ed.), *Economic Policy for the Arts*. Cambridge, Mass.: ABT Books.

MacCormack, C. and Strathern M. (1980), *Nature, Culture and Gender*, Cambridge: Cambridge University Press.

Magli, P. (1989), 'The Face and the Soul', in M. Feher (ed.), *Fragments for a History of the Body*, Part 2, New York: Zone.

Mahidol University Institute for Population and Social Research (1992), *Changing Roles and Status of Women in Thailand: A Documentary Assessment*, Nakhonpathom, Thailand: Mahidol University Institute for Population and Social Research.

Manderson, L. (1992), 'Public Sex Performances in Patpong and Explorations of the Edges of Imagination', *The Journal of Sex Research* 29 (4) (November):451–75.

Manderson, L. (1997), 'Parables of Imperialism and Fantasies of the Exotic: Western Representations of Thailand–Place and Sex', in L. Manderson and M. Jolly (eds), *Sites of Desire-Economies of Pleasure: Sexualities in Asia and the Pacific,* Chicago: The University of Chicago Press.

Mann, J. (1992), 'AIDS–The Second Decade: A Global Perspective', *The Journal of Infectious Disease,* 165:245–50.

Mansbridge, J. (1993), 'The Role of Discourse in The Feminist Movement', Paper presented at the 1993 Annual Meeting of the American Political Science Association, Chicago.

Mascia-Lees, F. and Sharpe P. (eds) (1992), 'Introduction: Soft-Tissue Modification and the Horror Within', in F. Mascia-Lees and P. Sharpe (eds), *Tattoo, Torture, Mutilation and Adornment,* Albany: State University of New York Press.

Masdit, S. (1991), *Politics in Thailand with Special Reference to the Role of Women,* IPS Regional Speakers Lecture Series, No. 4, Singapore: The Institute of Policy Studies/Times Academic Press.

McKinley, R. (1979), 'Zaman dan Masa, Eras and Periods: Religious Evolution and the Permanence of Epistemological Ages in Malay Culture', in A. Becker and A. Yengoyan (eds), *The Imaginaton of Reality: Essays in Southeast Asian Coherence Systems,* Norwood, NJ: Ablex.

Meyer, W. (1988), *Beyond the Mask,* Saarbrucken: Verlag breitenbach Publishers.

Mies, M. (1986), *Patriarchy and Accumulation on a World Scale,* London: Zed Books.

Mikell, G. (ed.) (1997), *African Feminisms: The Politics of Survival,* Philadelphia: University of Pennsylvania Press.

Milgram, L. (1998), 'Craft Production and Household Practices in the Upland Philippines', in S. Ilcan and L. Phillips (eds), *Transgressing Borders: Critical Perspectives on Gender, Household, and Culture,* Westport CT: Bergin and Garvey.

Mills, M.B. (1990), 'Moving Between Modernity and Tradition: The Case of Rural-Urban Migration from Northeast Thailand to Bangkok', *American Studies,* 2:52–70.

Mills, M.B. (1991), 'Modernity and Gender Vulnerability: Rural Women Working in Bangkok', in P. and J. Van Esterik (eds), *Gender and Development in Southeast Asia,* 83–92, Montreal: Canadian Asian Studies Association.

Mills, M. (1995), 'Attack of the Widow Ghosts: Gender, Death, and Modernity in Northeast Thailand', in A. Ong and M. Peletz (eds), *Bewitching Women, Pious Men: Gender and Body Politics in Southeast Asia*, Berkeley: University of California Press.

Mills, M. (1997), 'Contesting the Margins of Modernity: Women, Migration, and Consumption in Thailand', *American Ethnologist*, 24 (1):37–61.

Mills, M. (1999), *Thai Women in the Global Labor Force*, New Brunswick: Rutgers University Press.

Mitchell, T. (1988), *Colonizing Egypt*, Cambridge: Cambridge University Press.

Mohanty, C. (1991), 'Under Western Eyes: Feminist Scholarship and Colonial Discourses', in C. Mohanty, A. Russo and L. Torres (eds), *Third World Women and the Politics of Feminism*, Bloomington: Indiana University Press.

Moore, C.G. (1992), *Heart Talk*, Bangkok: White Lotus.

Moore, H. (1994), *A Passion for Difference: Essays in Anthropology and Gender*, Bloomington: Indiana University Press.

Moraga, C. and Anzaldua G. (eds) (1981), *This Bridge Called my Back: Writings by Radical Women of Color*, New York:Kitchen Table/Women of Color Press.

Morris, R. (1994a), 'Consuming the Margins: Northern Thai Spirit Mediumship and the Theatrics of Consumption in the Age of Late Capitalism', Unpublished Ph.D. dissertation, University of Chicago.

Morris, R. (1994b), 'Three Sexes and Four Sexualities: Redressing the Discourses on Gender and Sexuality in Contemporary Thailand', *Positions*, 2(1):15–43.

Morris, R. (1995), 'All Made Up: Performance Theory and the New Anthropology of Sex and Gender', *Annual Review of Anthropology*, 24:567–92.

Morris, R. (1997), 'A Ban on Gay Teachers: Education and Prohibition' in the 'Land of the Free', *Social Text*, 15(3/4):53–79.

Morris, R. (1998), 'Surviving Pleasure at the Periphery: Chiang Mai and the Photographs of Political Trauma in Thailand, 1976–1992', *Public Culture*, 10(2):341–70.

Morrison, L. and S. Guruge (1997), 'We Are a Part of that We Have Met: Women and AIDS', in D. Umeh (ed.), *Confronting the AIDS Epidemic: Cross-Cultural Perspectives on HIV/AIDS Education*, New Jersey: Africa World Press, Inc.

Moselina, L.M. (1979), 'Olongapos's Rest and Recration Industry: A Sociological Analysis of Institutionalized Prostitution – With Implications for a Grass-Roots Oriented Sociology', *Philippine Sociological Review*, 27(3):181–93.

Muang Boran (1980), *In The Ancient City*, Bangkok: Muang Boran Publishing House.

Muang Boran (1988), *Muang Boran: A Nostalgic Look*, Bangkok: Muang Boran Publishing House.

Muecke, M. (1992), 'Mother Sold Food, Daughter Sells Her Body: The Cultural Continuity of Prostitution', *Social Science and Medicine* 35(7): 891–901.

Mulder, N. (1978), *Everyday Life in Thailand: An Interpretation*, Bangkok: Editions Duang Kamol.

Mulder, N. (1983), *Java-Thailand: A Comparative Perspective*, Yogyakarta, Indonesia: Gadjah Mada University Press.

Mulder, N. (1992), *Inside Southeast Asia: Thai, Javanese and Filipino Interpretations of Everyday Life*, Bangkok: Editions Duang Kamol.

Mulder, N. (1997), *Thai Images: The Culture of the Public World*, Chiang Mai: Silkworm Books.

Murcott, S. (1991), *The First Buddhist Women: Translations and Commentary on the Therigatha*, Berkeley, CA.:Parallax Press.

Murray, S. (1994), 'Dragon Ladies, Draggin' Men: Some Reflections on Gender, Drag and Homosexual Communities', *Public Culture*, 6(2): 343–65.

Nagavajara, C. (1985), 'Literary Historiography and Socio-Cultural Transformation: the Case of Thailand', *Journal of the Siam Society*, 73(1&2):66–75.

Nagavajara, C. (1994a), 'Literature in Thai life: Reflections of a Native', *Journal of Southeast Asia Research*, 2(1):12–52.

Nagavajara, C. (1994b), 'Unsex me Here: An Oriental's Plea for Gender Reconciliation', in N. Masavisut, G. Simson and L. Smith (eds), *Gender and Culture in Literature and Film East and West: Issues of Perception and Interpretation*, Honolulu: East-West Center, University of Hawaii.

Nartsupha, C. (1991), 'The 'Community Culture' School of Thought', in M. Chitakasem and A. Turton (eds), *Thai Constructions of Knowledge*, London: School of Oriental and African Studies.

Norindr, P. (1996), *Phantasmatic Indochina*, Durham: Duke University Press.

Numnonda, T. (1977), 'When Thailand Followed the Leader', *Social Science Review*, 197–223.

Numnonda, T. (1978), 'Pibulsongram's Thai Nation-Building Programme during the Japanese Military Presence, 1941–1945', *Journal of Southeast Asian Studies*, 9(2):234–47.

Nyanatiloka. (1972), *Buddhist Dictionary*, Colombo: Frewin and Co.

O'Connor, R. (1989), 'From 'Fertility' to 'Order', Paternalism to Profits: The Thai City's Impact on the Culture-Environment Interface', *Culture and Environment in Thailand*, A Symposium of the Siam Society, Bangkok.

O'Connor, R. (1990), 'Place, Power and Discourse in the Thai Image of Bangkok', *Journal of Siam Society* 78(2):61–73.

O'Connor, R. (1991), 'Sukhothai: Rule, Religion and Elite Rivalry', in J. Chamberlain (ed.), *The Ram Khamhaeng Controversy*, Bangkok: Siam Society.

O'Connor, R. (1993), 'Interpreting Thai Religious Change: Temples, Sangha Reform and Social Change', *Journal of Southeast Asian Studies*, 24(2):330–9.

O'Connor, R. (1995a), 'Indigenous Urbanism: Class, City and Society in Southeast Asia', *Journal of Southeast Asian Studies*, 26(1):30–45.

O'Connor, R. (1995b), 'Agricultural Change and Ethnic Succession in Southeast Asian States: A Case for Regional Anthropology', *Journal of Asian Studies*, 54(4):698–996.

O'Connor, R. (1996), 'Rice, Rule and the Tai State', in P. Durrenberger (ed.), *State Power and Culture in Thailand*, New Haven: Yale University Southeast Asia Studies.

O'Connor, R. (1997), 'Review of *Siam Mapped* by Thongchai Winichakul', *Journal of Asian Studies*, 56(1):279–81.

O'Malley, J. (1988), 'Sex Tourism and Women's Status in Thailand', *Society and Leisure*, 11(1):99–114.

Odzer, C. (1994), *Patpong Sister: An American Woman's View of the Bangkok Sex World*, New York: Blue Moon Books.

Oetomo, D. (1996), 'Gender and Sexual Orientation in Indonesia', in L. Sears (ed.), *Fantacizing the Feminine in Indonesia*, Durham: Duke University Press.

Ogundipe-Leslie, M. (1991), 'Nigerian Scholar Talks of Feminism and Womanism, *Excaliber*, 26 Sept. 11:9.

Ohnuki-Tierney, E. (1990), *Culture Through Time*, Introduction, Stanford: Stanford University Press.

Ong, A. (1987), *Spirits of Resistance and Capitalist Discipline: Factory Women in Malaysia*, Albany: SUNY Press.

Ong, A. (1988), 'Colonialism and Modernity: Feminist Re-presentations of Women in Non-Western Societies', *Inscriptions*, 3(4):79–383.

Ong, A. (1989), 'Centre, Periphery, and Hierarchy: Gender in Southeast Asia', in S. Morgen (ed.), *Gender and Anthropology*, Washington D.C.: American Anthropological Association.

Ong, A. (1990), 'State Versus Islam: Malay Families, Women's Bodies, and the Body Politic in Malaysia', *American Ethnologist*, 17 (2):259–75.

Ong, A. (1995), 'Women Out of China: Travelling Tales and Travelling Theories in Postcolonial Feminism', in R. Behar and D. Gordon (eds), *Women Writing Culture*, Berkeley: University of California Press. (P. 350–372).

Ong, A. and Peletz, M. (eds) (1995), *Bewitching Women, Pious Men: Gender and Body Politics in Southeast Asia*, Berkeley: University of California Press.

Ortner, S. and Whitehead H. (1981), *Sexual Meanings: The Cultural Construction of Gender and Sexuality*, Cambridge: Cambridge University Press.

Ortner, S. (1990), 'Gender Hegemonies', *The Journal of the Society for the Study of the Multi-Ethnic Literature of the United States*, 15:35–80.

Owens, G. (1989), *Top Panha Hua Jai:* An Evaluation of 'Problems of the Heart': Newspaper Columns as a Data Source for Studies of Thai Social Behaviour, Honours Thesis, Faculty of Asian Studies, Australian National Unviersity, Canberra.

Packard-Winkler, M. (1988), 'Knowledge, Sex and Marriage in Modern Bangkok: Cultural Negotiations in the Time of AIDS', Unpublished PhD dissertation, American Unviersity.

Parker, A., Russo, M., Sommer D. and Yaeger P. (eds) (1992), *Nationalisms and Sexualities*, New York: Routledge.

Parnwell, M. (1993), 'Tourism and Rural Handicrafts in Thailand', in M. Hitchcock, V. King and M. Parnwell (eds), *Tourism in South-East Asia*, Routledge: London.

Peacock, J.L. (1968), *Rites of Modernization: Symbolic Aspects of Indonesian Proletarian Drama*, Chicago: University of Chicago Press.

Peleggi, M. (1994), 'National Heritage and Nationalist Narrative in Contemporary Thailand', Unpulished M.A. Thesis, Australian National University, Canberra.

Peleggi, M. (1996), 'National Heritage and Global Tourism in Thailand', *Annals of Tourism Research*, 23(2):432–48.

Peletz, M. (1995), 'Neither Reasonable nor Responsible: Contrasting Representations of Masculinity in a Malay Society', in A. Ong and M. Peletz (eds), *Bewitching Women and Pious Men,* Berkeley: University of California Press.

Pemberton, J. (1994), 'Recollections from Beautiful Indonesia: Somewhere Beyond the Postmodern', *Public Culture*, 6(2):241–63.

Phillips, H. (1965), *Thai Peasant Personality*, Berkeley: University of

California Press.

Phillips, H. (1987), *Modern Thai Literature.* Honolulu: University of Hawaii Press.

Phongpaichit, P. (1982), *From Peasant Girls to Bangkok Masseuses*, Geneva: International Labour Office.

Podhisita, C. (1985), 'Buddhism and Thai World View', in A. Pongsapich (ed.), *Tradition and Changing Thai World View*, Bangkok: Chulalongkorn University Social Research Institute.

Pongsapich, A. (1986), 'Status of Women's Activities in Thailand', *Women's Issues, Book of Readings*, A. Pongsapich (ed.), Bangkok: Chulalongkorn University Social Research Institute.

Pongsapich, A. (1990), 'Politico-economic Development Impacting on Society and Traditional Values', *American Studies*, 2:79–98.

Potter, S. (1977), *Family Life in a Northern Thai Village*, Berkeley: University of California Press.

Pramoj, K. (1981), *Si Phaendin* (Four Reigns), Vol. 1 and 2, Bangkok: Editions Duang Kamol.

Pratt, M. (1994), 'Women, Literature and National Brotherhood', *Nineteenth Century Contexts: An Interdisciplinary Journal*, 18(1):27–47.

Pritsdam P. (1989), 'Notes on Siamese Administration', in N. Brailey (ed.), *Two Views of Siam on the Eve of the Chakri Reformation*, Whiting Bay, Arran, Scotland: Kiscadale Publications.

Promta, S. (1993), 'A Buddhist Approach to the Contemporary Thai Prostitution Problem', Paper presented at the Fifth International Conference on Thai Studies, SOAS, London.

Pruksathorn, N. (1982), *We are Earth and Sand*, Bangkok: Buraphasan (in Thai).

Quaritch Wales, H. (1931), *Siamese State Ceremonies: Their History and Function*, London: Bernard Quaritch Ltd.

Quaritch Wales, H. (1983), *Divination in Thailand: The Hopes and Fears of a Southeast Asian People*, London: Curzon Press.

Rabibhadana, A. (1975), *The Organization of Thai Society in the Early Bangkok Period, 1782–1873*, Southeast Asia Program Data Paper No. 74, Ithaca, NY.

Raikes, D. (1990), 'Performances by 'National Living Treasures' at the Siam Society', *Journal of the Siam Society*, 78(2).

Rajadhon, P. (1961), *Life and Ritual in Old Siam*, New Haven, CT: Human Relation Area Files Press.

Ratarasarn, S. (1989), *The Principles and Concepts of Thai Classical Medicine*, Thai Khadi Research Institute, Thammasat University, Bangkok.

Reid, A. (1988), *Southeast Asia in the Age of Commerce 1450–1680*, Vol.

1 New Haven: Yale University Press.

Reynolds, C. (1977), 'A Nineteenth Century Thai Buddhist Defense of Polygamy and Some Remarks on the History of Women in Thailand', Paper prepared for Conference of the International Association of Historians of Asia, Bangkok, August.

Reynolds, C. (1987), *Thai Radical Discourse: The Real Face of Thai Feudalism Today*, Ithaca: Southeast Asia Program, Cornell University, Ithaca, N.Y.

Reynolds, C. (ed.) (1991), *National Identity and Its Defenders: Thailand, 1939–1989*, Monash Papers on Southeast Asia No. 25, Clayton: Monash University, Centre of Southeast Asian Studies.

Reynolds, C. (1994), 'Predicaments of Modern Thai History', *South East Asia Research*, 2(1):64–90.

Reynolds, C. (1995), 'A New Look at Old Southeast Asia', *Journal of Asian Studies*, Vol. 54, No. 2, 419–446.

Reynolds, F. (1978), 'Buddhism as Universal and Civic Religion', in Laos and Burma, B. Smith (ed.), *Religion and Legitimation of Power in Thailand*, Chambersberg, PA: Anima Books.

Reynolds, F. and Reynolds, M. (1982), *Three Worlds According to King Ruang: A Thai Buddhist Cosmology*, Berkeley: The Institute of Buddhist Studies.

Richardson, M. (1975), 'Anthropologist-the Myth Teller', *American Ethnologist*, 2(3):517–31.

Richter, L. (1989), *The Politics of Tourism in Asia*, Honolulu: University of Hawaii Press.

Rodman, M. (1992), 'Empowering Place: Multilocality and Multivocality', *American Anthropologist* 94(3):640–56.

Rojanapithayakorn, W. and R. Hanenberg (1996), 'The 100% Condom Program in Thailand', *AIDS*, 10:1–7.

Rosaldo, M. (1983), 'Moral/Analytic Dilemmas Posed by the Intersection of Feminism and Social Science', in N. Haan, R. Bellah, P. Rabinow and W. Sullivan (eds), *Social Science as Moral Inquiry*, New York: Columbia University Press.

Rosaldo, R. (1988), 'Ideology, Place and People without Culture', *Cultural Anthropology*, 3(1):77–87.

Roseberry, W. (1989), *Anthropologies and Histories: Essays in Culture, History, and Political Economy*, New Brunswick, NJ: Rutgers University Press.

Rubin, G. (1975), 'The Traffic in Women: Notes on the Political Economy of Sex', in R. Reiter (ed.), *Toward an Anthropology of Women*, New York: Monthly Review Press.

Rubin, G. (1984), 'Thinking Sex: Notes for a Radical Theory of the Politics of Sexuality', in C. Vance (ed.), *Pleasure and Danger*, Boston: Routledge and Kegan Paul.

Rugpao, S. et. al. (1997), 'Multiple Condom Use in Lamphun Province, Thailand: A Community Generated STD/HIV Prevention Strategy', *Sexually Transmitted Diseases*, 24(9):546–49.

Rutnin, M. (1983), *Transformation of Thai Concepts of Aesthetics*, Thai Khadi Research Institute, Thammasat University, Bangkok.

Rutnin, M. (1984), 'The Role of Women in Dramatic Arts and Social Development: Problems Concerning Child Prostitution in Thailand', in *Customs and Tradition: The Role of Thai Women*, International Conference on Thai Studies, Bangkok.

Rutnin, M. (1988), *Modern Thai Literature*, Bangkok: Thammasat University Press.

Saengtienchai, C. (1995), 'Women's Views on Extramarital Sex of Thai Married Men', Paper presented at the Conference on Gender and Sexuality in Modern Thailand, Canberra, Australia.

Said, E. (1978), *Orientalism*, New York: Vintage Books.

Samosorn, P. (1989), *E-Sarn Mural Paintings*, Khon Kaen: E-Sarn Cultural Center, Khon Kaen University.

Santasombat, Y. (1990), 'Traditional Values and Changing Thai Society', *American Studies*, 2:71–78.

Santasombat, Y. (1992), Prologue, in D. Walker and R. Ehrlich (eds), *Hello My Big Big Honey!: Love Letters to Bangkok Bar Girls and their Revealing Interviews*, Bangkok: Dragon Dance Publications.

Satha-Anand, S. (1996), 'Madsi: A Female Bodhisatva Denied?', Paper presented to the Sixth International Conference on Thai Studies, Chiang Mai, Thailand.

Sawicki, J. (1991), *Disciplining Foucault*, New York:Routledge.

Scharer, H. (1963), *Ngaju Religion*, The Hague: Marinus Nighoff.

Scharfstein, B.A. (1989), *The Dilemma of Context*, New York: New York University Press.

Scheper-Hughes, N. and M. Lock (1987), 'The Mindful Body: A Prolegomenon to Future Work in Medical Anthropology', *Medical Anthropology Quarterly*, 1:6–41.

Sharples, J. (1994), 'Her World in Bangkok', *Thailand Traveller*, 4(26): 44–9.

Singer, L. (1993), *Erotic Welfare*, New York: Routledge, Chapman and Hall.

Sivaraksa, S. (1988), *A Socially Engaged Buddhism*, Bangkok: Thai Inter-Religious Commission for Development.

Skrobanek, S. (1983), 'The Transnational Sex-Exploitation of Thai Women', MA thesis, Development Studies, The Hague.

Skrobanek, S. (1985), 'In Pursuit of an Illusion: Thai Women in Europe', *Southeast Asia Chronicle*, no. 96 (January):7–12.

Skrobanek, S. (1990), 'Child Prostitution in Thailand', *Voices of Thai Women*, 4:10–17.

Skrobanak, S., Boonpakdi, N. and Janthakeera, C. (1997), *The Traffic in Women*, London: Zed Books.

Soonthornthada, A. (1995), 'Understanding Adolescent Sexuality by the Discourses Approach: a case of urban youth in Thailand', Paper presented at the Conference on Gender and Sexuality in Modern Thailand, Canberra, Australia.

Spiro, M. (1970), *Buddhism and Society*, New York: Harper and Row, Publishers.

Sponberg, A. (1992), 'Attitudes towards Women and the Feminine in Early Buddhism', in J. Cabezon (ed.), *Buddhism, Sexuality and Gender*, Albany: State University of New York Press.

Srisambhand, N. (1988), *Research on Women in Thailand*, Bangkok: Chulalongkorn Social Research Institute.

Srisambhand, N. and Gordon, A. (1987), *Thai Rural Women and Agricultural Change: Approaches and a Case Study*, Bangkok: Chulalongkorn University Social Research Institute.

Stewart, S. (1984), *On Longing: Narratives of the Miniature, the Gigantic, the Souvenir, the Collection*, Baltimore: The Johns Hopkins University Press.

Stoler, A. (1977), 'Class Struggle and Female Autonomy in Rural Java', *Signs*, 3:74–89.

Stoler, A. (1991), 'Carnal Knowledge and Imperial Power: Gender, Race, and Morality in Colonial Asia', in M. di Leonardo (ed.), *Gender at the Crossroads of Knowledge: Feminist Anthropology in the Postmodern Era*, Berkeley: University of California Press.

Strathern, M. (1988), 'Concrete Topographies', *Cultural Anthropology*, 3(1):88–97.

Streckfuss, David. (1993), 'The Mixed Colonial Legacy in Siam: Origins of Thai Racialist Thought, 1890–1910', in L. Sears (ed.), *Autonomous History*, University of Wisconsin, Center for Southeast Asian Studies, Monograph No. 11.

Sturdevant, S. and Stoltzfus, B. (1992), *Let the Good Times Roll*, New York: New York Press.

Suehiro, A. (1989), *Capital Accumulation in Thailand: 1855–1985*, Tokyo: The Center for East Asian Cultural Studies.

Sunthraraks, P. (1986), 'Luang Wichit Watakan: Hegemony and Literature', Ph.D. dissertation, University of Wisconsin.

Support Foundation, (1985), *The Kings of the Chakri Dynasty in Nine Volumes*, Bangkok: Office of Her Majesty's Private Secretary.

Suttisakorn, O. (1990), *Dok Mai Khong Chat* (Flowers of the Nation), Bangkok: Duan Tad Press. (in Thai)

Suwannathat-Pian, K. (1995), *Thailand's Durable Premier: Phibun through Three Decades 1932–1957*, Kuala Lumpur: Oxford University Press.

Swaan, W. (1976), *Lost Cities of Asia*, London: Elek Books.

Symonds, P. (1999), 'From Gendered Past to Gendered Future: Hmong Women Negotiating Gender Inequity in Northern Thailand', Paper presented at the Seventh International Conference on Thai Studies, Amsterdam.

Synnott A. (1993), *The Body Social: Symbolism, Self and Society*, London: Routledge.

Tambiah, S.J. (1970), *Buddhism and the Spirit Cults in North-East Thailand*, Cambridge: Cambridge University Press.

Tambiah, S.J. (1976), *World Conqueror and World Renouncer: A Study of Buddhism and Polity in Thailand against a Historical Background*, Cambridge: Cambridge University Press.

Tambiah, S. (1984), *The Buddhist Saints of the Forest and the Cult of Amulets*, Cambridge: Cambridge University Press.

Tanabe, S. (1991), 'Spirits, Power and the Discourse of Female Gender', in M. Chitakasem and A. Turton (eds), *Thai Constructions of Knowledge*, London: School of Oriental and African Studies, University of London.

Tanchainan, S. (1987), 'Women in Thailand', *Seeds of Peace*, 3(3):4–8.

Tangchonlathip, K. (1995), 'Sexual Expectations of Thai Married Couples', Paper presented at the Conference on Gender and Sexuality in Modern Thailand, Canberra, Australia.

Tannenbaum, N. (1993), 'Anatta and Lack of Control: Shan Constructions of Buddhism', Paper presented at the Fifth International Thai Studies Conference, London.

Tannenbaum, N. (1995), 'Buddhism, Prostitution, and Sex: Limits on the Academic Discourse on Gender in Thailand', Paper presented at the Conference on Gender and Sexuality in Modern Thailand, Canberra, Australia.

Tantiwiramanond, D. and Pandey, S. (1989), 'Dutiful but Overburdened: Women in Thai Society', *Asian Review*, 3:41–53.

Tantiwiramanond, D. and Pandey, S. (1991), *By Women, For Women: A Study of Women's Organizations in Thailand*, Singapore: Institute of

Southeast Asian Studies.

Taylor, L. (1991), 'Articles of Peculiar Excellence: The Siamese Exhibit at the U.S. Centennial Exposition (Philadelphia, 1876)', *Journal of the Siam Society*, 79(2):13–23.

Teilbet-Fisk, J. (1996), 'The Miss Hailala Beauty Pageant: Where Beauty is More than Skin Deep', in C. Cohen, R. Wilk and B. Stoeltje (eds), *Beauty Queens on the Global Stage*, New York: Routledge.

Tejapira, K. (1992), 'Commodifying Marxism: The Formation of Modern Thai Radical Culture, 1927–1958', Unpublished Ph.D. dissertation, Cornell University, Ithaca, N.Y.

Tejapira, K. (1996), 'The Postmodernization of Thailand', Proceedings of the Sixth International Conference on Thai Studies, Chiang Mai, Thailand.

Terweil, B. (1975), *Monks and Magic*, Scandanavian Institute of Asian Studies Monograph Series No. 24, Bangkok: Craftsman Press.

Tettoni, L. and Warren, W. (1989), *Thai Style*, New York: Rizzoli.

The Entrance to Vinaya, Volume Two (1973), Bangkok: Mahamakut Rajavidyalaya Press.

Thitsa, K. (1980), *Providence and Prostitution*, Change International Reports, London.

Thitsa, K. (1983), 'Nuns, Mediums and Prostitutes in Chiengmai', *Women and Development in Southeast Asia*, Paper No. 1., University of Kent at Canterbury.

Thomson, S. (1990), *Gender Issues in Thailand Development*, Bangkok, Thailand: Gender and Development Research Institute.

Thongthai, V. and Guest, P. (1995), 'Thai Sexual Attitudes and Behaviour: Results from a Recent National Survey', Paper prepared for the 'Gender and Sexuality in Modern Thailand' Conference at the Australian National University, July (1995).

Tilley, C. (ed.) (1990), 'Michel Foucault: Towards an Archaeology of Archaeology', in C. Tilley (ed.), *Reading Material Culture*, Oxford: Blackwell Publishers.

Tingsabadh, C. and Tanchainan, S. (1986), 'Theories in Women Studies', in A. Pongsapich (ed.), *Women's Issues, Book of Readings*, Bangkok: Chulalongkorn University Social Research Institute.

Tinker, I. and Bramsen, B. (1976), *Women and World Development*, Washington: Overseas Development Council.

Tiyavanich, K. (1977), *Forest Recollections*, Honolulu: University of Hawaii Press.

Tobias, S. (1973), 'Chinese Religion in a Thai Market Town', Unpublished PhD dissertation, University of Chicago.

Trinh Minih Ha (1989), *Women Native Other*, Bloomington: Indiana University Press.

Truong, Thanh-Dam (1990), *Sex, Money, and Morality*, London: Zed Books.

Tsing, A. (1993), *In the Realm of the Diamond Queen*, Princeton, NJ: Princeton University Press.

Turton, A. (1987), *Production, Power and Participation in Rural Thailand*, Geneva: UNRISD Participation Program.

Ungphakorn, J. (1993), 'The Impact of AIDS on Women in Thailand', in M. Berer with S. Ray (eds), *Women and HIV/AIDS*: An International Resource Book, London: Pandora Press.

Usher, A.D. (1994), 'After the Forest: AIDS and Ecological Collapse in Thailand', in V. Shiva (ed.), *Close to Home*, Philadelphia: New Society Publishers.

Valerio, V. (1990) 'Constitutive History: Genealogy and Narrative in the Legitimation of Hawaiian Kingship', in E. Ohnuki-Tierney (ed.), *Culture Through Time: Anthropological Approaches*, Stanford: Stanford University Press.

Valverde, M. (1985), *Sex, Power and Pleasure*, Toronto: Women's Press.

Vance, C. (1991), 'Anthropology Rediscovers Sexuality: A Theoretical Comment', *Social Science and Medicine*, 33(8):875–84.

Vandergeest, P. (1993), 'Constructing Thailand: Regulation, Everyday Resistance, and Citizenship', *Comparative Studies in Society and History*, 35(1):133–58.

Van Esterik, J. (1977), 'Cultural Interpretation of Canonical Paradox: Lay Meditation in a Central Thai Village', Ph.D. dissertation, University of Illinois, Urbana.

Van Esterik, J. (1982), Women Meditation Teachers in Thailand, in P. Van Esterik (ed.), *Women of Southeast Asia*, Dekalb, IL: Northern Illinois University.

Van Esterik, P. (1973), 'Thai Tonsure Ceremonies: A Reinterpretation of Bahmanic Ritual in Thailand', *Journal of the Steward Anthropological Society*, 4(2):79–121.

Van Esterik, P. (1974), 'A Preliminary Analysis of Ban Chiang Pottery, Northeast Thailand', *Asian Perspectives*, 16(2):174–194.

Van Esterik, P. (1979), 'Symmetry and Symbolism in Ban Chiang Painted Pottery', *Journal of Anthropological Research*, 35(4):495–508.

Van Esterik, P. (1980), 'Royal Style in Village Context: Towards a Model of Interaction Between Royalty and Commoner', in C. Wilson, C. Smith and G. Smith (eds), *Royalty and Commoner: Essays in Thai Administrative, Economic and Social History*, Contributions to Asian

Studies, Vol. XV. Leiden: Brill. Pp.102–17.

Van Esterik, P. (1981), *Cognition and Design Production in Ban Chiang Painted Pottery*, Athens, Ohio: Center for International Studies, Southeast Asia Monograph Series, Ohio University Press.

Van Esterik, P. (ed.) (1982), *Women of Southeast Asia*, Dekalb, IL: Center for Southeast Asia Studies, Northern Illinois University (second edition, 1996).

Van Esterik, P. (1982), 'Laywomen in Theravada Buddhism', in P. Van Esterik (ed.), *Women in Southeast Asia*. Southeast Asia Monograph Series. DeKalb, Illinois: Northern Illinois University.

Van Esterik, P. (1984), 'Continuities and Transformations in Southeast Asian Symbolism: A Case Study from Thailand', *Bijdragen*, 140(1):77–92.

Van Esterik, P. (1985a), 'Imitating Ban Chiang Painted Pottery: Towards a Cognitive Theory of Replication', in J. Doughterty (ed.), *Directions in Cognitive Anthropology*, Urbana: University of Illinois Press.

Van Esterik, P. (1985b), 'The Cultural Context of Breastfeeding in Rural Thailand', in V. Hull and M. Simpson (eds), *Breastfeeding, Child Health, and Child Spacing: Cross-cultural Perspectives*. London: Croom Helm.

Van Esterik, P. (1986), 'Feeding Their Faith: Recipe Knowledge Among Thai Buddhist Women', *Food and Foodways*, 1(1):198–215.

Van Esterik, P. (1987), 'Ideologies and Women in Development Strategies in Thailand', in Proceedings of the International Conference on Thai Studies, 3(2):597–604. Australian National University, Canberra.

Van Esterik, P. (1988), 'The Cultural Context of Infant Feeding', in B. Winikoff, M. Castle and V. Laukaran (eds), *Feeding Infants in Four Societies*, New York: Greenwood Press.

Van Esterik, P. (1989), 'Deconstructing Display: Gender and Development in Thailand', Working Paper Series No. 2, Thai Studies Project, York University, Toronto.

Van Esterik, P. (1991), 'Linking Institutions: The Women in Development Consortium in Thailand and Canada', in A. Rao (ed.), *Women's Studies International: Nairobi and Beyond*. New York: Feminist Press. Pp.238–47.

Van Esterik, P. (1992a), 'From Marco Polo to McDonalds: Thai Cuisine in Transition', *Food and Foodways*, 5(2):177–93.

Van Esterik, P. (1992b), 'Thai Prostitution and the Medical Gaze', in P. and J. Van Esterik (eds), *Gender and Development in Southeast Asia*, Montreal: Canadian Asian Studies Association.

Van Esterik, P. (1994), 'Cutting Up Culture: Colonizing Costume', in L. Migram and P. Van Esterik (eds), *The Transformative Power of Cloth in Southeast Asia*, Montreal: Canadian Asian Studies Association.

Van Esterik, P. (1995), 'The Politics of Beauty in Thailand', in C. Cohen, R. Wilk and B. Stoelje (eds), *Beauty Queens on the Global Stage*, New York: Routledge, Pp.203–216.

Van Esterik, P. (1996), 'Nurturance and Reciprocity in Thai Studies', in P. Durrenberger (ed.), *State Power and Culture in Thailand*, New Haven: Yale University Southeast Asia Studies.

Vella, W. (1978), *Chaiyo! King Vajiravudh and the Development of Thai Nationalism*, Honolulu: University of Hawaii Press.

Vichit-Vadakan, J. (1990), 'Change and Continuity in Thai and American Values', *American Studies*, 2:27–51.

Vichit-Vadakan, J. (1994), 'Women and the Family in the Midst of Social Change', *Law and Society Review*, 28(3):515–24.

Vitebsky, P. (1993), 'Is Death the same Everywhere? Contexts of Knowing and Doubting', in M. Hobart (ed.), *An Anthropological Critique of Development: The Growth of Ignorance*, London: Routledge.

Vitson P. (1991), *People Centered Development: An Overview from Development Experience in Thailand*, Bangkok: People's Forum.

Wajuppa, T. (1992), 'Images of Women in Isan Folk Literature', Southeast Asia Paper, No. 36. Manoa: Center for Southeast Asian Studies, School of Hawaiian, Asian and Pacific Studies, University of Hawaii at Manoa.

Wakin, E. (1992), *Anthropology Goes to War: Professional Ethics and Counterinsurgency in Thailand*, Center for Southeast Asian Studies, Monograph No. 7. Madison: University of Wisconsin.

Walker, D. and Ehrlich S. (1992), *Hello My Big Big Honey!: Love Letters to Bangkok Bar Girls and their Revealing Interviews*, Bangkok: Dragon Dance Publications.

Warren, H. (1969), *Buddhism in Translations*, New York: Atheneum.

Warren, J. (1987), *At the Edge of Southeast Asian History*, Quezon City: New Day Publishers.

Wayne, V. (1994), 'A Denaturalized Performance: Gender and Body Construction in Thailand's *As You Like It*', in N. Masavisut, G. Simson and L. Smith, (eds). *Gender and Culture in Literature and Film East and West: Issues of Perception and Interpretation*, Honolulu: College of Languages, Linguistics and Literature, University of Hawaii and the East-West Center.

Wedel, Y. (with Paul Wedel) (1987), *Radical Thought, Thai Mind: The Development of Revolutionary Ideas in Thailand*, Assumption Business Administration College.

Weisman, J. (1997), 'The Emperor's Lady Transformed: Race, Gender and Shifting Embodiments of the Nation in Contemporary Thailand', Paper presented at the annual meetings of the American Anthropological Association, Washington D.C.

Weniger, B. And T. Brown (1996), 'The March of AIDS through Asia', *The New England Journal of Medicine*, 335(5):343–344.

Whitam, F. and Mathy, R. (1986), *Male Homosexuality in Four Societies*, New York: Praeger.

White, L. (1990), *The Comforts of Home: Prostitution in Colonial Nairobi*, Chicago: The University of Chicago Press.

Wijeyewardene, G. (1986), *Place and Emotion*, Pandora: Bangkok.

Wilayasakpan, J. (1992), 'Nationalism and the Transformation of Aesthetic Concepts: Theatre in Thailand during the Phibun Period', Unpublished PhD dissertation, Cornell University.

Winichakul, T. (1994), *Siam Mapped: A History of the Geo-Body of a Nation*, Honolulu: University of Hawaii Press.

Wolf, D. (1988), 'Female Autonomy, the Family, and Industrialization in Java', *Journal of Family*, 9(1):85–107.

Wolf, N. (1991), *The Beauty Myth*, Toronto: Vintage Books.

Wolters, O. (1982), *History, Culture and Region in Southeast Asian Perspectives*, Singapore: Institute of Southeast Asian Studies.

Wood, R.E. (1980), 'International Tourism and Cultural Change in Southeast Asia', *Economic Development and Cultural Change*, 28(3): 561–81.

Wyatt, D. (1982), *Thailand: A Short History*, New Haven: Yale University Press.

Wyatt, D. (1994), 'Voices from Southeast Asia's Past', *Journal of Asian Studies*, 53(4):1076–91.

Young, K. (ed.). (1993), *Bodylore*, Knoxville: University of Tennessee Press.

Zwilling, L. (1992), 'Homosexuality as Seen in Indian Buddhist Texts', in J. Cabezon (ed.), *Buddhism, Sexuality, and Gender*, Albany: State University of New York Press.

Index